Shamanism

SHAMANISM

THE TIMELESS RELIGION

Manvir Singh

Alfred A. Knopf
NEW YORK
2025

Published by Alfred A. Knopf, a division of
Penguin Random House LLC, 1745 Broadway, New York, NY 10019.

Knopf, Borzoi Books, and the colophon are registered trademarks of
Penguin Random House LLC.

Some material in this text was previously published in *Vice* and *Wired*.

Library of Congress Cataloging-in-Publication Data
Names: Singh, Manvir, author.
Title: Shamanism : the timeless religion / Manvir Singh.
Description: First edition. | New York : Alfred A. Knopf, 2025. | "This is
a Borzoi book published by Alfred A. Knopf." | Includes bibliographical
references and index.
Identifiers: LCCN 2024023735 | ISBN 9780593537541 (hardcover) |
ISBN 9780593537558 (ebook)
Subjects:
Classification: LCC BL2370.S5 S529 2025 |
DDC 201/.44—dc23/eng/20241029
LC record available at https://lccn.loc.gov/2024023735

penguinrandomhouse.com | aaknopf.com

Printed in the United States of America
First Edition

The authorized representative in the EU for product safety and
compliance is Penguin Random House Ireland, Morrison Chambers,
32 Nassau Street, Dublin D02 YH68, Ireland, https://eu-contact.penguin.ie.

To the people of Madobag, Ugai, and Buttui
Surak sabeu

And to my Evelyns,
Nina and Zora, for the ecstatic

Contents

AUTHOR'S NOTE

In order to respect the privacy of certain individuals mentioned in this book, some names have been changed.

Shamanism

Introduction

Opa, a man of about fifty, was to be initiated. His nephew had trekked upriver to share the news, arriving at my house just as I was waking up. He explained that Opa had been sick for weeks, debilitated by a savage blend of fever, diarrhea, and an icy body pain that spidered through his joints. His eyes had turned yellow. He could barely pick himself up. His family had summoned shamans, hunted for herbs, visited the clinic, even invited a pastor to muster the benevolence of the Christian god. But until yesterday, nothing worked.

"Sounds like witchcraft," my assistant Rustam said.

"No," said Opa's nephew. "*Kerei.*" Shaman.

He explained that, two days before, the shamans stopped trying to heal Opa and started to initiate him. They suspected his illness might be a sign that his spirit longed to become a shaman. And they were right, it seemed. Like a soul returning to its body, a new vitality possessed Opa, energizing him to participate in the first of many trance dances required for initiation.

"Will you join?" asked the nephew.

"Of course," I replied.

By this point, I had made four trips to the Indonesian island of Siberut, spending nearly a year in total with its inhabitants, the Mentawai. I had lived with shamans, studied healing rituals, and interviewed people about gods, black magic, and deprivation. I spoke the Mentawai language and had a small house. To observe an initiation was a dream.

The nephew told us to come at midday. "Bring some money for the shamans," he said. "And we need fuel for the generator."

"No problem."

"And bring *oleh-oleh*," he added, using the Indonesian word for gifts and referring to market-bought goodies like tea, sugar, coffee, and cookies. "This will be good."

———————

Through his initiation, Opa would ascend from *simata*, a word that refers to both non-shamans and uncooked food, to *sikerei*, a shaman. Like other *sikerei*, he would be able to see people's souls and the legions of spirits that occupy our world. He would enter trance in nighttime ceremonies. He would learn the plants for treating infections and the songs for calling souls to feverish bodies. He would be expected to wear a loincloth and, depending on his commitment, tattoo his body and grow out his hair. The process would imbue him with spiritual power. As a result, he would have to forgo some of the tastiest animal flesh and have considerably less sex. Violate these prohibitions, the Mentawai say, and one invites illness, bad luck, and even death.

When I first visited the Mentawai, in 2014, I knew to expect shamans. I had seen photos of them, the so-called flower men, shirtless and loinclothed, decked out in leaves and headbands and red and white blossoms, their wiry bodies contoured by trim charcoal-ash tattoos. But I didn't appreciate how important they were. Mentawai shamans are healers, of course, but they are also diviners, spiritual guides, feared sorcerers, and walking archives of cultural knowledge. They are entertainers, alone permitted to perform some of the most riveting routines. Their tattoos and ceremonial garb—including not just leaves, flowers, and heaps of beads but also face paint and a turmeric body coating—make them particularly attractive. When conflicts arise, they arbitrate. When they speak, people listen.

The Mentawai aren't unique in having shamanism. To the

contrary, similar practices have appeared around the world. Inuit *angakok* coaxed illness-causing ghosts into igloos before slaughtering them with snow knives. Zande *ira avure* in Sudan ate medicines and danced before entering altered states and divining. Some Kalahari hunter-gatherers held all-night ceremonies in which ecstatic healers were said to nearly die from the boiling upsurge of spiritual energy. Unique among animals, we humans cultivate altered states of consciousness in our efforts to contact the beyond.[1]

When I tell people I study shamans, I usually encounter one of two views. The first is that shamanism is "primeval wisdom"—a repository of ancient knowledge, a remnant of our once-true spirituality and genuine connection to nature. With the shift to modern industrialized societies, the story goes, people abandoned this wisdom, subjecting themselves to depression and meaninglessness.

According to the alternate view, shamanism is "superstitious savagery"—a relic of a backward era, a spectacle produced by crafty showmen to exploit naïve credulity. For this camp, the apparent decline of shamanism represents a triumph—of science over magic, reason over irrationality.

The clash between primeval wisdom and superstitious savagery is about more than shamanism. It is a disagreement about Western industrialized societies and their relationship to human history. Are we—the people of these societies—corrupted? Or are we enlightened? Have we divorced ourselves from nature and true understanding? Or have we overcome irrationality, harnessing science to improve our well-being? These two views serve as political props, casting industrialized societies as either failures in need of fixing or achievements to be defended.

Whatever their disagreements, both sides agree that industrialized societies depart radically from the rest of humanity. Each is committed, in other words, to a story of extreme exceptionalism, to a yawning chasm separating them from us. On one side, we find not just shamanism but also magic, myths, nature, and tribal communalism. On the other side, we find the exemplars of modernity: reason, science, capitalism, Abrahamic religions.

As an anthropologist, I tend to be skeptical of stark lines like this. Yes, rich Western societies differ in important ways from the rest of humanity. But flashy differences blind us to the ever-present expressions of human nature. They tempt us to see the history and institutions of Western societies as utterly unique, devoid of cross-cultural parallels. If you're looking for a thesis for this book, turn to Ecclesiastes, chapter 1. The famous line is "There is nothing new under the sun," but I prefer what comes next:

> Is there anything of which one can say,
> "Look! This is something new"?
> It was here already, long ago;
>   it was here before our time.

This is a book about an institution that was here long before us and will survive long after. Shamanism, I argue, is neither primeval wisdom nor superstitious savagery. Rather, it is a near inevitability of human societies—a captivating package of practices and beliefs that appears over and over because of its deep psychological appeal. It characterized the earliest human religions, echoes in industrialized societies today, and will perpetually re-emerge. In their eagerness to limit shamanism to archaic or far-away societies, commentators have denied the universality of its principles and the intrinsic needs it addresses.

While working on this book, I was sometimes asked about my view on the morality of shamanism. Are shamans good or bad? Helpful or exploitative? Yet the question is based on a false premise. It's like asking if artificial intelligence is bad, or if blockchain is bad, or if drones are bad. Shamanism is like most technologies. Its morality depends on how it's used and the value system you adopt when considering it. As we'll see, Kalahari trance healing is an egalitarian, communal institution that seems well designed to alleviate anxiety. From many perspectives, it is good. Some CEOs, meanwhile, use shamanic techniques to cultivate personas of extraordinariness, misleading themselves and others about their usefulness. Many people, I'm guessing, would see this as bad. To insist that shamanism is either good or bad is to impose a singular morality on a practice that is far more dynamic.

Another question I often got was whether I believe in shamanism. I am trained as an empiricist and, as you will see, do not think we can conclude that shamans heal, divine, or change the weather by interacting with gods, ghosts, ancestors, or any other non-ordinary beings. Yet I have also tried to inhabit the worlds of shamans, their clients, and their communities. I have been transported by the drumming and throat singing of a Tuvan shaman. I have inhaled psychedelic snuffs and been propelled into parallel realms. I have soul journeyed with neo-shamans and stood on the brink of spirit possession during all-night dances with the Mentawai. And, perhaps most importantly, I have seen patients leave shamanic healing ceremonies feeling less distressed. I have tried to write this book both as a scientific researcher and as someone who appreciates the experiential profundity of shamanism.

One of my favorite things about anthropology is its power to turn the strange familiar and the familiar strange—and this is nowhere clearer than with shamanism. For many people, shamans are quintessentially strange. Depending on the culture, they may be said to fly, turn invisible, speak to the dead, or transform into jaguars. They may walk on fire, swallow hot coals, fire deadly pellets at each other, or claim to have been swallowed and regurgitated by a bear. They may, as among the Yanomami of Venezuela, snort a hallucinogenic powder and call upon tiny beings that pirouette down invisible trails, the males wearing fiery haloes, the females with glittery wands protruding from their vaginas. They may become prophets and trumpet new religions.[2]

And yet: take some time, and this strangeness makes sense. Like so much of culture, shamanism adapts to the contours of the human mind. And just as studying popular foods can teach us how taste works, journeying into shamanism provides us with a new lens to understand human nature—a lens that alters how we see the world around us.

This book is the culmination of a decade spent researching the psychological origins of religion. Aside from living with the Mentawai, I have combed through ethnographies and databases, mapping out patterns in myth, witchcraft, and shamanism. I have studied healing songs and sought out curers and diviners in India, the Andes, and the northwest Amazon, observing music, drug use, and healing ceremonies wherever I could. I have chased modern resurrections of shamanism, from Harvard Square to the Nevada deserts.

———————

This book is organized into two parts. The first is a shamanic orientation. We'll begin in 2014, when I first landed on Siberut Island. I will acquaint you with the *sikerei* I first met, as well as with the thrills and anxieties of arriving in a remote community with little more than a backpack. We will then zoom out from Siberut, locating in this corner of Indonesia an echo of a puzzling human tendency. The *sikerei*, it turns out, share striking similarities with specialists around the world. They enter altered states. They commune with unseen realities. And they channel that connection for ends like curing and prophecy.

What is it about our minds and societies that leads shamanism to develop over and over? Across three chapters, I propose an answer. The secret of the shaman's success, I argue, is psychological resonance. People are inclined to believe in unseen forces and to rely on rituals for control. They want their fevers to subside, their crops to grow, and their hunts to succeed. They want to know whether it will rain next week and whether their business will prosper. As they seek this control, specialists discover and incorporate the most attractive services, driving the evolution of shamanism almost everywhere humans go.

Like the best virtual reality technology, shamanism creates an enthralling, simulated experience. Through combinations of dance, touch, music, theater, and psychotropic drugs, shamans and their communities construct mystical realities in which a specialist appeals to otherwise unseen worlds for blessings, protection, and information. Key to this performance is transformation: the shaman appears to become a different kind of entity—one possessed with powers normal humans lack.

My use of the word "performance" might bother some readers. It might evoke images of crafty magicians fooling a gullible clientele. But this is a limitation of language. Shamans aren't scammers, and their clients aren't suckers. Rather, people understand the reality of shamanic practices in ways that are much more nuanced. On the one hand, people are often skeptical of shamans' abilities. Shamans and their clients recognize that they use sleight of hand, and they often question the authenticity of trance. On the other hand, clients and specialists experience the power of shamanism. A shaman might see their colleagues use stage tricks on Monday and then visit them on Tuesday after falling sick. Moreover, shamans and their communities collaborate to create as moving a healing experience as possible. In trying to reconcile these contradictions, we will go beyond familiar notions of belief to better understand the sophisticated ways people think about the supernatural.

This new view of shamanism explains many curious patterns, from self-denial to intense initiations. Yet the feature I'll spend the most time on is trance. Although they disagree on the function of altered states, leading writers like Michael Harner and Michael Winkelman have insisted that shamans across the globe enter a similar trance state, which they call the "integrative" or "shamanic state of consciousness." Shamans themselves describe wildly varied experiences, however, and the evidence we'll review suggests that Harner and Winkelman have been mistaken. Like a global legion of psychonauts, shamans have discovered innumerable ways to tweak their consciousness, from dancing to darkness to deliriants.

This diversity forces us to reconsider the function of trance, and, again, I'll emphasize transformation and performance. For now, suffice it to say that, like other shamanic practices, altered states create stirring experiences for both specialist and audience. A shaman who communes with a sky god in a normal voice looks like a fraud. One who loses consciousness, froths at the mouth, and then speaks in a spirit tongue is more conceivably doing something us normal humans cannot. Altered states can also feel divine, of course, and we will explore in rich detail the link between shamanic trance and mysticism.

Part 1 ends with the most common question about shamanism: Does it work? Given what we know, I'm not convinced that shamans contact beings from the beyond to cure, prophesy, and change the weather. But do they heal? For years, I was doubtful. Speaking to the most ardent proponents, I noticed that their conviction was grounded less in empirical research and more in a rosy image of archaic wisdom. Yet my views have since changed, and I'll present some of the people and evidence that have convinced me otherwise. Through this survey, we will confront a paradox of shamanism: when it comes to healing, the stronger the illusion, the more potent the effects.

<hr>

With shamanism's appeal established, I spend part 2 tracing it across time and social contexts. We journey into its timelessness. We behold its relentless drive to exist.

The material here roughly follows the arc of history and religious evolution, beginning with Paleolithic hunter-gatherers. Deciphering our deep past is like reading a book with all but one of the pages torn out, and this applies just as much to studying ancient shamanism as to anything else. We'll visit a cave in southwest France that supposedly holds one of the earliest signs of shamanism before turning to other standard pieces of evidence, like trippy rock art and impressive burials. None of it is conclusive, and, in fact, most of it is flimsier than often claimed. This doesn't mean Stone Age religion is unknowable, however. Combing history for the pristine emergence of shamanism, I'll present complementary evidence for its antiquity—evidence that not only corroborates archaeological findings but also pushes estimates of shamanism's debut to the origins of cognitively modern humans, if not earlier.

For many people, the story stops somewhere between here and the rise of world religions. Shamans, they assume, are confined to ancestral societies and premodern tribes. I call this the "Pokémon theory" of religious history: like Squirtle or Bulbasaur, shamans are treated as an evolutionarily earlier stage, replaced by more sophisticated forms such as priests, bishops, and ayatollahs.

The next three chapters show how misguided this view is, starting at the beginnings of organized religions. Shamans, it so happens, have a knack for becoming prophets. Survey world history, and you'll see that messianic movements often have shamans at their helms. Leveraging their supernatural connection, possessed healers promise salvation and renewal. They amass followings that destabilize the social milieu. They inspire self-sacrifice and become shrouded in myth.

Messianic shamans featured in contexts ranging from New Guinean cargo cults to Japanese millenarian movements, but the ones I spend the most time on are Judeo-Christian prophets. Many people reject efforts to examine these figures through a comparative lens, especially ones that stress similarities with shamanism. Others assert that shamanism "loses meaning" as soon as it applies to hallowed Western figures. But drawing on a revisionist turn in biblical scholarship, I'll show that this resistance is hard to justify. Hebrew prophets like Samuel, Elijah, and Elisha qualify as shamans. The early Christian church was shamanic, and Jesus likely was, too. The impulse to view Abrahamic prophets as beyond comparison is driven less by empirical evidence and more by a prejudice that separates Western heritage from the rest of humanity.

From their origins, we will track the rise of organized religions, where, again, the Pokémon theory turns out wrong. Rather than superseding shamanism, organized religions have been locked in an unending battle to subdue it. As ecstatic provocateurs, shamans threaten religious authority. They emerge constantly and offer access to the supernatural that is more direct, more engaging, and aimed at everyday goals. The most successful among them siphon adherents away from organized religions and introduce competing takes on doctrine and divine will. To check these firebrands, officials condemn shamanism, or at least delegitimize it among laypeople. The Spanish Inquisition attacked shamans, as did Polynesian chiefs. Even today, new religions undergo a predictable evolution, starting out shamanic before turning on their ecstatic origins. But shamans persist, as they always have.

Still, the prognosis for religion in Western countries seems dire. Between 2012 and 2017, 11 percent of the U.S. population stopped describing themselves as "religious." The situation is grimmer in European countries like Sweden and the Czech Republic, where roughly three-quarters of people have no religious affiliation. In a curious turn, though, shamanism seems to grow stronger. New practices, collectively known as "neo-shamanism," are flourishing. For the first time in the history of the British census, in 2021, thousands of respondents declared their religion to be "shamanism." Surveys in the United States suggest that hundreds of thousands of Americans consult shamans regularly. We'll visit some of these practitioners and discover that, despite accusations of inauthenticity, varieties of neo-shamanism are as shamanic as anything else covered in this book. Sure, they have their quirks, but these exemplify the blend of universal tendencies and local idiosyncrasies that characterizes so much of human culture.

Many readers might still be skeptical. They might acknowledge everything to this point but maintain that they never interact with shamans. This may be technically correct, but I will present the unrecognized ways that elements of shamanism appear in seemingly enlightened spaces. We'll probe the reliance on what I call "hedge wizards," or experts who promise control over uncertainty despite no evidence of efficacy. Epitomized in money managers, these figures compete among themselves to convince clients they can control the uncontrollable. Although they don't enter trance, their models, degrees, personalities, and superhuman work schedules assure clients of their abilities to discern otherwise opaque forces. We are all endowed with the same cognitive architecture, all captivated by promises that forecasters with special gifts can tame uncertainty. Recognizing this not only reminds us of shamanism's ubiquity—it also reveals the strangeness of institutions we so easily take for granted.

Part 2 concludes by addressing the hype. No book on shamanism, especially one on its modern expressions, can ignore psychedelics. In the last decade or so, psychedelics have gone from the fringe to the mainstream, from countercultural playthings to medical marvels. At the center of this renaissance is the figure of the shaman. According to numerous proponents, psychedelic therapy is not a newfangled practice but a recapitulation of an ancient, worldwide shamanic tradition. This narrative might feel good, but we'll see that it mangles history in service of ideology. In so doing, it reinforces a distinction between primitive and civilized while projecting images that are Western-centric and attention-grabbing onto the diversity of the world's spiritual practices. The final stop of our journey into shamanism leaves us with an important lesson. Elements of shamanism may always recur, but comparison needs to be done with care. We should be wary of hallucinating similarities in contexts where they don't exist.

Opa's house was teeming with activity when we arrived. Guests wearing T-shirts and beaded necklaces gossiped on the front veranda. Inside, the shamans' wives tucked flowers into their hair and wrapped meters of beaded strings around their wrists, elbows, and necks. The oldest one teased me about my feet—how do I always end up with so much dried mud caked on them? In the kitchen, two boys rapped on snakeskin drums as their cousins beat bamboo tongs on a cauldron. On the back veranda, a pile of tubers sat waiting to be cooked. Beside it, two monstrous boars bound in palm fronds wriggled in agitation.

Opa arrived shortly after us, accompanied by five shamans. He had clearly come close to dying. Before his illness, he had bronze skin and muscular legs. Now he looked like a ghost on stilts: as pale as a palm grub with bird-bone legs.

Opa's main teacher was Teu Rami, a chocolate-colored goofball who liked to crack penis jokes and always squeezed my biceps when I ran into him, needling me for tobacco. Teu Rami was a shaman but, aside from his loincloth, didn't fully look the part. His hair was short, and he hadn't yet tattooed his body. Yet none of that mattered. No one healed like Teu Rami. In ceremonies, he was serious and professional—but also much more. When spirits approached him after a bout of dancing, he became sacred yet obscene, a hollow cadaver possessed by a wild, inhuman force— jerky, bizarre, ancestral. To watch him was to be invited to believe in something powerful and beyond ourselves, like seeing a corpse come back to life. It was little wonder he had been selected to be Opa's instructor.

For the next two hours, I followed Opa and the shamans like

a preteen trailing his older brother's friend group. I assiduously chronicled everything they did, snapping photos, jotting down notes, waving around my audio recorder. Each action had significance. Opa and his wife ate in a doorway rather than inside. They ate smoked meat rather than recently netted fish. The shamans collected in the kitchen, where they examined Opa's *salipa*, the trunk containing a shaman's amulets and other magical curios. They recited protective mantras and tied leaves to one another's necklaces. They sacrificed a chicken and sang together.

Eventually they collected in a large room, where they pulled out their trunks and started to get dressed. They fastened cloth skirts around their waists and tied bundles of chicken feathers to their hair. They tucked flowers into their headbands and red- and yellow-veined leaves into their loincloths. Draped in beads, nature, and bold-colored fabrics, they were beautiful, not just for humans but for spirits and wandering souls, as well.

They were getting dressed, my assistant explained, for perhaps the most important ceremony during a shaman's initiation. This one wasn't about learning songs or having the right items. Rather, it was Opa's transformation—the very genesis of his shamanic powers—and all of us would get to watch.

Part One

SHAMANISM

Anciently, human beings and spirits did not mix. But certain persons who were so perspicacious, single-minded, reverential, and correct that their intelligence could understand what lies above and below, their sagely wisdom could illumine what is distant and profound, their vision was bright and clear, and their hearing was penetrating. Therefore the spirits would descend upon them.

—FROM THE FOURTH-CENTURY BCE CHINESE TEXT *Kuo-yü*

CHAPTER 1

Setting Off

It was morning when Siberut first came into view. The date was June 21, 2014; I was barely twenty-four. I remember seeing the island in the far-off distance—an oasis of rain forest in a vast, violent ocean. I had just spent fourteen hours on a creaky wooden ferry with an Indonesian man who grinned a lot and referred to me only in the third person. ("Is this the first time Manvir is in Indonesia?") His aim, I think, was to be polite, but I was new to Indonesian norms and found him hard to trust.

I met the man—I'll call him Happy—the day before at a university in the Sumatran city of Padang. A professor introduced us, explaining that Happy was headed to a community in Siberut's interior. Did I want to join him? Sure. The professor and Happy made a flurry of phone calls—to whom, I had no clue—and by the end of the day, Happy and I were on the deck of the ship, rolling out sleeping pads under the stars and going over Mentawai vocabulary.

The ferry pulled up at Siberut's southern port and disgorged the passengers. Most were not Mentawai. Rather, they were merchants, administrators, and family members from elsewhere in Indonesia, mostly Sumatra. They had colonized Siberut's southern port, turning it into a generic facsimile of semi-urban Indonesia. There were some Mentawai people, too—although I couldn't point them out yet—as well as a gang of Western surfers, who used Siberut as a jumping-off point to visit the world-class waves nearby.

I felt unmoored getting off the ferry. Everything was unfamiliar. The air was wet and salty and had the faint scent of incineration. I didn't trust Happy but had to rely on him. I knew nine hundred words of Indonesian, and even those I had trouble discerning. People greeted one another. They exhaled smoke that smelled like spicy trees; they yelled and laughed and coughed and pushed past and climbed onto motorbikes. I felt like I was in the way. My backpack, heavy with gifts, was the size of a baby dolphin, but I felt wary of putting it down. I had been told to look out for thieves.

Happy pulled me to two men standing next to motor scooters. They were athletic and had prominent cheekbones. Happy said that they were Mentawai. He handed his bags to one of them and climbed onto his scooter. I did the same with the other man. We set off, the sea to our left and a blur of jungle to our right. We rode over a crumbling cement road and, after several turns, ended at a thatched house. Happy went and sat on the porch. I was rushed inside, where I met a crew of five people: a woman, a baby, an older man, one of the motorbike guys, and, most memorably, a man named Lala.

I knew about *sikerei* at this point. And Lala, I could tell, was a *sikerei*. He seemed to revel in the shaman look. He wore a loincloth along with a T-shirt featuring a grinning Balinese demon— a gift, presumably, from a tourist who passed through. His face, arms, hands, and legs were decorated with a cobweb of tattoos. His ears were pierced. In one earlobe, he wore a small hoop. In the other, he had inserted a half-smoked hand-rolled cigar.

"*Anda sikerei?*" I asked in my bare-bones Indonesian. ("You *sikerei?*") Lala smiled, squinted, and arched his eyebrows. This is a facial expression I have encountered only with the Mentawai, but even then I recognized the mix of confirmation and self-satisfaction.

The conversation shifted to practicalities. I explained as best as I could that I was a student and that I wanted to stay with one of the communities in the island's interior for the next six weeks. I also said I was looking for Rustam. Another American anthropologist, Chris Hammons, had told me to find Rustam, who he said was trustworthy and knew some English. But I was out of luck. They knew Rustam but did not know where to find him. Instead, they said, one of the motor-scooter guys could take me. He would be my cook and porter and would charge 250,000 rupiah—about $20—per day. When I finally found Rustam, I could hire him as well. Both would take me to a region called Attabai, but they would have to accompany me for the entire six weeks. Naturally, they added, I would also have to pay for food, gifts, and accommodations, as well as the cigarettes for both of my guides.

It seemed like a scam, or at least like way more than I needed. I wondered whether Happy had set me up and distrusted him even more. I needed more information. After struggling to negotiate, I declined their offer and paid for the motorbike ride. The sun bore down like punishment as I walked to the port town.

———————

This is book about shamanism. It is a book about the timeless appeal of a particular package of practices and beliefs, and how that appeal challenges assumptions we make about the arc of history and how different societies compare. Before we get to the argument, though, it helps to understand what shamanism is and how I came to study it—which brings us to Siberut.

Siberut is the largest and northernmost island in the Mentawai archipelago. It is a wet, wild place, receiving more than four times as much rain annually as Seattle and nearly eight times as much as London. Lying seventy miles off the west coast of Sumatra, the archipelago is fabled among surfers for its hard-hitting, glassy swells fed by Indian Ocean storms. The waves, some more than a story high, have carved steep cliffs on Siberut's west coast. Boats are not safe there. The east coast, which is what I saw for the first time that morning in 2014, is a checkerboard of coral beaches and spidery mangroves. The hilly interior is carpeted with dense jungle, much of it swampy and crammed with palm trees. Rivers snake through the valleys and empty into the sea.[1]

The seafloor separating the Mentawai archipelago from Sumatra runs nearly a mile deep. With a few possible exceptions, then, the islands have remained detached from the rest of Indonesia for hundreds of thousands of years and perhaps much longer. Visit them, and you will find creatures that live nowhere else, including an owl that's the height of a pencil and five unique primate species, three of which are monogamous.[2]

The Mentawai archipelago is named for its Indigenous inhabitants. Exactly how they came to be called Mentawai is a mystery, although Malay-speaking traders have used the label since the late 1700s. Curiously, the Mentawai lacked many technological innovations of their neighbors. They did not weave, grow rice, work metal, or make pottery. They lacked the political stratification of the west Sumatran kingdoms or even the chiefly villages of the Nias Islanders farther north. Relations were small-scale and egalitarian. People lived in longhouses and hunted with bows and poison-tipped arrows. They raised pigs and chickens and lived on fruits, taro, and the starchy pith of the sago palm. Apart from metal introduced by trading, the main tool-making materials were wood, bamboo, and rattan. By the time I arrived, the agents of global acculturation—in this case, missionaries, Dutch colonialism, the Indonesian state, and the market—had long transformed Mentawai lifeways, although I had heard that, in the archipelago, interior Siberut remained the most buffered.[3]

In the months leading up to my trip, I consulted other anthropologists' descriptions of the Mentawai people. The Swiss-Dutch anthropologist Reimar Schefold first visited Siberut in 1967 and has done more than anyone to document and share Mentawai culture. His legacy lives on in the students he has trained, including Juniator Tulius, who is himself Mentawai.[4]

Schefold was preceded by a handful of scholars and missionaries, among them Edwin Meyer Loeb, who, through his mother Rose, was a scion of the Guggenheim family, one of the world's wealthiest dynasties at the time. Loeb arrived in the Pagai Islands, the southernmost in the archipelago, in 1926 and spent five months there. He had by then conducted fieldwork in California, New Zealand, and the South Pacific island of Niue and had studied initiations and sacrifice around the world. More than Schefold, Loeb saw the Mentawai through a comparative lens—as one of many manifestations of human culture, linked to the rest of the world through both shared history and shared humanity.[5]

This was especially true in his observations of Mentawai *sikerei*. They were healers, uniquely equipped with powers to see and hear spirits. Loeb listed the many ways people seemed to become *sikerei*: sky abductions, spirit dreams, rituals that transformed their eyes. But he also saw the *sikerei* in a larger context. As with specialists everywhere, he observed, *sikerei* healed patients by communing with spirits. From northern Japan to southern Africa, the Andaman Islands to the American Great Plains, specialists acquired supernatural powers that allowed them to interact with the beyond and serve their communities. Sure, the details varied, but even the variation seemed patterned. Some specialists were possessed. Others, like *sikerei*, summoned spirits and spoke to them. A large group sent their souls out from their bodies. "If religion, by definition, be limited to the knowledge of the unseen world," he wrote, "then the shamans and seers, who in all periods have been the main instruments in depicting this department of nature, have been its chief creators." From a curious practice in a wave-battered corner of Indonesia, Loeb saw a pervasive tendency in human culture—perhaps even a glimpse into the origins of religion itself.[6]

I eventually found Rustam. Or rather: he found me. One of the many lessons I learned that first day on Siberut was that word travels fast. When I started asking about him, around eight in the morning, he was in a village upriver. By seven p.m., he had not only heard that a foreigner was looking for him; he had trekked thirteen miles to the port town and found me. Curiously enough, I learned that the people I had met that morning were his in-laws; Lala, the tattooed *sikerei*, was his father.

Rustam is about five feet tall—short, perhaps, by many readers' standards but unexceptional for the Mentawai. He guessed that he was twenty-nine years old when we met, although we later figured out that he was closer to thirty-five or forty. Like most Mentawai people, he has many names. His Mentawai name is "Boroiogok," which translates as "Throw Flower." "Rustam" is his Muslim name. (His Muslim identity is largely nominal. Like almost every Mentawai person I know, he loves pork.) The Mentawai are teknonymous, meaning that people are referred to by the names of their children, typically their firstborn. Rustam's dad is known as Aman Boroiogok, or "Father of Boroiogok." He also goes by Lala. Rustam, meanwhile, prefers the name "Aman Tak Jeujeu," or "Father of Tak Jeujeu."

Understanding Rustam's story requires a brief history lesson. In the 1960s, the Indonesian government decided the Mentawai were a *suku terasing*, an "isolated ethnic group" that had to be absorbed into the Indonesian nation. By the 1970s, the state kicked off a brutal acculturation campaign. Tattooing, teeth sharpening, and other Mentawai practices were prohibited. Longhouses were demolished, and *sikerei* were forbidden from practicing. As a result, traditional culture declined in the Mentawai Islands, although it survived in Siberut's interior, partly because it was so hard to keep officials in the malarial rain forests and partly because several clans fled to ever more remote areas.[7]

Rustam's clan, Sakaliou, briefly settled in a government-built village before returning to their ancestral land in the 1980s. But by rejecting state-enforced modernity, they ironically welcomed other global forces. In their tattoos, loincloths, and longhouses, Sakaliou became a prototype of authentic Mentawai culture. They were also easy to visit. They lived next to a government village and closer to the coast than other clans. It didn't take long for tourists to find them. By the 1990s, Sumatran guides hosted "tribal tours" for foreigners to visit Sakaliou and glimpse a living Stone Age culture.[8]

Rustam, along with other young members of Sakaliou, was hired as a porter and cook. He learned to speak English and eventually solicited tourists on his own at the port. Raised in the forest, he became an ambassador of worlds, a status still visible on his skin. His chest bears four small tattoos in the traditional Mentawai style, in the shapes of a sun, a flower, a water droplet, and a gecko. His back, meanwhile, is covered with an eagle and

a lifelike depiction of a naked woman with globular breasts plea-
suring herself.

When I met Rustam, his success had long faded. Younger
Mentawai people, literate and tech-savvy, now dominated the
tourism scene. Our second day together, we walked the thirteen
miles back to his house. He lived in Madobag, the government
village that Sakaliou had fled so many decades ago. We walked
past the houses of his cousin and his nephew, each built with lavish incomes from tourists, and arrived at his place, a one-room
shack with a crumbling porch and a small kitchen attached to the
back. While his wife brought me pork and spongy bread made of
sago-palm flour, I saw holes in the thatch roof. They had tried to
patch them with leaves and tarp, but rain inevitably got through,
decaying the floorboards at our feet. He brought out a tin-can
oil lantern, lit it, and introduced me to his talkative son Deni, his
quieter older daughter Tak Jeujeu, and his newborn Rangga.

Even now, I feel like a child with the Mentawai—slow in the
forest, uncertain with a machete. But there have been few periods in my life when I remember feeling as awkward or helpless
as I did those first days in 2014. The morning after we arrived
in Madobag, I awoke to the sounds of people speaking in Mentawai, a language that, to my uninformed ears, seemed a blend of
Chinese and breathy Italian. I felt then, as I felt so many times
afterward, that learning the language would be impossible.

Those first days were also filled with cultural misunder-
standings, one of which sticks out especially. Seeing that older
men and younger shamans went shirtless and wore loincloths, I
decided to wear only underpants. The rain forest is hot, after all,
and I wanted to be comfortable. I emerged from Rustam's shack
and greeted his visitors, including Lala, who had followed us up.
They looked at me with a kind of intrigued amusement, like I was
a dog behaving in a weird but not necessarily threatening way.
Rustam pulled me to the side. He told me to fish out cigarettes
for the guests—and then he asked why I was not wearing pants.
After I explained my reasoning, he said that Mentawai men either
wear loincloths (which, I swear, are far more revealing than the
boxers I was wearing) or Western-style garments, like shorts or
swim trunks. I am not sure which of us was more confused.

Rustam and I decided that I would spend six weeks in Attabai, a several-hour hike from his house in Madobag, but he said we needed time to prepare. So I spent time with his family, who gave me my two most enduring Mentawai names: "Sibulungungu," which translates to something like "Bearded One," and "Bakla Bilou," or "Gibbon Chin." Both reflect the fact that my beard and mustache are anomalies in Mentawai—orders of magnitude longer and denser than anything the average Mentawai man is capable of growing. The names ended up being helpful because they were answers to the question, "What is your name?" (*Kasei onim?*) that made people laugh and established a human connection, which is something one desperately craves when deprived of language and basic abilities.

One of the first activities I joined was collecting durians, the spiky, football-sized fruits infamous for smelling like a mixture of uncooked fish and sweet but raunchy French cheese. I put on worn-out Adidas sneakers, the only shoes I brought that summer, and followed his relatives into the jungle. A tangle of paths zigzagged through the rain forest. Logs served as platforms over the swampy mush. While I struggled to balance on them, the others scampered across with ease. "*Moile, moile,*" they said—"Slowly, slowly"—whenever I slipped and landed a foot in soggy mud. We eventually came to what looked like a cliff and climbed it using ledges smoothed out by countless feet. At the top was an enormous durian tree. At its base were a husband and wife.

As with Lala, I knew immediately that the man was a *sikerei*. He wore nothing but a loincloth and beaded necklaces. He had long hair. He had the face of a fifty-year-old but the physique of a marathon runner in his prime. His body was adorned with the tattoos typical of *sikerei* and older men in this part of Siberut. Ladders of parallel lines climbed his quadriceps. Four lines extended from each shoulder; two arced under the collarbones and joined somewhere around the Adam's apple; the other two swept across his pectorals. His upper arms were bedecked with what looked like swaying vines. A line followed his spinal cord, running from the bottom of his back to the base of his neck. It was crossed by another, which ran from one shoulder blade to the other. Dots decorated the point of intersection. An intricate checkerboard of swirls and streaks enveloped his hands like gloves. On his face, plain lines traced the hollows of his cheeks. The overall impression was of a minimalist skeleton sketched upon the skin—a reduction of the human form into dots, rays, and loops. Beyond this standard set, the *sikerei* had another design that is otherwise uncommon: a small trident-like shape on his forehead. His name, I learned, was Salomo, and he was Rustam's grandfather's youngest brother.

Salomo also goes by "Teu Jala Mati," "Jala Mati" being one of his sons and "Teu" being a term of respect that is used, among other contexts, when referring to someone who recently lost a child. He introduced his wife, who was also called Teu Jala Mati. Like a dwindling proportion of Mentawai people, her incisors had been sharpened into canine-like V's. She, too, was shirtless, revealing a distinct set of tattoos.

That interaction left a lasting impression. The Mentawai are viciously egalitarian, at least among people of the same sex. It is not unusual to see a youngster teasing an older man about his penis. (They are also refreshingly crude.) Yet the two Teu Jala Matis were clearly respected. They had a kind of social gravity, as if the fabric of reality bent toward them. I introduced myself to many people that morning, yet my conversation with them was special; I felt people's eyes on us—a palpable interest in the interaction between outsider and *sikerei*.

It took Rustam and me longer than anticipated to get to Attabai. The trek lasts only a couple of hours, but we failed on our first attempt. My body, unaccustomed to both the hilly terrain and the tropical climate, sweated profusely, and I guzzled all our water within the first hour of our hike. That didn't matter for Rustam, but I had to turn back. We set out again the next day. We brought four liters this time, but they ended up being unnecessary. It rained so heavily that I barely drank what we brought. By the time we arrived at the longhouse in Attabai, I felt overwhelmed. My belongings were drenched. My feet were soggy. I was covered in mud from slipping so many times. And here we finally were. Disappointment bubbled up. I had expected a vibrant community—houses, laughter, curiosity, pointing—but we stood before a single longhouse. Pigs nibbled on the pith of sago palms. Inside, a mother catered to her four children. A couple hours later, the father, a *sikerei*, came home. No one seemed to know Indonesian, let alone English. Over the next twenty-four hours, not a single person came by, except for the *sikerei*'s brother.

Everything felt deeply lonely. Although I couldn't admit it to myself, I was scared of spending six weeks there, alone, without Rustam. I told myself that research here would be impossible. The vision I had been chasing—a traditional-living community in the forest—was misguided. Perhaps it was real once, I said to myself, but tourism and the state had reconfigured the island: anything traditional was dead; everyone was modernized; everyone had clothes; a man who walks around in his boxers is a fool. Yes, there were scattered shamans. And yes, there was a longhouse like this one. But they were fragments, memories, the fragile, solitary, disconnected remnants of a transformed world, kept alive by fear and tourist dollars, and anything that I had hoped to study here—law, religion, taboo—would be impossible.

After a day or two more in the longhouse, I told Rustam that I wanted to leave—not just Attabai, but Siberut altogether. So he made an excuse and bought a chicken. The *sikerei* held the clueless bird near me while chanting a mantra, then broke its neck. Rustam singed its feathers off, butchered it, and handed it to the shaman's wife, who cooked it. We ate together, and I noticed I was starting to get the hang of things. I hungrily devoured the different chicken parts—skin, intestine, whatever—and dipped sticks of cooked sago flour into a coconut shell filled with communal chicken broth. Every couple of bites, I looked around and said, "*Mukop ita*" ("We eat").

When we were finished, the *sikerei* performed what felt like a ghost song. He began with a heady vibrato, shifting occasionally to a high, mournful falsetto that evoked a benevolent but broken older woman. Other times, he swung into a deeper chest voice, his tone becoming more commanding, although he always came back to that heady vibrato, his voice quivering on long vowels like a tense string about to snap. The performance seemed supplicating yet alien, like he was calling to a past self or even to a deep emotion. When he finished, Rustam explained that the song was for summoning souls who had been offended. I understood.

That performance was my first exposure to the experientially powerful world of the *sikerei*. It suggested a lush, mystical realm to explore, and I briefly wondered whether my decision to leave was the wrong one. But I had made up my mind. The next morning, Rustam and I retraced our steps: we hiked back to Madobag and, after a night or two there, walked back to the port town. We shared a room at a hotel. I gave Rustam my phone, a Nokia I bought in Malaysia, and boarded the ferry. On the morning of July 4, after two weeks on the island, I left Siberut.

What is shamanism? Decades before my first trip to Siberut, another scholar was pondering this question. Indeed, he had read Loeb's work on the similarities between Mentawai *sikerei* and practitioners in other societies, although he would build on Loeb's proposal in a way that no other writer had.

That scholar, Mircea Eliade, himself had a shamanic air. Born in Romania in 1907, he was, according to one writer, "breast-fed by a gypsy woman." One of his earliest memories was of staring into the eyes of a turquoise lizard. "Both of us were dumbfounded," he later recalled. He claimed to sleep four hours a day and to have eaten soap, toothpaste, and caterpillars to encourage "absolute freedom." By eighteen, he had written more than a hundred articles. At twenty-one, he left for India for three years. He studied Sanskrit for twelve hours a day and ended up living as a yogi in a cave near Rishikesh. At thirty, he had published, depending on whom you ask, either twelve or seventeen books, including a monograph on yoga and a novel about his love affair with the Indian poet Maitreyi Devi.[9]

Although he considered fiction to be his master craft, Eliade is known outside Romania mostly for his work on comparative religion, including on shamanism. Anticipating the rise of the

Romanian communist regime, he moved to Paris in 1945 in a self-imposed exile. It was there, between 1946 and 1951, that he wrote *Le Chamanisme et les Techniques Archaïques de l'Extase*, later published in English as *Shamanism: Archaic Techniques of Ecstasy*.[10]

Eliade began his book with two premises—that shamanism is widespread and that its quintessential forms appeared in Siberia. From there, he set out what he believed to be the practice's defining features. The most important was soul journeying. For Eliade, not all traditions involving altered states were shamanic. A medium who is possessed by an ancestor? Not a shaman, in his eyes. Someone who consumes medicines and then sees spirits in an ecstatic state? Not a shaman, either. Rather, Eliade wrote, the true shaman "specializes in a trance during which his soul is believed to leave his body and ascend to the sky or descend to the underworld."[11]

Although he treated soul journeying as definitive, Eliade proposed other common features of shamanism, including flight, mastery over fire, mastery over spirits, and death-and-rebirth initiations. He described a shamanic cosmology consisting of three realms: the sky, the earth, and the underworld. The realms, he said, connect via a central axis, often a world tree or sacred mountain, which runs through holes or openings. Gods and the souls of shamans travel through those holes in skyward and subterranean journeys.

Eliade's claims guided decades of work on shamanism. They also seeped into the mainstream, shaping neo-shamanic practices.[12] Yet scholarly scrutiny has since identified numerous flaws. Take his focus on soul journeying. If we follow Eliade, we are forced to exclude many traditions often deemed shamanic. Korean shamanism centers on possession, not soul journeying. So do many practices throughout sub-Saharan Africa.[13]

More inconvenient for Eliade, Siberian practitioners used many techniques to communicate with the beyond—not just soul journeying. The Finnish folklorist Anna-Leena Siikala found that peoples in different parts of Siberia preferred different techniques. In the northwest, soul journeying was popular. In central and eastern Siberia, specialists favored spirit possession. At the opposite extremes of Siberia, among the Chukchee near the Bering Strait and the Turkic groups near central Asia, healers and diviners summoned spirit beings and spoke to them. Even this grouping clouds more interesting variation. An Evenk practitioner, for example, used all three in a single session—he was possessed by spirits, then he ejected them and talked to them, and then his soul flew off.[14] An Eliade fan might fire back that Evenks did not have true shamans. But it is the Evenks, a Tungusic people, from whom the word "shaman" originated in the first place.[15]

Other elements of Eliade's shamanic prototype have the same problems: they vary not just across regions but within Siberia itself. A telling example is the structure of the universe. Eliade stressed a three-tiered scheme, but Siberian cosmologies were far more wide-ranging and imaginative. According to the English folklorist Ronald Hutton, the Chukchee believed in a stack of nine worlds. Some Altai tribes imagined seven or nine levels in the heavens alone; others described the world as a disc on the back of a great fish. Hutton concluded that Eliade "highlighted material which supported his arguments, and disposed of the rest," with the result that "an ideal type" was imposed on "a very diverse and complex set of phenomena."[16]

Even so, Eliade's contribution shouldn't be trivialized. He showed that shamanism was pervasive—that spiritual practices found in Siberia resemble those in places as far-flung as Tibet, Australia, the Americas, and Indonesia. And although he overstated parallels, he nevertheless demonstrated that specialists from distant societies settle on stunningly similar techniques, like death-and-rebirth rituals.

Following Eliade, anthropologists have tried to be more systematic when studying shamanism's ubiquity. As a PhD student in the mid-1980s, for example, Michael Winkelman read more than a hundred books and articles covering forty-seven diverse nonindustrial societies. Although he looked at a relatively small number of societies, he designed the sample to cover human geographic and cultural diversity, allowing him to generalize his findings to all nonindustrial societies. For each specialist class he found, like Zuni priests or Shuar shamans, he recorded 260 variables, including whether the specialist massaged clients, ingested drugs, and oversaw funerals.[17]

Winkelman published his database nearly forty years ago, yet it remains one of the richest cross-cultural resources on shamans and other religious specialists. We will revisit it throughout this book, but for now, the important point is that he found trance practitioners in nearly all the societies—forty-three of the forty-seven—that he surveyed. Recent research corroborates his findings. In 2016, a team led by Hervey Peoples (who has the perfect surname for an anthropologist) recorded shamanism among twenty-six of thirty-three hunter-gatherer groups. I looked at the seven that presumably lack it. Three, it seems, have had shamans. Of the remaining four, the members of one society, the Mbuti of central Africa, visited "the local witch doctor" of nearby farmers. Reports about another, the Tiwi, lack descriptions of shamans, although anthropologists did mention that some "clever men" could foretell the future while others figured out who used magical poisons. Finding a society without trance practitioners is harder than it seems.[18]

———————

In the decades since Eliade's book, people have bickered over exactly what shamanism is. They agree that there are curious similarities across societies but struggle to draw boundaries. Does shamanism require healing? Possession? A hunting and gathering economy? A three-part universe? Many definitions end up omitting traditions that seem shamanic and have been studied as such, including those in Siberia. At the same time, each new proposal carries the risk of repeating Eliade's mistake—that is, of distorting cultural practices to fit our expectations.[19]

Given those challenges, some experts have converged on inclusive yet precise definitions. Most of them go something like this: *A shaman is a specialist who, through non-ordinary states, engages with unseen realities and provides services like healing and divination.*[20] This is the definition I prefer and that I will use throughout this book. It consists of three important parts:

A "non-ordinary" or "altered" state—also described as "trance" or "ecstasy"—is any state that looks distinct from normal waking functioning. Hypnotic stillness. Drug-induced raving. Quaking and dissociation after hours of dancing. All these qualify as non-ordinary.

"Engaging with an unseen reality" means interacting with agents that are invisible or work through invisible means. As with non-ordinary states, these can be stunningly diverse. Some Zande witch doctors saw trails of witchcraft floating like untethered candlelight. Nepali *bombo* extracted ghosts from people's bodies and threw them far away. Other shamans have battled witches in spiritual combat, become possessed by salty ancestors, and gone on soul journeys to commune with gods.[21]

A "service" is an act performed for someone else's benefit. Aside from healing and divination, popular shamanic services include changing the weather, improving harvests, boosting business success, and raining down afflictions on one's enemies.

Not everyone is comfortable with this definition. Some specialists urge that we restrict shamanism to Siberian practices.[22] At first, this choice seems to vibe with history. The word "shaman" comes from northern Asia. It first appeared in print in 1672, in the memoirs of a Russian clergyman, and entered central and western Europe two decades later through the writings of several Dutchmen. Yet the decision isn't so straightforward. For one, Siberia is a diverse place, filled with many language families, most of which did not use the term. For some Turkic-speaking peoples, the corresponding word was *kam;* for Samoyedic speakers, *tadibei;* for the Buryats, *bö.*[23]

Beyond that, limiting "shaman" to its seventeenth-century usage ignores its history before then or the changes since. The word may actually derive from the Sanskrit *sramana,* having arrived in central Asia via Chinese or Tocharian Buddhists, who used it to mean "monk." Meanwhile, "shaman" has expanded in the last century to the point that many people use it to refer to specialists worldwide. To insist on its usage in the 1670s is to treat that snapshot as the only authentic moment, rather than as one point during an ongoing conceptual evolution.[24]

A related approach is to reject the terms "shaman" and "shamanism" altogether. Critics warn that, by using the same word for wildly different contexts, we invite people to project a simplified picture onto the diverse expressions of human spirituality and politics.[25] This is fair and seems partly a hangover from Eliade's mistake. But it doesn't mean that patterns do not exist, and it shouldn't doom cross-cultural comparisons. The same criticism can be leveled at terms like "myth," "music," "justice," "religion," "marriage," "property"—in fact, any aspect of our social and cultural lives that pops up often and matters. An awareness of our preconceptions urges us to study humanity carefully and thoughtfully, not to eschew comparison.

———————

None of this was on my mind when I first came to Indonesia. I had just finished the first year of a PhD at Harvard and was concerned mostly with deciding whether Siberut was the kind of place I could return to for longer-term fieldwork. Back on Sumatra, then, I tried to go through my options.

I started by writing an email to five "experts on Mentawai." I am still ashamed of the message—in fact, I hadn't read it for years before writing this chapter—but it honestly reflects what I expected. After barely any time in Siberut, I laid out my impressions of how things worked. Most people lived in government settlement villages. Some families, chiefly those of *sikerei*, still lived in the forest, but they were "lone satellites of settled, quickly modernizing communities." I wrote that "my hope in visiting Mentawai was originally to find entire communities that continued to live quite traditionally in the forest, that self-governed and had their own religion that related to how people should behave. I didn't really find that in Sarareiket."

I didn't appreciate how delusional—or offensive—my expectations were until I got a response from Tulius, the anthropologist of Mentawai ancestry. Tulius is fluent in Dutch and Indonesian, in addition to the Mentawai language, but he chose to respond in English to make sure I understood. "We are living in 21st century and still in the same globe," he wrote. I needed to look beyond the documentaries and coffee-table books that show the Mentawai as untouched rain-forest people. "If you are looking something totally isolated and pure traditional Mentawaians, you are not going to find them because they are not living museum. They are human being who want to change and adjust their life to what they assume or perceive suitable to them."

I spent six days in Sumatra. I emailed an anthropologist who works in the Bolivian Amazon asking if I could join him for the summer. He said no. I thought about going to the tribal belt in India. I even considered visiting the Amish, the plain-clothed Anabaptists who live scattered throughout the midwestern United States. But too much of the summer had already passed; no one could accommodate me in time.

I also thought about my decision to leave Siberut. I told myself and my mentors that a research project there would be impossible, that acculturation had been inescapable and totalizing. But there was clearly more involved in my departure. Research had been hard. I was, by all approximations, a nerdy kid from suburban New Jersey, unaccustomed to leeches, moldy belongings, and wounds that never heal. After nearly a week in Sumatra, I realized that I had conflated the possibility of doing research with my personal discomfort. I wondered whether fear, and not reason, had guided my decision. "i logically believe that i can't do a project here," I wrote to my friend Feini on July 10. "but i can also acknowledge that my organism freaked out in that second, and i can't fully trust myself."

It was hard, but I knew what I needed to do. Eight hours after I sent that email, I boarded a ferry. I was heading back to the Mentawai Islands.

It wasn't long before I found Rustam again. We scrapped the old plan. I would not live with a single family. Instead, we would travel up and down the Rereiket River, visiting as many longhouses as we could. I told him that I had three goals, aside from seeing more of southern Siberut. The first was to study *keikei*, or taboo-like prohibitions. This was actually my research interest at the time—what better way to understand a society's workings, I thought, than to study what it forbids. Second, I would learn as much as possible of the Mentawai language. If I ended up coming back to do research, this would be the best investment of my time: a necessary tool for studying Mentawai culture as well as a medium for forging social connection. Finally, I wanted to live with *sikerei*.

So, we adventured. We headed to Rustam's clan's ancestral land, an area once choked with tourists. We stopped by his father's abandoned longhouse, then trekked a short distance to visit one of his grandfather's brothers, a cheery older *sikerei* named Tarason. In typical *sikerei* fashion, Tarason wore a loincloth and beaded jewelry, as well as a metal wristwatch. His skin was completely tattooed. This included his feet, which are the final parts of the body to be inked and indicate a person's advanced age.

In the evening, after Tarason fed his numerous pigs and Rustam cooked the rice and noodles we brought, we lit a kerosene lamp and talked. I wanted to discuss *keikei* and Tarason's initiation as a *sikerei*, but the conversation meandered. Tarason recalled the many tourists who used to come through, pointing to laminated photos showing bohemian white people posing next to him. While I pushed for a semi-structured interview, he preferred a more mythical discourse, explaining how the four major groups as he saw them—the Mentawai, the Arabs, the Sumatrans, and the Europeans—ultimately descended from a single common ancestor named Pagetasabbau. (I don't remember where I, of South Asian ancestry, fit in.)

Rustam and I left after a breakfast of bananas and sago. From there, we went farther and farther up the Rereiket River, replenishing our supply of gifts at stores in government villages. We developed a routine: arrive at a longhouse; pull out tea, coffee, sugar, and cookies; pass time until dinner; prepare noodles and rice; eat with the family; talk with the *sikerei*; sleep. As this was durian season, some of our days were spent following people to large trees and picnicking on the smelly fruit. Each night, I tried to guide the discussion toward *keikei* and *sikerei*. But conversation is like a child—no matter how much you try to shape it, it will decide its own fate—and each night, we ended at unexpected places. People told me about the spirits and souls they saw, about the violent campaigns past governments had waged on Mentawai culture, about the disturbing images newly printed on cigarette cartons, about how the water spirit had punished foreigners who refused to share, about the strange contrast between Mentawai *keikei*—which, they said, truly protected people from harm—and the Islamic prohibition on pork, which they saw as pointless.

I glimpsed many healing ceremonies with Rustam, but always in passing and from a distance. I saw turmeric-coated *sikerei* decked out in leaves and beads. I heard the dissonant clanging of bells and the hellish squeals of sacrificed pigs. I even watched kids imitating *sikerei*, dancing on loosened floorboards and singing shaman songs in prepubescent tones.

We eventually stayed with a family living at the headwaters of the Rereiket River, beyond the reach of tourists. The forests here were so empty of human settlement that gibbons still inhabited them, and we awoke to the apes' sunrise songs. Yet I knew there was more to see. Siberut has around eleven major rivers; Rereiket was just one—and the one most popular among tourists. So Rustam handed me off to his friend Martinus, who knew no English and hailed from another river valley farther north. Martinus and I took a boat up Siberut's east coast, to the mouth of the Saibi River. From there, we rode motorbikes and a canoe as far as they could take us, then tramped through the rain forest carrying gasoline to his home village near the Simatalu River. Like Rustam, Martinus walked fast through river and jungle. But he had little interaction with foreigners, and trailing behind him, I remember constantly yelling *"Ale!"* (Dude!), afraid that he would make a quick turn and leave me in a morass of green. We spent two nights with his family, then took a motor-powered dugout to a more remote longhouse.

Those first two months in Siberut were hard. I felt hot, tired, teased, beseeched, bored, and clumsy. I capsized a canoe and had to swim to shore. I fell off two motorbikes. I left the island with athlete's foot and two infected wounds. But it was also eye-opening. It turned out that I was right, to some degree. No part of the island was untouched by modernity. There was no strict line separating government settlement villages and jungle longhouses; *sikerei* who kept to the forest had houses next to schools and clinics, as well. They wanted their children to learn to read and write, to get jobs that would provide them with soap and clothing and chain saws. But I was also very wrong. The search for a pristine jungle tribe was not only delusional, it was unnecessary. No cultural tradition is stagnant; everything, even the most ostensibly "traditional" element, is a moment in a living, evolving dynamism. Culture lives. It adapts. This was true for the *sikerei*. Much of what passed as authentic elements of Mentawai shamanism—their handbells, dancing skirts, and beaded necklaces—had entered Siberut through trade with outsiders.

I came away entranced by more than the history of the *sikerei*, however. Throughout that summer, I searched for the best analog. Were they like doctors? Priests? By the end, I saw that they were much more. *Sikerei* lay at the nexus of so much of society—of law, medicine, politics, ritual, entertainment. They were treated as different from normal humans, and they embraced their special status, decorating themselves in the most beautiful designs and accessories they could find.

I didn't realize it then, but those *sikerei*—and the worldwide phenomenon they embodied—would possess me for years. I would come to know Siberut intimately and would devote years to studying shamanism and witchcraft. And I would become fixated on a simple but foundational question: *Why?* What fates this remarkable practice to emerge so often when we lanky primates get together, from the Mentawai Islands to the Siberian taiga? The best way to start answering this question, I eventually concluded, is with human psychology.

CHAPTER 2

The Mind Behind the Magic

I have complicated feelings about fieldwork. I enjoy it. People seem to like me, and it often feels like an adventure. I have never regretted going on a trip. Yet in the mornings, when I am waking up, and at night, as I fall asleep, I sometimes feel what I call the Longing. It takes time to settle in, but after a few weeks, quiet hours can be filled with an all-consuming, almost painful desperation to go home. I know exactly how many days are left—five, twelve, thirty, whatever—and count that many days backward to get a sense of how much longer until my departure ("Twenty days ago, I fell off that motorbike; okay, so twenty days isn't so far off").

After that first summer, I spent another two months in Indonesia in 2015 before returning for a much longer trip in 2017. I made it my goal to subdue the Longing. I would exercise every day. I would have more control over my diet. I would leave Siberut to visit Sumatra once a month. The biggest change, however, would involve where I lived. During my first two summers, I had always stayed with families, either for brief stints (summer 1) or for longer stretches (summer 2). This gave me intimate glimpses into people's lives, but for someone accustomed to personal privacy, it was exhausting. My only time alone had been while pooping. This time around, I would have more autonomy. With one or two research assistants, I would live in a small house.

I got to Siberut on April 11, after which it took more than a month to organize and construct the house. In the meantime, I began attending healing ceremonies. With Rustam and some local *sikerei*, I came up with a plan. The ceremonies, called *pabetei*, are normally off-limits to nonrelatives, but as a curious foreigner, I was in a strange category. The deal we agreed to was as follows: If a family and the *sikerei* were comfortable with me joining, I would bring refreshments (tea, coffee, sugar, cookies) and provide the family and *sikerei* with "tobacco money" (a euphemism for paying them cash). In return, I would be able to observe, record, and interview; the family would also share any meat from sacrificed animals with me and my research assistants.

I attended my first healing ceremony early in May, but it is the second one that has stuck with me. I had never seen someone so close to death. In an email to my friend Sandeep, then a medical resident in the United States, I described his condition.

"There's a kid here who has yellow skin and a cough and is skeletal-skinny," I wrote. "He looks like he's gonna die. He's been sick for a month. Do you have any sense of what this might be?"

I was emailing from a middle school, some two hours from where we were building my house. I had just watched five *sikerei* treat the boy in a seven-hour healing ceremony. He was sick, they suspected, because someone in the clan hadn't shared meat. Angered by the stinginess, the crocodile spirit, Sikameinan, had presumably snuck into the clan's longhouse and settled on the shelf above the kitchen fire. It radiated its sickness-causing energy, sapping the boy of strength and turning him jaundice yellow. At night, it was said to climb on top of him, the weight of this invisible river god suffocating the tiny boy, explaining why he had so much trouble breathing and sleeping.[1]

This was bad, but the *sikerei* could treat it. After the boy's father sacrificed a pig and two chickens, they put out items to attract Sikameinan: fabric, a fishing net, a beaded headband, a small piece of meat. They acknowledged that someone did not share but promised the spirit that this was accidental. They sang an eerie, spectral song, inviting Sikameinan into a small bowl of water. I imagined it, this shape-shifting crocodilian, flitting down into the basin like a genie swirling into a lantern.

The *sikerei* picked up the bowl and carried it to the river, careful not to let water spill lest Sikameinan escape. When they returned, we ate together, and the family asked everyone to recite a Christian prayer. Afterward, the shamans left with the best pieces of meat.

When the *sikerei* lured Sikameinan into the water, they partook in a pervasive human activity: engaging with the supernatural to control life's uncertainties. Such engagement is at the core of shamanism wherever it occurs. Shamans are believed to summon souls, channel ancestors, and struggle against witches. They call upon spirit familiars who travel across time and space. They leave their bodies to journey to heaven or hell, to barter with gods over the fates of their communities. Yet such appeals also transcend shamanism. In *The Promise of Salvation* (2010), the sociologist Martin Riesebrodt argues that supernatural appeals define religion. Look across the world's religious traditions, from Daoism to Hinduism to Christianity, and the golden thread linking them is engagement with the beyond. We want blessings, salvation, and to overcome misfortune. In fighting and pleading with supernatural forces to get them, we create religion.[2]

To understand shamanism, then, we need to begin with supernatural engagement. Why do we believe in supernatural forces? Why do we try to engage with them? And why does such engagement so often center on life's uncertainties? Pursuing such questions will carry us far beyond shamanism, to the origins of religion itself.

On September 29, 2009, two large earthquakes struck the Tonga Trench in the South Pacific, launching walls of water four stories high. "The wave, it reached the sky," remembered one Samoan. "Oh my god. We ran. We thought we would die."[3]

Samoa was demolished. Like enraged leviathans unleashed onto some unwitting country, the waves flattened shores indiscriminately. Dozens of villages were wiped out. Some three thousand people were left homeless. Beach resorts were crushed, and the eastern part of the country's main island was left without power. At least 149 Samoans died in the tsunami, many of them kids. "God gave me the most beautiful children," said a Samoan woman to Australian reporters. "And now he took them back."[4]

As locals struggled to make sense of the destruction, the Norwegian anthropologist Sanne Holmgaard noticed two main explanations develop. The first was that God had sent the waves as punishment. Popular in more traditional churches, this narrative blamed sinful Sabbath breakers. An elderly woman explained:

> They come over here on Sunday and have an entertainment, a barbecue, a band making lots of noises without singing a hymn from God. But they are Samoans! They know God, they know Sunday, this is the one day for them to go to church, but they take Sundays to entertain themselves over here. That's why I say, it's a punishment for those people.[5]

The second explanation prevailed in newer, less hierarchical churches. Here, the tsunami was considered a warning of the Second Coming of Christ—one of many signs, along with earthquakes, global warming, and violence in faraway places, urging people to turn to God before it's too late. A Samoan missionary described an ecstatic thrill at seeing the tsunami: "I saw everything shaking, it was so powerful, and I raised my hands and yelled 'praise God! The Lord is coming and I'm ready to be united!'"[6]

These reactions illustrate an important human tendency: we attribute unpredictable events to agents. We come down with a cough; our house burns down; a tsunami devastates our communities—and the first questions are *Who did it?* and *How?* Sometimes we point at doctors, immigrants, or the government. But just as often, we suspect the supernatural.

Such supernatural finger-pointing has been going on as long as humans have kept records. When Athens was beset with plague three years into the Peloponnesian War, its citizens couldn't help but wonder whether the gods had sided with Sparta.[7] After Mount Vesuvius exploded with the thermal energy of one hundred thousand World War II–era atomic bombs, destroying the ancient cities of Pompeii and Herculaneum and producing a hellish heat capable of turning brains into glass, the Roman Jewish writer Josephus suspected that God was punishing the emperor Titus for sacking Jerusalem.[8] Even today, people argue that Pompeii's destruction was divine retribution. Reviewing the raunchy art, phallic figurines, and many brothels discovered in Pompeii's ruins, a writer for the Armstrong Institute of Biblical Archaeology concluded, "Small wonder, then, that the area suffered the same fate as Sodom and Gomorrah."[9]

Of course, people turn to the supernatural to explain more than just devastation. The Siberian Chukchee said that spirits were responsible for mushroom-induced hallucinations. The Mbuti of the Ituri Forest in central Africa considered dreams, goose bumps, and confusion the work of Toré, the lord of the forest. And peoples in many societies have seen spirits in stars, rainbows, and other cosmic phenomena.[10]

Still, supernatural explanations gravitate toward unexpected events, especially misfortunes like illness. When the anthropologist George Murdock studied 139 societies around the world, from the Babylonians to Tanzanian hunter-gatherers, he found that all of them believed that some illnesses were caused by supernatural forces. Many cultures pointed to lost souls and broken taboos, yet the most common belief, which popped up in all but two societies, was "spirit aggression"—the idea that maladies are caused by invisible agents. The heavenly father smites you for partying. A ghost slips inside you and devours your organs. The crocodile god crawls into your house and suffocates you because Cousin Billy hogged all the pork.[11]

Just as people suspect gods and spirits, they also blame one another for misfortune. Often, this means seeing adversity through the lens of witchcraft. Rivals are accused of using evil spells. In-laws are suspected of spreading illness through envious stares. The misshapen pariah is charged with transforming into a snake and striking the schoolboy who laughed at him. During my PhD, I read through anthropological reports of sixty diverse societies to identify the misfortunes people connect to witchcraft. The most common ones were as you'd expect: death, illness, disasters, economic trouble. The full list, meanwhile, was a lengthy catalog of hard-to-explain annoyances: bald spots, bad dreams, broken stools, falling while playing basketball, one's spouse suddenly become sulky and unresponsive. We have a predisposition for localized paranoia, spotting agency in seas of randomness.[12]

Stepping back, it seems that the bigger, badder, and more uncertain an event—epitomized in sickness, death, and catastrophe—the riper it is for supernatural thinking. Why is this the case?

A common answer is that supernatural beliefs are intuitive. We can't help but latch on to them given quirks of our psychology. This is a leading explanation of religiosity, at least in more scientific circles, and cognitive scientists have proposed laundry lists of psychological ingredients supposed to underlie our beliefs in the beyond. We remember and pay attention to categorical anomalies. We instinctively think of minds as separate from bodies. We use unfalsifiable statements to signal group identity.[13]

The cognitive quirk most often discussed is agency detection. Humans are social organisms, the idea goes, so natural selection has equipped us with mental machinery for spotting other minds. Like an overly sensitive smoke detector, however, this machinery goes off at the slightest hint of a signal, leading us to hallucinate agency everywhere. We notice faces in the clouds and emotions in the weather. We get annoyed at our computers and impute richer inner lives to squirrels. We have, as one psychologist put it, a "hyperactive agency detection device," and beliefs in gods, ghosts, and other disembodied minds emerge as incidental by-products.[14]

Intuitionist explanations like these are elegant. They provide naturalistic explanations for religious beliefs without pushing patronizing pictures of religious people as delusional or irrational. Yet they run into some hurdles. The biggest, the anthropologist Tanya Luhrmann told me, is that believing can be hard.

Luhrmann grew up steeped in the puzzles of belief. Her maternal grandparents were Baptist missionaries in what is now Myanmar. Her paternal grandparents were Christian Scientists. Both her parents rebelled, yet neither gave up on religion, and as a child, she attended a Unitarian church. She spent years growing up in an Orthodox Jewish neighborhood in New Jersey and often served as the Shabbas goy, a non-Jew tasked with performing jobs prohibited by Jewish law during the Sabbath. "I could tell that all these smart, good people had very different understandings of what was real," she once said, reflecting on her upbringing. "And that really grabbed me."[15]

Luhrmann's fascination with subjective reality led her to study self-identified witches, American psychiatry, and people who conjure up imaginary beings.[16] Between 2003 and 2012, she focused on charismatic Christianity, attending churches first in Chicago and later in the San Francisco Bay Area. She began her research trying to understand how evangelical Christians experience God. But after a while, she noticed something surprising. "These Christians—they believed in God," she told me. "But they didn't believe in God as earnestly or as much or as deeply as they wanted to."

Luhrmann watched as Christians constantly expressed frustration at their lack of faith. They confessed to forgetting about God between Sunday services. They admitted to prioritizing other activities over prayer. They came home from a church service, yelled at their kids, and felt like fools for forgetting to be like Jesus. She once saw a man weep in front of a congregation. "When I lost my job, I didn't trust that God was going to help me, even though I know that God can do everything," she remembers him saying.[17]

Luhrmann's observations look like a hitch for intuitionist explanations. They suggest that religious ideas are not as sticky as they first appear, that they need something else to become ingrained in human minds. Yet do the experiences of charismatic Christians generalize to humanity more broadly? The Christians Luhrmann worked with may be devoted, but they are still surrounded by a skeptical, rationalist, Enlightenment culture. They live in a society rocked by atheism and the Scientific Revolution—one in which books like *The God Delusion* and *God Is Not Great* have become airport bestsellers. Presumably, if we looked at non-literate societies without Enlightenment views, we would find much less doubt. Right?

Many anthropologists have thought so. Or at least they've written sentences like this:

> God's existence is taken for granted by everybody. (Evans-Pritchard, on the Nuer of East Africa)[18]

> I think the Ifugao's religious attitude is simply a traditional acceptance—that is to say, the firmest and toughest kind of attitude. (Barton, on the Ifugao of the Philippines)[19]

> The Mundurucú believe that the rains are their children and that atmospheric disturbances are the results of their activities. (Murphy, on the Mundurukú of the Amazon River basin)[20]

But declarative statements like these hide pockets of skepticism. Read through reports of the world's societies, and you find much more doubt. A great demonstration was by the cultural anthropologist Melford Spiro, who visited a small Burmese village in the early 1960s. As part of his research, Spiro studied local spirits called *nats*. At first glance, everyone in the village seemed to believe in the spirits. Of the people he interviewed, all but one performed rituals to appease them. Yet after a bit of digging, he found more uncertainty. Two people denied that *nats* existed, a larger group doubted that they could harm good people, and an even larger proportion said that *nats* were incapable of doing good. What appeared to be unquestioning belief was layered upon flickers of skepticism.[21]

Then there are children. Proponents of intuitionist explanations often treat children as avid believers in the supernatural. This was the thesis of the book *Born Believers* (2012) by the psychologist Justin Barrett.[22] Richard Dawkins made a similar point in his book *Outgrowing God* (2019). As he put it:

> Natural selection simply builds into the child brain the rule "Believe whatever your parents tell you." And that rule will come into force even when "what your parents tell you" is actually silly or untrue.[23]

Snappy. Yet it doesn't fully line up with the research. In 2006, the psychologist Cristine Legare interviewed rural Sesotho speakers in South Africa about why hypothetical individuals got sick. Everyone, regardless of age, endorsed biological explanations, like that the illness was contagiously transmitted. Yet while adults unanimously entertained supernatural explanations, such as witchcraft, only about half the children did. Researchers working in India, Madagascar, the United States, and Manus Island near New Guinea found a similar contrast between naturalistically minded children and supernaturally focused adults. For children, it seems, supernatural explanations are harder to accept than natural ones.[24]

Luhrmann suspects that the missing ingredient here is experience. Firsthand encounters are powerful teachers. People feel God's presence. They see spirits and catch glimpses of witches' magic. When older Garifuna people on the Caribbean island of Saint Vincent encountered youngsters who doubted the existence of dead spirits, they would tell them, "Someday [they] will catch you. Then you *must* believe."[25]

Luhrmann admitted that people can doubt these experiences. They might "hear God speaking and then say, 'Well, that was a mistake. That was, you know, a bit of burrito from lunch.'

"But," she went on, "the more people have those experiences, the more it helps to shore up and make more visceral the sense that claims in the Gospels or the Quran are real." If you want to convince someone of the supernatural, don't tell them about it. Let them experience it for themselves.

Exactly what counts as an experience of the supernatural is more complicated. It depends partly on local attitudes. The Mentawai say that ghosts look like normal people, except that they are all white. So seeing a pale figure in a cemetery becomes a weighty, metaphysical encounter.* People also develop personal ways of sensing the divine, which their church or community can train and encourage. In the Christian communities Luhrmann worked in, people learned to experience God through goose bumps, warm tingling, and mental images evoked during prayer, any of which became a sign of God's presence.[26]

One of the experiences that most consistently boosts super-natural belief is misfortune. Your friends might have told you that God condemns Sabbath breakers or that the crocodile god attacks the stingy. But it isn't until the tsunami hits or your child suffers that this impression becomes a belief. The missionary-anthropologist Alex Rödlach noticed this effect while working in Zimbabwe in the early 1990s. Whereas everyone struggled to understand where HIV came from, the people who most confidently connected it to witchcraft were either those infected with HIV or their closer family members. For rural Zimbabweans, agony crystallized rumors into reality.[27]

Thinking about misfortunes helps reconcile Luhrmann's focus on experience with psychologists' emphasis on agency detection. We are not born believers. Experience clearly matters. Yet because of how our minds work, certain experiences can push us toward belief. When something happens—especially something bad—and it's hard to know why, we feel a conviction that something, some*one*, was behind it. This conviction can reinforce our faith in the supernatural.

———————

By the time Sandeep replied to my email, the boy from the healing ceremony had died. The *sikerei* failed. Weeks later, one of them—a spry older man with a single tooth—complained that

* As it turns out, I was riding home on a motor scooter one night in Siberut and, as I zipped past a cemetery, saw something ghostlike: a humanoid figure that glowed faintly like a light bulb. It was probably one of Luhrmann's proverbial lunch burritos. But it's a go-to story whenever people ask me whether I've had extraordinary experiences.

his colleagues messed up the procedure. I knew neither the Mentawai language nor the details of the ceremony well enough yet to understand what his qualms were. But he assured me: perform the ceremony correctly, and the boy would have lived.

We started this chapter asking why people turn to the supernatural to control life's uncertainties. Having journeyed from Pompeii to Zimbabwe, we've assembled part of an answer: supernatural forces help us make sense of uncertainty, especially when it's big and bad. But this is only half an answer. Why appeal to them? Why pray? Why pursue rituals like the healing ceremony I saw, particularly when a good number of them do not end in success?

We do not have to visit the Mentawai to answer these questions. To the contrary, we can look at the people around us—athletes like Tiger Woods, for example. Say you catch the golfer on the last day of a tournament. He'll wear a red shirt. He'll have three tees in his front right pocket, ChapStick in the front left, and a glove in the back left. If he's carrying a yardage book, it'll sit in his back right pocket. He'll also be carrying a 1932 quarter. "It was the year my dad was born," he once said. "He taught me how to putt. So my dad is always there with me when I play."[28]

Tiger isn't alone. Soccer superstar Cristiano Ronaldo steps onto the field with his right foot first and kisses his shin guards after each match. Throughout his career, basketball god Michael Jordan played with his university practice shorts under his professional uniform. And tennis maestro Serena Williams has a long checklist of rituals, any of which, she says, can cost her a game. "I didn't tie my laces right and I didn't bounce the ball five times and I didn't bring my shower sandals to the court with me," she said in 2007 after losing to Justine Henin in the French Open quarterfinals. "I didn't have my extra dress. I just knew fate, it wasn't going to happen."[29]

These are all examples of magical rituals. They are techniques used to influence a course of events through esoteric means. Magical rituals appear worldwide, deployed by everyone from gamblers to fishermen. And like supernatural explanations, they overwhelmingly target big, uncertain events. An easy quiz that doesn't affect anything? Bring it on. A final exam that covers months of thorny material and determines whether you graduate? You'll probably engage in a ritual or two.[30]

The connection between ritual and uncertainty is clearest in sports. In the game of baseball, for example, uncertainty rules. Whether you win a division championship after a 162-game season often hinges on just one or two games. Luck plays such a big role that, according to statisticians, the best team finishes first only between 20 and 35 percent of the time.[31]

With so much left to chance, players turn to rituals with a staggering devotion. In 2005, the American psychologists Jerry Burger and Amy Lynn distributed questionnaires to the players of eight major league baseball teams—five in the United States and three in Japan. They found magic everywhere. Three-quarters of the players admitted to using rituals to induce luck. Of these, half used rituals in every game. The techniques were varied and idiosyncratic. One player always ate chicken. Another chewed three pieces of gum. A third drew four lines in the dirt before getting into the batter's box. Lucky items of clothing, from cups to batting gloves, were widespread. One player said he wore the same jockstrap four years straight.[32]

Two results stand out. First, as expected, the researchers found that uncertainty breeds rituals. The more a player thought luck was important, the likelier they were to use magic rituals. Second, players were iffy about whether their rituals worked. Despite the popularity of rituals, players rated their average effectiveness somewhere between "hardly ever has an impact" and "sometimes has an impact." They scarfed down chicken, chewed their gum, and wore the same underwear for years, yet they were only half convinced their actions made a difference.

Burger and Lynn refer to the rituals as "superstitions," which, according to Google's English dictionary, implies "excessively credulous belief" or "a widely held but irrational belief."[33] These definitions miss the point, however. For one, using rituals does not mean excessive credulity. As the baseball players demonstrated, belief is nuanced, not binary. We are not simple automata who either believe or do not. Rather, we are sophisticated creatures who assign degrees of confidence to claims about the world.

We have rich understandings of how stuff works. Even when we act in ways that might violate those understandings, we do not accept those actions unthinkingly but treat them with doubt and curiosity.

Nor is it fair to say that rituals are "irrational." Quite the opposite. One of the best explanations of ritual behavior suggests that they reflect an underlying rationality.[34] This idea, which we can call the "bet-hedging theory," is captured best in a little thought experiment. Imagine you're a baseball or softball player about to compete in a big game. You're wearing new flamingo-print underwear, and you happen to chew three sticks of gum before the game. And then you triumph. You hit nine home runs and pitch a perfect game and your hair looks great, and the next day you appear on the cover of *The New York Times* with the headline "SOVEREIGN OF SWING."

The underwear and gum probably didn't make a difference. But the cost of trying them out is so low, and the potential benefit so high, that you figure you might as well stick with them. And so a ritual is born.

I described this process as happening deliberately, but much of it occurs beyond conscious awareness. Our minds are wired in such a way that we're prone to use low-cost behaviors to control big, uncertain outcomes. It's a psychological quirk responsible for lots of ineffective actions—pregame chicken, stinky underwear, lines drawn in the dirt—yet it every so often lands on something that works, a behavior that truly sways uncertainty in our favor, making it worth it in the first place. What looks like irrationality is a necessary hiccup of a strategy that, over the long term, is exceedingly rational.

We can again turn to the example of the smoke detector: we're willing to accept some false alarms because that means the device detects occasional faint but useful signals. We tolerate the alarm when the veggies sizzle because that means catching the burning Christmas lights. Rituals are stabilized by an error-prone psychology that, like smoke detectors, is designed to pick up subtle but useful information.[35]

———————

It took just over a month to figure out all the house logistics—to find land, negotiate a yearlong lease with the clan who owned it, buy any trees standing there, and have the house constructed. We chose a location at the edge of a government settlement village: a patch of banana trees a stone's throw from a peaceful, pebbly river. Cross the river and follow the muddy path, and you would reach, one by one, the houses and longhouses of several *sikerei* and their families. Rustam had full control over the architectural design of the house. When it was finished, it was beyond anything I could have imagined.

Our house was made mostly of mango wood. When we moved in, it was a subdued red, like the color of early dawn. Its roof was thatched with sago palm leaves. Like all Mentawai houses I've seen, it was raised off the ground, its wooden stilts perched on stones shaped like thick encyclopedias. The main part of the house consisted of two rooms, one for me and one for Rustam and any other research assistants. My room contained two shelves, my backpack, a mosquito net, a basket where I kept my dirty clothes, and a rattan mat that I slept on every night. The rooms opened onto a kind of veranda with a large bench. Visitors liked to lounge there, gossip, drink sweet tea and coffee, and gaze at the river. At one end of the veranda was an attached one-room kitchen. The other end looked out onto a wooden platform, which connected to a path of logs leading down to the water.

I chose to live in this region of Siberut partly because of the *sikerei*. Nowhere in the Mentawai archipelago can you find as many, at least on a per capita basis. In my survey of 265 residents, 24 of them were male *sikerei*—more than four-tenths of the adult male population. The overrepresentation partly reflected the many traditionalists living in the area. Many other Mentawai considered this to be pig country, inhabited by families who had opted out of the government settlement program. But the state is a powerful and single-minded specter. ("Wherever we go, it knows," a man once said, comparing the government to Sika-meinan, the water spirit.) In 2010, rows of identical settlement houses popped up. They were followed by a clinic, an elementary school, and the arrival of an Islamic development organization.

We moved into the house on May 22. After going through the typical housewarming customs (planting magical cuttings, hosting a ceremony involving meat sharing), I interviewed a local *sikerei* whom I'll call Mangga. He was an old man, perhaps in his sixties or seventies. His voice was soft and had a slight squeak. His small head reminded me of a turtle's. But it was his legs that were most noticeable. His ankles had swelled up. The skin around them looked raw in places, but also scaly and dry, as if covered with a lattice of tiny scabs. Mangga asked me what the affliction was and whether I had any medicine. I said that I didn't know but that I could take photos and ask a friend.

Before I could send off the pictures, I heard from one of Mangga's nephews. They had called three *sikerei* to treat Mangga's legs. It would be an all-night healing ceremony, and we were invited.

Rustam and I stocked up on refreshments, packed our belongings, and headed to Mangga's longhouse. We arrived early and so helped his nephews ensnare one of his large female pigs to sacrifice.

The ceremony started around six p.m. While the women prepared sago and taro, the shamans administered standard treatments, including massaging, applying an herbal paste, sweeping away bad spirits, and protecting against everyday taboo violations. Around seven p.m., the pig's throat was slit. Another of Mangga's nephews recently became a father, and the family took a moment to conduct a ritual for the infant, holding her while passing beneath the pig. Afterward, they butchered the animal. The women cooked sago. Men divvied up around fifty shares of meat for the attendees and other relatives who could not make it. Each share had a roughly equivalent amount of skin, fat, organ meat, and skeletal muscle. Rustam and I got one share each, stuffed into bamboo to take home.

Then platters of meat and cooked sago were brought out. Guests collected around each platter and indulged. The vibe was festive, and people intermittently called to me to "continue eating" or to remind me that "we eat," assurances that help cement the social bonds established through communal feasting. As people finished, they retired to the sidelines or benches, sometimes picking fibers of dried sago leaves from the overhanging thatch to use as toothpicks.

Once dinner was over, around 1:30 a.m., the python-skin drums were pulled out. The *sikerei* tied dancing aprons around their waists and tucked stalks of leaves into their loincloths like green tail feathers. Thus commenced *kut kerei*, a kind of dance medicine performed expressly for healing other *sikerei*. Much of it was familiar: The musicians tapped out beats on the python-skin drums while the *sikerei* hammered their feet on the floorboards, adding another layer of rhythm. The *sikerei* trotted in a circle, but rather than entering trance, as often happens during healing dances, they acted like animals. In the first dance, the most experienced shaman scurried away from the other two, squatting and grabbing one of the poles of the longhouse. "A monkey!" yelled Mangga. The other two *sikerei* crowded around him before they all laughed and gave one another reassuring squeezes. Then they returned to dancing.

On paper, this was a religious ritual. Yet more than anything, it felt like a party. Mangga's ankles looked like they were decaying, but the attitude was neither solemn nor serious, but amusing and playful. Full from pig and sago flour and sweet coffee, we laughed and chatted during dance breaks. It felt less like Mangga had called these shamans to cure him and more like he was hosting an all-nighter for his younger relatives.

Eventually, the *sikerei* retired to the sidelines, and others replaced them on the dance floor. I fell asleep sometime around four a.m. When I woke up at dawn, Mangga was on the python-skin drum, banging out staccato beats. I interviewed him shortly after, but even before we chatted, I intuited the ritual's effects. His feet looked the same, but he was bubblier during our second conversation and said he was feeling better.

Mangga's improvement suggested to me that rituals can be therapeutic, especially when enhanced with other mechanisms of social bonding, like touch, dancing, and feasting. I later came across other research corroborating my impressions. In July 2006, when war broke out between Israel and the Lebanese paramilitary organization Hezbollah, the American anthropologist Rich Sosis found that Israeli women living in bombed areas experienced lower anxiety when they recited psalms. (No one ran similar surveys with Lebanese women, although there's good reason to suspect that they, too, turned to religious ritual and found some relief.) At the same time, a growing collection of experiments, including studies conducted in Mauritius and the Czech Republic, demonstrates that ritualized behaviors lower self-reported anxiety and its physiological correlates. Even without the intensity of Mentawai healing ceremonies, rituals worldwide seem to bring solace.[36]

Every ritual we have looked at—psalm recitation, sports superstitions, the ceremony to entice Sikameinan—is a snapshot of an endless process of winnowing and shaping. Rituals, like all technologies, evolve. People design them, tweak them, and pass them on. When they preferentially choose and retain the versions they like best, they direct the evolution of rituals so that they become better adapted to our psychology.

In his book *How the Mind Works* (1997), the psychologist Steven Pinker famously explored the analogy between a cultural phenomenon—in his case, music—and cheesecake. As we experiment with recipes and keep the tastiest ones, we shape cheesecake so that it becomes, in his words, "an exquisite confection crafted to tickle the sensitive spots of . . . our mental facilities."[37] We can think about rituals similarly. Just as cheesecake (and perhaps music) has culturally evolved to hack our mental and physiological sweet spots, so have we fashioned rituals into their most psychologically powerful forms.

Humans share psychological predispositions that guide how rituals evolve. Imagine, for example, that you desperately need rain. Your neighbor comes over and gives you a choice between two rituals. One, called drizzle-blitz, involves drawing a circle on the ground representing where you want the rain to fall. You then spritz water on the circle while making thunder sounds. Drizzle-blitz can be performed only early in the morning, when the air is moist and rainfall is most likely. The other, called long-face, requires that you stare at a wall, scrunch up your eyebrows, and stick out your tongue. You can long-face whenever you want, for however long you want.

Most readers, I'd wager, would choose to drizzle-blitz. This isn't a baseless guess: psychologists find that people expect rituals with certain features—including more steps, greater repetition, and a specific time—to be more effective. Drizzle-blitzing also conforms to what's called "the law of similarity": the action you produce (sprinkling water on the circle) resembles the outcome you desire (rain falling on your field). Researchers still puzzle over why people prefer rituals with these elements. But they clearly do, and, as a result, rituals that incorporate them are adopted and passed on more often.[38]

This brings us to the intersection of the psychological ingredients explored in this chapter. People turn to rituals to deal with the uncertainty of the world. But they do not choose randomly. Rather, they drift toward rituals that seem appealing, and one of the most important determinants of appeal is the supernatural. We tend to believe that invisible beings oversee uncertain events and, as a result, prefer rituals that involve engaging with those beings. If I'm desperate to heal my wife, a ritual that deals with the spirit who caused her illness would be ideal.

Religion—and shamanism, too—emerges from a dance between these tendencies: our desperation to manage fortune and misfortune, combined with our belief in unseen forces, means that we preferentially turn to the beyond for blessings and salvation.

This all provides the foundations of a theory of shamanism. As people seek ways to interact with the beyond to manage uncertainty, specialists compete to provide the most appealing services. Across time and space, those specialists discover and hone techniques to assure people they can probe, tackle, and speak to the beings responsible for big and unpredictable events. What those techniques are and why people find them compelling are the subjects of the next two chapters.

Nina Sreshta

MANVIR SINGH is an assistant professor of anthropology at the University of California, Davis. He holds a bachelor's degree from Brown University and a PhD in human evolutionary biology from Harvard University. He is a regular contributor to *The New Yorker,* and his writings have also appeared in *Wired, Vice, Aeon,* and *The Guardian,* as well as in leading academic journals, including *Science, Nature Human Behaviour,* and *Behavioral and Brain Sciences.* He has studied the use of psychedelics in the rain forests of Colombia and, since 2014, has conducted ethnographic fieldwork with Mentawai communities on Siberut Island, Indonesia, focusing on shamanism and justice. He lives with his wife, Nina, and daughter, Zora, in Davis, California.

CHAPTER 3

The Xenized

I'm not a picky eater with the Mentawai. At home I waffle between vegetarianism and pescatarianism, but on Siberut I eat whatever's in front of me—a decision that has resulted in some adventurous eating. Staying with families, I've had fried grubs, boiled pangolin, and pig testicles. I've eaten the wings of flying foxes and civet meat with cooked sago palm flour. My absolute favorite item, however, is eel. During my second summer, when I spent weeks living in a large longhouse with a family of fifteen, the women would bring home big eels, as long and thick as human arms, and cook them in bamboo. Unlike the fatty pigs, bony chickens, and sinewy monkeys we sometimes had, eel meat was almost all soft skeletal muscle.

It was because I loved eel so much that I was stunned to see that my *sikerei* hosts never ate it. When I asked why, I was met with a puzzled stare. Of course they can't eat eel. They would die. Mentawai shamans, I was reminded, are not like the rest of us. Consider the terminology. We regular folk are *simata*, a word that also refers to uncooked food and unripe fruit. Shamans, in contrast, are *sikerei*, a word that implies a fundamental transformation. They are matured, cooked, ripened versions of us regular folk. Their bodies are special, and they alone have special sight. For the rest of their lives following their initiation, *sikerei* must refrain not just from eels but also from flounders, gibbons, and white simakobu monkeys—as well as, quite often, from sex. Engaging in any of these pleasures will corrupt a shaman's hallowed body.[1]

In the last chapter, we saw that the structure of our minds predisposes us to turn to rituals to control uncertainty, especially rituals that involve engaging with supernatural forces. Yet how do we go from everyday rituals to shamanism? How do we go from lucky underwear to visiting trance-dancing witch doctors who deprive themselves of food and sex? Why do we create such an elaborate, compelling, mystifying tradition if our goal is just to control uncertainty? In other words: Why are there shamans?

This is a big question. It has obsessed anthropologists since they started comparing societies yet has remained fiendishly hard to answer. As Jeremy Narby and Francis Huxley wrote in 2001, "Even after five hundred years of reports on shamanism, its core remains a mystery."[2]

In this chapter, I'll try to start to resolve this mystery. At the center of my explanation will be the concept critical for the family's explanation of the eel taboo: the fundamental difference between shamans and the rest of humanity. Before we get to that, however, it helps to step back and get a better sense of what shamanism looks like.

———————

Shamanism is as diverse as its practitioners. Some Arikara shamans in the American Great Plains wore the scalps and horns of bison before summoning others to be killed. Among Hausa speakers in Nigeria, women are sometimes possessed, or "mounted," by the spirits of sickly Muslim scholars. In tracts of the Colombian Amazon, a specialist led the communal consumption of a psychedelic brew to help a group of men travel beyond the Milky Way to the beginning of creation.[3]

Critically, this diversity coexists with deep commonalities. Most important are the three defining elements of shamanism: non-ordinary states, engagement with unseen realities, and services like healing and divination. These constitute shamanism.

They represent its beating heart, the vibrating strings whose resonance manifests in shamanic traditions everywhere.

Layered around this beating heart are what we might call
secondary commonalities. Shamans are outfitted with special
powers. They sing and dance and undergo initiations. They wear
costumes and ingest substances and deny themselves food and
sex. These elements aren't necessarily universal, although they
pop up reliably enough that they deserve some attention.

Take special powers. We defined shamans partly on the basis
of special abilities—namely, engaging with unseen realities. Yet
as Duncan Pryde observed with the Inuit, many shamans' powers
seem to go far beyond inter-realm interactions.

Pryde was an unconventional source of anthropological
observations. Born in 1937, he spent his childhood in orphanages
across Scotland. At fifteen, he joined the merchant navy. Three
years later, in 1955, he noticed an ad in the Scottish *Sunday Post*
placed by the Hudson's Bay Company in Canada. Headlined "Fur
traders wanted for the far north," it sought "single, ambitious,
self-reliant young men" who were "prepared to live in isolation"
and "willing to learn native language."[4]

Pryde got the job. He spent his first three years in northern Ontario and Manitoba, where he learned Cree. He found
life "too soft and civilized for my liking," he later wrote, and,
in 1958, demanded to be transferred to the Arctic. Pryde stayed
there for more than a decade thereafter, achieving an integration
surpassing that of most Arctic anthropologists. For years, the
Inuit were his people. He fought, hunted, and celebrated with
them. He went stretches of eight to ten months without seeing
another "whiteman" and admitted to fathering at least three children with Inuit women. He became fluent in Inuktitut, an Inuit
language. Despite having only an elementary school education,
he was eventually considered a "legendary Inuktitut linguist" and
was hired at the Inupiat University of the Arctic to teach Inuit
languages. When he died in 1997, he was still working on his
dream project, a dictionary of twenty-six Inuit tongues.[5]

Pryde recorded his story in his memoir, *Nunaga: My Land,
My Country* (1972). In the same book, he introduced Alikammiq,
an Inuit shaman with renowned powers. What made Alikammiq

respected was not his ability to walk on water. Mere insects could do that, the Inuit observed. Nor was it his capacity for flight. "Shamans have always been able to go to the moon," said an Inuit man when Pryde told him that the United States had landed a rocket on the moon. Rather, it was his ability to cut off his own leg, wave it in the air, then reattach it and mosey away.[6]

With one exception, everyone on Perry Island, the small island where Pryde was stationed for four years, swore that they either witnessed Alikammiq's feat or knew someone who saw it. They also recounted the story of the white policeman who insisted that it was a ruse. "Now, if you don't believe me, go ahead and cut my leg off right here," Alikammiq said, pointing to his knee and handing the policeman a snow knife. Unnerved, the policeman dropped the knife and never doubted Alikammiq's powers again, at least not publicly.[7]

Powers like these have been reported around the world. I analyzed Michael Winkelman's cross-cultural dataset. In roughly three-quarters of the societies he studied, shamans were said to have at least one of the following powers: flight, fire immunity, animal control, and animal transformation. Sanema shamans in Venezuela sometimes returned to their communities with blood covering their mouths, a sign that they had killed vultures and sparrow hawks on the journey from earth to heaven. They were also said to float a foot or so off the ground. When the anthropologist Johannes Wilbert said that they seemed to walk like everyone else, he was told, "That is because you don't understand." The Austrian missionary Martin Dobrizhoffer got a similar response when, in the mid-1700s, he insisted to Abipón people in Paraguay that shamans could not transform into jaguars: "You fathers don't understand these matters."[8]

———————————

Aside from special powers, another common element of shamanism is selection. Wherever there is shamanism, people suspect that some individuals make better shamans than others. Sometimes this is because of extreme or sensitive behavior. When, as a child, the Yanomami shaman Davi Kopenawa awoke screaming or sobbing, his shaman stepfather told him, "Abandon that dream, come back from that ghost state! Don't be scared! It is the animal ancestors that you are seeing. If you want, when you grow up I will let you drink the *yãkoana* [psychedelic snuff] and they will build their house near you. Then you will be able to call them in your turn."[9]

In many northern Asian cultures, people look for signs of shamanic power from birth, including restless behavior, a tendency to swallow objects, an en-caul birth (where the baby is born in an unbroken amniotic sac), and physical abnormalities, like bony projections, extra teeth, or extra fingers. In fact, for years—and perhaps still now as you're reading this book—the main photo on the Wikipedia page for "Shamanism" featured a Siberian shaman with two thumbs fused on his right hand.[10]

Just as often, however, cultures develop initiations. To become a shaman, you need to go through a formalized procedure. To outsiders, these can seem incredible—hallucinatory blends of the dramatic, agonizing, and nightmarish. In parts of southern Nigeria, neophyte shamans underwent a four-day ceremony in which their eyes were treated with plant medicines and hot pepper juice. On the final day, in front of everyone and to a chorus of drumming, men killed a dog, removed its eyes, and then retreated to a tent, where they were said to replace the initiate's eyes with the animal's.[11]

Especially evocative are descriptions from Australia. Around 1902, an aboriginal Australian man named Ilpailurkna explained to two anthropologists how he had become a shaman. An old man had approached him with a spear-thrower, he said, and hurled crystals at him. Some hit him on the chest. Others tore through his head, killing him. The old man then cut up Ilpailurkna's corpse. He removed all the innards—heart, lung, liver, intestines—and left the body out all night. After returning in the morning, the old man inspected Ilpailurkna's body and placed more crystals inside. He sang until it swelled up like an inflatable raft, filled it with a new set of organs, and planted even more crystals. When he patted the corpse on the head, Ilpailurkna came back to life.

"I think I am lost," he said. He didn't know who or where he was. He didn't remember anything about his past life.

"No, you are not lost," said the old man. "I killed you a long time ago."

The old man escorted Ilpailurkna back to camp and reintroduced him to his wife. Everyone saw how dazed he was, how incoherent and confused. They knew he had become a shaman.[12]

Aside from vivid initiations, becoming a shaman often includes a lot of learning. Novices need to learn myths, songs, and dances. They need to learn plant knowledge and the appropriate ceremonies. They need to learn rosters of taboos and tomes of ritual knowledge.

Most importantly, they need to learn how to master nonordinary states. In 1989, the filmmaker Diana Lee and anthropologist Laurel Kendall observed the initiation ritual of Chini, a thirty-two-year-old Korean woman. She was possessed by a series of spirits—the Buddhist Sage, the Heavenly King, even her sister at one point. But for the most part, her performances were demure. "She doesn't have the power of inspired speech," her teacher said. "She isn't ready to earn money as a shaman." Chini failed the initiation. Her teacher later explained, "It isn't as if anyone could become a successful shaman right when they got the calling. They must make a great effort and change completely. If it happened automatically, then wouldn't everyone be making their living as a shaman?"[13]

———————

There are many other common elements of shamanism, from music to psychotropic drugs, but for now, let's end with the one I found so intriguing that summer with the Mentawai: deprivation. After I returned home from Siberut, I was obsessed with the eel prohibition. The shamans could just make up taboos, I thought. People trust their supernatural expertise. What prevents them from telling everyone that the previous rules are outdated? Why not rewrite the record and say that, in fact, *non*-shamans are tabooed, so everyone should hand over all the tasty eel flesh to the *sikerei*?

This might seem cynical. Yet profiteering like this happens all the time. Across societies, taboos tend to favor people in power, especially older men.[14] Mentawai people say that women are tabooed from leaving their house or accepting visitors while their husbands are out hunting, conveniently restricting women's movement. Violate this prohibition, people tell me, and the hunt can fail or the hunter might hurt himself.

Shamans are humans, and like humans everywhere, they take advantage of their position for self-serving ends. Michael Harner, the late anthropologist and neo-shamanic guru, noticed this working with the Shuar of Ecuador. Fearing "the bewitching power of the shamans," he wrote, fathers married their daughters to shamans without demanding bride payments. Shamans accepted gifts from laypeople with little plan to repay them. In fact, he said, shamans "often boasted to me how well they (compared to non-shamans) were fed when visiting neighbors' houses."[15]

Shamans extort people for more than gifts and reduced bride payments. Male Inuit shamans encouraged sex as a form of payment, sometimes threatening hesitant women with supernatural consequences like becoming pregnant with a seal. A shaman in the Sora tribe in eastern India took a different approach. Working with an attractive widow, he channeled her dead husband and told her, "I want to sleep with you again, but now the only way I can do so is through this shaman's body."[16]

Keen to figure out the eel taboo, I rummaged through old anthropological reports. Immediately I saw: deprivation is everywhere. Among Yanomami living in Venezuela, "the induction of shamans involves drug-taking, fasting and meditation." For the Ulithi of Micronesia, magical specialists "may not eat certain foods, touch a corpse, dig a grave, come into contact with a menstruating woman, or have sexual intercourse." Years later, a Jiw shaman in eastern Colombia told me that he abstained from meat, various fish, and other hot foods while training to become a shaman. When I asked him what he ate for all those years, he named psychotropic drugs: "Tobacco. Yagé. Yopo."[17]

The best evidence for the ubiquity of deprivation comes from Winkelman's dataset. Analyzing it, I found that shamans in more than 80 percent of the societies surveyed refrained from food, sex, or social contact. Given that Winkelman collated his data from reports by travelers and anthropologists, they are probably an underestimate. Self-denial by Mentawai shamans is less a local peculiarity and more a manifestation of a ubiquitous shamanic practice.[18]

Shamans, we can now appreciate, are more than trance specialists. They are, to use the Western Apache translation, "people with power."[19] They are endowed with incredible abilities, marked by fasting and deprivation, and separated by initiations and idiosyncrasies. They are special. This leaves us better equipped to return to the questions from the beginning of this chapter: Why do humans create such an elaborate, compelling, mystifying tradition if our goal is just to control uncertainty? Why shamanism?

I will answer this question. To do that, however, we first need to consider a very different class of special beings: superheroes.

In January 1933, a pair of Cleveland high-school students, Jerry Siegel and Joe Shuster, published the third issue of their fanzine *Science Fiction*. You couldn't tell from looking at it, but this is among the most sought-after fanzines in history. In 2006, a copy went for nearly $50,000 in an auction in Dallas, Texas.[20]

The reason for the issue's popularity is a story called "The Reign of the Superman." As was typical for their collaboration, Siegel wrote it and Shuster illustrated. The story is a grim mirror of its Depression-era origins. A wealthy professor approaches the "vagrant" Bill Dunn in a bread line, promising him food and clothing in exchange for work. The professor assures Dunn that his intentions are "purely humanitarian," but they're not. Siegel writes:

> Some time previous [the professor] had secured a fragment of a meteor and upon subjecting to chemical analysis found the presence of what he suspected to be a new element. Upon further investigation he had learned that

it exerted a strange influence up on the laboratory animals to whom it was administered.[21]

The professor offers Dunn a hearty meal, spiking the poor man's drink with the alien element. Soon after, Dunn feels queasy and flees through a window. He resembles an "escaped lunatic." He babbles incoherently, dashes through the streets at full speed, and has "roving, frantic eyes"—descriptions reminiscent of the frenzies common to shamanic trances and initiations.[22]

In his hysteria, Dunn crashes into a tree, at which point his powers kick in. Suddenly, he can read others' thoughts, even control them. He can see anything anywhere, even on Mars. He can glimpse the future and, while sleeping, absorbs "all the knowledge that exists in the universe." Following the transformation, Siegel rarely calls his protagonist Bill Dunn, opting instead for descriptors like "the thing that had been Bill Dunn" or, more commonly, "the Superman." Unlike their later creation, Shuster and Siegel's first Superman was a power-hungry fiend, bent on enriching himself and ruling over humanity.[23]

In the months and years that followed, Shuster and Siegel refashioned their Superman. They made him good, named him Clark Kent, and swapped mental superpowers for physical ones. By June 1934, Siegel decided that Superman should come from the future, an infant babe strapped into a time machine by "the last man on earth." By the 1938 debut of *Action Comics* number one—the first true Superman comic and widely considered the most valuable comic book ever—the origin story had changed again. The very first panel of *Action Comics* number one explains, "As a distant planet was destroyed by old age, a scientist placed his infant son within a hastily devised space-ship, launching it toward Earth!" Lower down on the same page, the reader learns that "Kent had come from a planet whose inhabitants' physical structure was millions of years advanced of our own. Upon reaching maturity, the people of his race became gifted with titanic strength!"[24]

Through Superman, Shuster and Siegel inaugurated the superhero genre, setting the stage for a kaleidoscope of marvelous superhumans, from the half-demon Hellboy to the web-slinging Spider-Man. Like Superman, almost all had an origin story laying out how they could do things the rest of us cannot. Some were beset by mishaps, like a bite from a radioactive spider. Others, like the X-Men, had outlandish genetic mutations. Still others, like Thor and Wonder Woman, are simply not human.[25]

The popularity of the origin story reveals something simple about human psychology: we find superpowers more reasonable when their possessors deviate from humanity. To be sure, we don't accept just any deviation. Peter Parker didn't get the Spidey-Sense from dyeing his hair green or wearing vintage pants. Rather, he and other superheroes undergo fundamental transformations. Putting aside characters who have magical gifts or ridiculous technology, most either get their essences reconfigured or start out nonhuman.

These transformations make sense. Psychologists insist that humans are essentialists. We assume that living beings have essences that give them an identity and that only certain transformations affect those essences. Tell a child that you shaved a dog or put a tiger costume on it, and they'll respond that it's still a dog. But tell them that you removed everything inside its body, and they'll assure you that it's no longer a dog and no longer capable of doing dog things. New identities require modified essences.[26]

Exactly which transformations affect essences differ depending on the culture. Even if we focus on the United States during the twentieth century, we see that people's understandings of essential change were constantly evolving. Consider the DC Comics character the Flash, who possesses superspeed. DC Comics actually created a couple of superheroes called the Flash, so let's focus on the first one, the college student Jay Garrick. When introduced in 1940, Garrick gained his powers by inhaling vapors of hard water, or water with a high mineral content. It turns out that hard water is safe to drink. So this was later changed to heavy water, or water that contains heavy hydron isotopes. But this apparently didn't seem transformative enough. So it was later implied that the inhalation had activated a "metagene," a genetic variant that can catalyze widespread genetic change. As readers' understandings of essential transformation evolved, so did Jay Garrick's story.

What exactly do origin stories tell us about shamans?

Recall that people want to control the uncertain. They want the rain to start, their vomiting to stop, and their investments to yield profits. Specialists promise this control by offering to engage with the invisible forces believed to oversee the unpredictable. They assure clients that they will speak to rain goddesses, battle the demons behind disease, and channel ancestors who know about tomorrow.

But there's an obvious limitation: skepticism. Imagine your next-door neighbor, let's call her Jyotika, promised to stop a drought by bargaining with a rain goddess. You'd be dubious. How could this regular Jyotika possess such superpowers? You know the abilities of a normal human—you are one, after all—and bargaining with a rain goddess is not among them.

Such skepticism is a major obstacle for ritual specialists, and shamans overcome it partly through transformation. Like superheroes, they deviate from the rest of humanity. They die and come back to life. They ingest magical substances. They say older shamans disemboweled them and filled their bodies with crystals. Such transformations even apply to body parts. When asked why an Igbo initiate should have his eyes replaced with a dog's, a Nigerian man explained, "Now he will be able to see spirits just as dogs see spirits." Whether in the realm of Marvel or Mentawai, transformation makes special powers tenable.[27]

Self-denial is one of the tools shamans use to look powerful. If you're like most people, you already have this intuition. "No pain, no gain." "What doesn't kill you makes you stronger." In many societies, people say deprivation cultivates not just shamanic power but greater power in general, including the power to do evil. For the Barama River Caribs of Guyana, to become a *kanaima*—a heinous, shadowy figure who could turn invisible—a person had to subsist on rainwater, white fungus, a spiky palm called *kosako*, and a single bird species. Endure, we assume, and power will follow.[28]

Shamans feel and understand this. A Japanese shaman told the British scholar Carmen Blacker that living off pine needles was "conducive to the development of second sight and clairaudient perception." Other shamans told her that it was only when cold, hunger, and sleeplessness pushed them to the verge of collapse that they felt both transformed and endowed with new strength. "With this access of power," she wrote, "they feel themselves to be different people from those they had been in the past."[29]

In 2017, to feed my obsession, I studied Mentawai people's inferences about self-denial. I presented people with two hypothetical shamans and asked them a series of questions about them. One shaman denied himself food or sex; the other did not. People said that self-denying shamans were more dissimilar from normal people and, critically, more supernaturally powerful. Without eels and sex, *sikerei* grow stronger.[30]

There isn't a good word that captures the transformative effects of shamanic practices. So I propose the term "xenize," from the Greek prefix *xen*, meaning "foreign" or "other." We can say, then, that asceticism, magical surgeries, and death-and-rebirth rituals all xenize a specialist—that is, they apparently turn the specialist into a different kind of entity, one more credibly endowed with special powers.

Many characteristics can xenize a shaman. Some of the most powerful involve gender and sexuality.

To start, shamans come in all genders. There seems to be a skew toward male shamans across societies, although, surprisingly, this seems strongest in small-scale, relatively egalitarian communities, as with the Mentawai. As societies become larger and more stratified, we see a greater representation of female shamans. The *wu*, or shamans of ancient China, were mostly female, as are the *mudang* of Korea and the *miko* of Japan. The *zar* cults found in the Horn of Africa and throughout much of the

Middle East have overwhelmingly been led by possessed women shamans.[31]

Yet shamans, more than any other class, also confound gender binaries. Approximately 1,400 miles east of Siberut lies the Indonesian island of Sulawesi—a mountainous, coral-fringed jumble of peninsulas shaped like an angelfish or fleeing octopus. Its size and topography supported a diversification of cultures, several of which connected sacred abilities with gender nonconformity. Before Dutch colonization, for example, the Pamona of the central highlands recognized a group of people they called *bajasa*. According to missionaries, *bajasa* were sexually male but preferred to be called "mother" or "aunt." They performed women's work and avoided warfare. Some were rumored to have penises "no longer than half a finger joint," and at least one was uninterested in sex. This gender ambiguity imbued them with spiritual sway. As priests, they spoke a special language. Unlike gender-typical males, but like some women, they could call spirits and direct them skyward to recover the souls of sick people. Unfortunately, we know little about the *bajasa* beyond these basic observations. By the time missionaries recorded Pamona culture in the 1910s, the tradition had been erased by Christian moralizing, surviving only in memories.[32]

Farther south and closer to the sea, a similar tradition has survived, although barely. The Bugis people, who for centuries ruled kingdoms in Sulawesi's lowland plains, revered specialists known as *bissu*. Fabled to have been created by the moon near the beginning of the world, the *bissu* defied a simple gender binary. In the earliest historical account, a Portuguese bishop introduced them as "priests of these kings" who married men, spoke and dressed like women, and kept long, braided hair. They conducted rituals, especially rites of passage, for nobles. They were also considered formidable shamans. A seventeenth-century Bugis manuscript describes a *bissu* who fell into trance. Their soul escaped their body and climbed a rainbow to the edge of heaven, where they met the Creator in his Palace of Shining Mirrors. They acquired weapons and supernatural plants, rode the rainbow back to earth, and shared the prizes with the ruler. In other rituals, *bissu* became vessels of gods, stabbing themselves with swords to prove the reality of their possession.[33]

Unlike the *bajasa*, the *bissu* coexisted with an Abrahamic religion—in this case, Islam—for centuries. With the dissolution of the Bugis kingdoms following the creation of the Republic of Indonesia, however, the *bissu* lost their royal patrons. In the 1960s, they became the targets of an Islamic fundamentalist movement that scorched southern Sulawesi. They were branded un-Islamic. Their sacred objects were burned, their rituals forbidden. A *bissu* leader, Sanro Makgangke, was beheaded; others were forced to behave like "normal men" or suffer the same fate. Despite attempts to revitalize *bissu* practices, the tradition today is a whisper of its historic glory.[34]

Like extra fingers, bouts of abstinence, and death-and-rebirth ceremonies, nonbinary gender identities can xenize specialists, promoting perceptions of mystical gifts. But as the histories of the *bajasa* and *bissu* demonstrate, culture matters. There are many forms of otherness. How they are perceived varies with context. The Pamona understood ambiguous gender expression very differently from the Dutch missionaries who sought to convert them. Even seventeenth-century Bugis nobles thought of transgenderism unlike their twentieth-century descendants. Power lies in difference, but cultural mores deem some forms of difference more acceptable than others.

On Siberut, initiations help xenize new shamans. I remember when this happened for Opa. Onlookers had packed onto his veranda, an excited anticipation buzzing through the crowd. I jostled to the front, just behind a row of children, and pulled out my camera to record as much as I could.

Dressed in beads, leaves, and fabrics, Opa and the five shamans had gathered in a clearing next to his house. They formed a circle, placing a hunting bow and powerful plants in the middle to invite the spirits of their ancestors. Then they started to sing. Clanging small handbells, they produced a hypnotic, white-noise cacophony—similar, I imagined, to the sound of sleigh bells played out of sync. They crooned over the noise, bellowing long syllables (*aaaa-eeee*) while abruptly changing pitch. The performance was bewitching and forceful, as if the power of their singing pulled the spirits toward them.

Eyes shut with neck veins bulging, Teu Rami sang the hardest. He also tilted forward and taught Opa the song as they performed it, feeding his trainee words before the group sang them together. The other shamans lacked his intensity, but none seemed less invested than Aman Joji, Teu Rami's brother. Aman Joji didn't bend forward, didn't sing with the same gusto, and seemed more concerned with swatting away ants than with summoning spirits. I wondered if he was invited because it would've been rude to call one shaman brother and not the other.

The shamans sang for about fifteen minutes. I don't know how long exactly because my camera died ten minutes into the performance. As I panicked and asked to use Rustam's phone, the shamans sacrificed a chicken and handed it to someone to take inside. By that point, not only was Opa's house packed, but the adjacent house was, too. And everyone's eyes were on Opa.

When I had first arrived that day, Opa and the shamans were out in the forest. They were conducting secret shaman activities, I was told, including a ceremony to transform his eyes. This was key for his initiation. Mentawai shamans know songs and herbal remedies, but the biggest difference between them and normal folk is that they are said to see souls and spirits. This special sight starts with the modification of their eyes.

Damn, I had thought. I wanted to see them transform his eyes, but it seemed impossible to finagle my way into a secret shaman meeting, especially one happening that very moment in the jungle. But one of Opa's clanmates assured me I had another chance. "They will treat his eyes again," he said, "in front of us."

Now that moment had come. Opa squatted next to the offerings. Teu Rami walked over carrying a magical green concoction. He rubbed his fingers in the substance and applied it to Opa's eyes. He massaged them briefly. Then he stepped back.

I looked around. *Is that it?* I wondered. The moment passed with little fanfare. Opa's eyes may have watered a little. Otherwise, he didn't seem affected.

As it turns out, the eye treatment was merely the palate cleanser for a much more haunting main dish. Opa and the shamans returned to the house and formed a circle on the veranda. Next to them sat three men, the percussionists. One had a plastic jug. The other two held cylindrical drums with lizard-skin heads.

The percussionists drummed a *turut*, or Mentawai dance, beat, which sounds something like a slow jackhammer with syncopated embellishments. The shamans started dancing, moving in a circle while stamping out beats on the floorboards. Teu Rami sang and waved around the magical concoction. As is typical for *turut* performances, the dancing shamans resembled flying birds, their arms flapping like wings beside them.

After a minute and a half, Opa entered trance, a sign that spirits had arrived. He shut his eyes. His legs trotted to the beat while the top of his body went rigid. Still dancing, the other shamans held him, the six of them ambling about like a large, chaotic spider. His wife, who was watching from a bench, also entered trance. She rocked violently. Her face became anguished, and she put her hands to her head. The percussionists were playing faster. One of the shamans pulled Opa to the ground and held him. Three others—all except Aman Joji—had also entered trance by now. The beat continued to speed up—no syncopation anymore, just a strong, unadorned rhythm. Aman Joji grabbed one of the trancing shamans, then another. But no one could get hold of Teu Rami, who was spinning. With a tortured grimace and the green potion still in hand, he spun and spun, dodging shamans and audience members before collapsing into the drummers.

I had seen this before. It was called *lajo simagre*, and its function was to invite spirits. This was not the main event. It was performed merely to fill the house with ghosts. Now that they were here, however, the strangest part of the ceremony could take place.

Teu Rami placed the magical herb concoction on the floor with a mirror next to it. The *sikerei* squatted around and started singing, but in a mournful tone. Then, to my surprise, they began to cry. Teu Rami's face contorted like a squeezed fist. The *sikerei* next to him wept with his whole body. They wiped their eyes. After about thirty seconds, Aman Joji jumped into trance. Opa followed, announcing himself with a clap, although his trance looked less convincing and elicited laughter from the children watching. A third *sikerei* joined them, stamping and swooshing across the floor, his arms extended in front of him.

It took a moment to get the *sikerei* under control. They returned to the circle and went back to singing and weeping. This time, however, they started to resemble birds. Never stopping their mournful song, they flapped their arms at their sides. Then they put their hands at their waists and stuck their elbows behind them, stepping toward and away from the mirror and concoction like moseying chickens. The tiny bells secured around their arms clinked as they fluttered. Finally, in a single moment, as if teeming with spiritual energy, four of them burst in trance, their bodies shaking, their faces knotted into grimaces.

On our walk home, Rustam explained as best as he could. The ghosts the *sikerei* had called had been their own relatives. Seeing them was traumatic and emotional, but especially so for Opa, who had never before seen the spirits of his dead relatives. By weeping for us, he proved that his eyes had been transformed, that he could finally contact the beyond.

CHAPTER 4

Dramas of Otherness

Somewhere near the border of Colombia and Venezuela, a shaman held a small tray of powder in front of me and handed me an *inhalador*. It was shaped like a Y and made from the bones of a turkey-like bird called a curassow. I cleared as much air from my lungs as possible, put the bones to my nostrils, and inhaled powder. It rushed into my airways, mixing with my snot to create a sandy paste that collected at the back of my throat. My eyes watered. I sat back, exhaled deeply, then bent forward and inhaled more powder, sweeping the *inhalador* across the tray like a miniature vacuum. Sandeep, my friend, was able to clear the tray in three snorts, but my nose was stuffy, so each inhalation was a struggle. After six tries, most of the powder was gone, and I returned to my plastic lawn chair. My wife, Nina, took my place on the stool and began to inhale.

Nina is a psychiatrist and psychotherapist. When we met, in 2018, she was finishing her residency and preparing to move to Rwanda to work for the medical nonprofit Partners in Health. She's intrepid and curious about the many contexts in which healing occurs, which has made her a natural traveling companion on my journey to understand shamanism. Along with Sandeep—by this point, a psychedelics researcher and psychiatry professor at Johns Hopkins—we were trying yopo, a hallucinogenic snuff made from the beans of the *Anadenanthera peregrina* tree. There are trace amounts of DMT and 5-MeO-DMT in yopo, although the main psychoactive compound seems to be bufotenine, another serotonergic psychedelic similar in structure to DMT and psilocin. Bufotenine is little known outside South America; Western researchers still argue over whether it has psychoactive effects. (I can assure you, it does.) But peoples in South America have used it for generations, apparently in shamanic contexts. Archaeologists found evidence of bufotenine-containing snuffs in small woolen pouches at an oasis in Chile dated to between 1,100 and 1,700 years ago. A millennium-old leather bundle discovered in the Bolivian Andes held a cornucopia of ritual paraphernalia, including a woven headband, a pouch made from three fox snouts stitched together, and a carved snuff tray with traces of bufotenine. With each snort, I saw myself reproducing an ancient practice.[1]

Today, yopo use occurs mostly in the Orinoco basin, a mosaic of steamy forests, wetlands, and savannas covering eastern Colombia and much of Venezuela. This was our second time in the region, and the snuffs were part of the reason we had come. Unlike ayahuasca or the San Pedro cactus, bufotenine snuffs have mostly escaped the transformative tsunami of psychedelic tourism. Thus, we hoped, we could better understand how these substances were used in ritual contexts without meddling from Western markets.[2]

Within moments of inhaling yopo, a terrible physical discomfort took over. I was hot. I started to breathe deeply through my mouth. I felt agitated, as if nanobots had been slitted into each cell of my body and were shaking violently. My muscles felt like they had been blended and were being stimulated with an electric current. I rubbed my arms, not for pleasure but to cope with the tension.

Then the visuals started. At first, I saw them only when my eyes were closed: an array of rectangles enclosed within one another. In my notes afterward, I described them as both lime green and black and white. Soon, I saw them with my eyes open. I tried to figure out what exactly about my vision was distorted, but something fractured in my psyche, and the observer was separated from the experiencer. Nausea took over. I saw that Sandeep had asked for a bowl. I gestured at it and said, "*Yo también*" (Me too). Someone handed me a plastic basin, and I heaved. I felt relief for the tiniest flicker before heaving again, and again.

I needed to lie down. I searched for the words in Spanish, struggling to string together a sentence, when I noticed that Nina had made it to the floor. I looked to the shaman's son and gestured at Nina, then at myself. He nodded, which I took as permission that I could also lie down. As I got down from the chair, I spilled some vomit on my arm. I didn't care.

———————

There are many names for the non-ordinary states that shamans enter: trance, ecstasy, hysteria, inspiration, dissociation. What each of those means, unfortunately, is often far from clear. For the French ethnomusicologist Gilbert Rouget, "trance" implied a state of raucous movement, while "ecstasy" entailed silence, solitude, and immobility. The scholar of Japan Carmen Blacker wrote about a similar contrast—violent shaking, on the one hand, and inanimation, on the other—although she used "trance" to talk about both extremes.[3]

This conceptual murkiness connects to a larger question in the study of shamanism: How similar are shamans' experiences across societies? Michael Harner, the anthropologist turned neoshamanic guru, insisted that all shamans enter what he called the "shamanic state of consciousness."[4] Michael Winkelman, the anthropologist whose database has uncovered many crosscultural patterns, goes further. He maintains that all shamans enter an "integrative mode of consciousness." Dancing, hallucinogens, sensory deprivation—all of them, he argues, connect brain networks that normally do not communicate, allowing specialists to think creatively, mediate conflict, and better locate animals for hunting.[5]

The idea that shamanic trance states look similar around the world—what I'll call the "ecstatic equivalence hypothesis"—is widespread.[6] Yet research on altered states tells a different story.

Shamans are psychonauts. As they seek to commune with the beyond, they map out the limits of the human condition, showing just how diverse subjective experiences can be.

This was partly why I had come to South America. After spending more than a year in total with the Mentawai and studying the *sikerei* institution in depth, I knew I needed more perspective. The altered states of *sikerei* are brief affairs—momentary bursts of dissociation that occur during bouts of dancing and to accelerating rhythms. Despite the insistence of writers like Harner and Winkelman, they seemed to differ in important ways from shamanic performances in other societies, including the drug-inspired visions of many South American communities. To properly understand the nature of shamanism, I had to witness it firsthand in a very different context.

Even before I came to South America, I had discovered a large literature challenging the ecstatic equivalence hypothesis. The most comprehensive study was conducted by a team of thirteen English and European scientists. Led by Dieter Vaitl, a psychologist at the University of Giessen, the team identified twenty methods of inducing altered states, including dancing, sleeping, starvation, deep breathing, meditation, and sensory deprivation. They collected all the research they could find on the psychobiology of those states. Their findings, which I've reproduced partially in Table 1, show that non-ordinary states are far more different than often assumed.[7]

Compare, for example, the effects of deep breathing ("Respiratory maneuvers," in the table) and those of drumming and dancing ("Rhythm-induced trance"). Deep breathing relaxes people. It narrows their attention, amps up their self-awareness, and dampens their sensation. Drumming and dancing, meanwhile, tend to have the opposite effects. They are arousing. They expand people's awareness and pull them to a point where they lose themselves. They enhance sensation, making the world richer, closer, and more moving.

Vaitl and his colleagues opted not to consider psychoactive drugs. Once we probe their effects, however, we again find difference rather than unity. We can appreciate this simply by con-

TABLE 1. Some altered states of consciousness along with their subjective experiences. "Sensory dynamics" are sensory and perceptual changes; altered states with increased sensory dynamics exhibit synesthesia, hallucinations, and otherwise richer and more vivid sensory experiences. For the full table, see "Psychobiology of Altered States of Consciousness," by Vaitl et al. (2005).

Induction method	Activation (+ aroused – relaxed)	Awareness span (+ wide – narrow)	Self-awareness (+ present – absent)	Sensory dynamics (+ increased – decreased)
PHYSICALLY AND PHYSIOLOGICALLY INDUCED				
Extreme environmental conditions	+	–	+	+
Starvation and diet	+	–	+	–
Sexual activity and orgasm	+	–	–	–
Respiratory maneuvers	–	–	+	–
PSYCHOLOGICALLY INDUCED				
Sensory deprivation	–	+	+/–	–
Sensory homogenization	–	+/–	+/–	+
Sensory overload	+	–	–	+
Rhythm-induced trance	+	+	–	+
Relaxation	–	–	+	–
Meditation	+/–	+/–	+/–	+/–

sulting shamans, who often have sophisticated understandings of how different substances compare. Zulu healers in South Africa, for example, separate vision-inducing plants into two categories: those that produce hallucinations and those that induce vivid dreams. Hallucinogens, like the fan-shaped *Boophone disticha*, are compared to mirrors or televisions. Diviners consider their visions to be impure and arbitrary, although they still ingest them and give them to patients seeking hidden knowledge. Dream-inducing plants, meanwhile, like the African dream herb *Silene undulata*, are said to produce true visions. These can be disturbing for initiates, yet trained healers trust them as genuine gateways for connecting with ancestral spirits. For Zulu healers, there are two classes of visionary states, not one.[8]

One of the best resources for comparing the effects of drugs is PsychonautWiki, a self-described "community-driven online encyclopedia that aims to document the emerging field of psychonautics (i.e., the exploration of altered states of consciousness) in a comprehensive, scientifically-grounded manner." PsychonautWiki has the standard drawbacks of wikis: articles are works in progress; anyone can create or edit them; they can be vandalized. Nevertheless, it is closely monitored and has two advantages that most academic studies lack.[9]

First, it is ambitious, aspiring not only to study as wide a range of psychoactive substances as possible but also to capture what it feels like to use those substances. It synthesizes far-flung accounts of non-ordinary states, including trip reports on websites like Erowid. Second, it characterizes each substance using a standard list of subjective effects—called, quite fittingly, the Subjective Effect Index, or SEI. The SEI is huge. As of March 2023, it comprised some 240 subjective effects and included everything from "double vision" to "orgasm depression." Combined with the website's scope and careful editing, the SEI makes PsychonautWiki ideal for our purposes. Using it, we can investigate what, if anything, is shared across shamanic trance states.[10]

I analyzed the entries for three psychoactive substances: tobacco, ayahuasca, and datura. Each is used by shamans in the Americas to enter altered states and engage with unseen agents. Tobacco contains nicotine, a highly addictive stimulant. Ayahuasca, at least as I use the term here, is a psychedelic brew commonly made from the *Banisteriopsis caapi* vine and the DMT-containing chacruna plant. Datura, also known as devil's trumpet or jimsonweed, refers to nine species of poisonous nightshades that, when consumed, act as deliriants, pulling people seamlessly into profound and often unpleasant hallucinations.[11]

Contrary to the ecstatic equivalence hypothesis, I found little overlap in the experiences induced by the three substances. Of the eighty-one effects that accompany ayahuasca, a mere twenty-two are observed with datura or tobacco, as well. Only four effects occur with all three substances: stimulation, sedation, nausea, and wakefulness. None embody the kinds of "integrative" experiences emphasized by Winkelman. In fact, many of the effects that some researchers associate with a shamanic state of consciousness—like ego death, creativity enhancement, pattern recognition enhancement, and feelings of unity, interconnectedness, and eternalism—occur only with ayahuasca. It's as if researchers, moved by transformative experiences with classic psychedelics, have eagerly interpreted their trips as glimpses into the true and universal nature of shamanism.

———

There is, of course, a crucial feature shared across all the nonordinary states shamans seem to enter: their non-ordinariness. As a man told me after we watched a shaman become possessed by a local deity, "He was different. He was not himself." He brought up the man's voice. "Did you hear him? That was something else."

We were in Mangalore, a coastal city in the South Indian state of Karnataka, and had just witnessed a ritual called *bhuta kola*. A high-caste family had invited a low-caste shaman to a roadside temple. He was much darker than they were but still painted his face black. His bare chest and arms were covered in white markings. He sported a palm-leaf skirt over royal red pants and was clad in glamorous metal objects, including silver armlets and thick anklets that clanged when he moved. A strand of fire-colored flowers encircled his face; atop his head, he wore a golden skullcap and a garland of jasmine flowers. A priest, naked from the waist up except for gold jewelry, handed him two glistening scepters. A kaleidoscope of royal and sacred imagery, the shaman had transformed himself into a receptacle of a god.

A small band started playing drums, trumpets, and shakers. It sounded like procession music and was far more jovial and celebratory than I had expected. The shaman danced, his movements becoming stranger with time. After a while, he was twitching his legs, lifting and lowering the scepter to the beat, and laughing. Someone turned him ninety degrees, then another ninety degrees, and so on until he completed a full circle. All the while, he continued laughing. It was somewhere between the loud gaiety of Santa Claus and the unhinged mania of a supervillain—a sign, I was later told, that the local god Koragajja had entered him.

The purposes of the ceremony were blessing and divination. The shaman, normally of a social stratum that would draw little respect from the high-status family, became divine. The family draped garlands over his neck. They touched him. Some forty other people came to see him. They bowed on their knees, threw flower petals on him, and gave offerings, including bottles of alcohol. Eventually, the shirtless priest interceded, asking questions to the possessed shaman—or to the god possessing him, depending on whom you ask. He was still shaking, as if tweaked from ten cups of coffee, and responded in a rapid, booming voice. They went back and forth in Tulu, a local language that I do not understand; afterward I was told that he divined about health and a child's education.

My wife's family is from Mangalore. They knew that we wanted to attend a *bhuta kola*, and two of them, her aunt Joy and family friend Sheila, brought us to the ritual that night. But Nina's family is Catholic. Her ancestors were converted by Portuguese missionaries many generations ago. They are forbidden from believing in rituals like *bhuta kola*, let alone paying offerings for possessed shamans to divine their future. Yet this didn't stop them from entertaining an open curiosity. "The Hindus believe in it," one of them told me earlier that day. "And it works for them."

Talking to Mangalorean Catholics, I found that they were especially intrigued by the shaman's strange behavior. An urbane woman speculated that the shamans must have gotten drunk beforehand, thinking that only intoxication could explain their outlandish behavior. But Sheila wasn't so sure. "The voice changes," she said after the ceremony. "I don't know how they could manage that."

Sheila's comment reflects an important intuition about non-ordinary states: the more foreign a state is from normal behavior, the more it demonstrates special powers and supernatural contact. A shaman who chitchats with an audience in their everyday voice is likely to be considered a fraud. One who thrashes violently, speaks in a strange voice, and then doesn't remember anything afterward is more conceivably doing something we regular humans cannot.

This intuition is crucial for understanding why shamans enter non-ordinary states. In the last chapter, we covered the Regular Jyotika Problem—the fact that people are skeptical when an apparently normal human claims special powers. We saw that specialists partly overcome this skepticism through practices like self-denial, magical surgeries, and death-and-rebirth rituals. By transforming a specialist into a different kind of entity, by supposedly changing their essences and endowing them with magical body parts—in short, by xenizing them—these practices make claims of superpowers more tenable.

Non-ordinary states seem to do something similar. They xenize a specialist, albeit on a shorter time scale. Their difference from normal behavior and experience makes them compelling. Just as we visit miracle workers who diverge from the rest of humanity, we are enthralled by supernatural acts that look and feel nothing like typical human behavior.

―――――――――

The intuition that otherness signals supernatural contact is common. Dig through descriptions of prophecy and divine healing, and you often find people associating extreme altered states with otherworldly powers. A telling example comes from Carmen Blacker, the British scholar who studied Japanese shamanism.

Blacker's work on Japanese culture is legendary. Born in 1924, she started learning Japanese from a grammar book at the age of twelve. By seventeen, she was taking private lessons with her friend's father, Major-General Francis Piggott, who had just returned from serving at the British embassy in Tokyo. Her Japanese advanced so quickly that, when the war broke out in 1942, she was one of twenty British young people recruited as Japanese codebreakers. She was paid £2 a week, "partly," she later explained, "due to my age, 18, and partly due to my being a woman."[12]

After the war, Blacker continued to study Japanese language and culture, eventually landing a lectureship at Cambridge. Although she wrote extensively about Japanese folklore, literature, and intellectual history, she is remembered best for her research on religion, particularly her magnum opus, *The Catalpa Bow: A Study of Shamanistic Practices in Japan* (1975).

One of the incidents presented in *The Catalpa Bow* is a shamanic séance from 1963. Blacker was in Ōkura, a tiny village in Japan's eastern hills, then consisting mostly of a few farmhouses strung along a stream. She came for Hayama Matsuri, an autumn festival devoted to the mountain god Hayama. During the festival, a *miko*, or shaman, channeled Hayama and answered questions about the coming year's harvest, like: When should we plant rice? How big will the next harvest be? Will the silkworms produce a good yield? Afterward, everyone escorted the god to the summit of a mountain, where he stayed until the rice planting in the spring.[13]

The festival that year turned out to be disappointing, at least for the attendees. "The general verdict the next day was that the *miko*'s performance had been so languid that it was difficult to realise that she was possessed at all," wrote Blacker. The attendees contrasted her possession with that of a shaman five years earlier, who levitated, screamed answers in an odd bass voice, and flailed on the floor "in a convincingly frenzied manner." They had been so taken with the other shaman's performance that they bombarded her with questions until dawn. The festival Blacker attended, in contrast, ended before midnight.[14]

As Blacker wrote later, "In every case we noticed that a trance was approved by the village as 'good' and genuine when the medium's behaviour was violent, inhuman and strange. Behaviour ordinary or human—as in the decorous waving of the wand or a polite use of language—was instantly condemned as weak and unconvincing."[15]

We do not have to go to Japan to discover an association between startling behavior and supernatural contact. Indeed, it lurks in our language. In English, we say that someone who produces something unexpectedly creative is "inspired" or has a flash of "inspiration." This comes from the Latin *inspirare* and originally referred to moments in which spirits or divine beings breathed ideas into people. Likewise, we say that someone with exceptional intellectual ability is a "genius," the word originally denoting a spirit assigned each person at birth.[16]

In other contexts, strange behavior is linked to possession or a loss of identity. *She is not herself! Something has gotten into her! He is out of his mind! He is beside himself! What has gotten hold of you?* These statements all conjure up images of a person's identity leaving them or another taking its place, exactly the kinds of claims that many shamans make. Similar idioms appear in other languages. Spanish speakers say *"fuera de sí,"* or "out of oneself." Mandarin speakers say *"shī hún luò pò"* (失魂落魄), or "lose one's soul and fall apart." In Arabic, people say that a person's mind has flown away (*"taar a'qluh,"* طار عقله), while in Vietnamese, they say a person has a ghost in their head (*"trong đầu có ma"*). Whether aware of it or not, humans often have similar intuitions about unusual behavior.

Why, then, do shamans enter altered states? Winkelman sees them as cognitive enhancements useful for healing, finding animals to hunt, and organizing social activity. Harner, in contrast, described them as many shamans do: as the work required to access non-ordinary reality and commune with spirits. These views are different, but they agree that shamanic states exist because they "work"—that is, because they help shamans solve the problems for which people seek them out.[17]

Everything we have reviewed suggests another function of altered states, however. More than methods to aid in healing or social coordination, altered states bolster the simulated reality of supernatural contact. They are divine dramas—performances of otherness that make the experience realer for clients, as well as, in many cases, for shamans themselves.

This perspective might bother some people. It might seem to strip shamanism of its authenticity, to denounce it as gawdy artifice. Yet this is the wrong conclusion. The performative nature of trance does not deny its power. As we will see in the next chapter, the simulated reality that shamans construct—the vivid experience of another person making contact with divine forces—can be a powerful healing tool. Just as importantly, the methods of inducing altered states can be profound. Some shamanic trance is bogus. But much of it truly feels otherworldly. In convincing audiences and themselves of unearthly contact, shamans have invented mystical traditions worldwide.

The anthropologist Rusty Greaves has written about the subjective effects of taking yopo snuffs. At first, the eyes redden and water. The body feels warm. Hallucinations appear as geometric lines, with nausea kicking in around the same time.[18]

Then begins what he calls "mental confusion," which lasts anywhere from twenty minutes to an hour. To quote one of his unpublished manuscripts, "Even when not frightening, disassociation from normal thinking can be extreme. Contact with spirits of the dead and non-human entities are stated by the Pumé [another yopo-using people of the Orinoco basin] to occur during this stage."[19]

For me, mental confusion started as I lay down. I recall glimpses of lucidity. I sensed Nina near my feet. I searched every so often for the basin to vomit in. I clutched Sandeep's legs and sometimes looked up at his face. But most of my thoughts from that time are obscure. I remember only outlines of them, like shadowy creatures sensed but never seen. I remember repeating the phrase "*al frente, afuera*," meaning "to the front, outside." I remember thinking of myself as a time being, as someone who could transcend present and future. I remember that the shaman approached me playing a maraca. He touched my hair. I felt deeply insightful in that moment and thought that he could sense it.

Then, with the immediacy of waking up, my trip ended. I

became aware of my surroundings. People were watching us through the doorway. Vomit was everywhere. It stained my shirt, and a puddle had formed around my face on the floor. Sludgy nasal discharge covered my mustache, mouth, and beard, and streaked down my right arm. After I got back to my chair, Sandeep told me that I had been muttering nonsensical Spanish words like "*afueramente*" (outsidely) and "*profesionamente*" (a bastardization of *profesionalmente*, or "professionally"). I had presumably said, "What? What? I'm like, what?" and, gripping his leg, exclaimed, "What time is it even anyway?" When he asked me to "please shut up," I replied, "For sure," stretching out the "u" with the relaxed assurance of a car salesman, before repeating "*básicamente*" (basically) over and over.

I saw everything more clearly: I had been rolling around on the floor, barfing and babbling absurdities. The others had vomited, too, but my response had clearly been the most extreme and, from the outside, the most unpleasant. I felt embarrassed. Yet no one seemed to care. The shaman's son (who, unlike his father, spoke Spanish) asked me if everything was normal again. I said yes, and he gave me a thumbs-up. When I insisted that I clean up the vomit, he forbade me.

On the boat ride out of the community, I asked our guide, a leader of a nearby community, "After watching our experience, do you want to try yopo?" I meant the question sincerely, but he took it as a joke. How could witnessing a bunch of foreigners lose their minds and stomachs ever inspire a non-shaman to inhale this sacred powder? So rather than answering my question, he assured me that our experiences were typical, that all first times were like that.

Others—the shaman, his son, a teacher with a mystical bent—told us the same thing. First times with yopo are rough. The Yanomami shaman Davi Kopenawa described a similar loss of control during his early experiences with *yākoana*, a psychedelic snuff whose main active ingredient is 5-MeO-DMT:

> I rolled and thrashed on the ground like a ghost. I could no longer see anything around me, neither my house nor its inhabitants. I whimpered and called for my mother:

"Napaaa! Napaaa!" My skin remained sprawled on the ground but the *xapiri* [spirits] took hold of my image [spirit/soul]. They sped away with it, far into the distance. It flew with them onto the sky's back, where the ghosts live, or in the *aõpatari* ancestors' [carnivorous ancestors'] underground world. In the end they brought me back to where my skin was lying and I came to my senses.[20]

Chatting with longtime yopo users, we discovered a nuanced discourse about how to use it. The teacher with a mystical bent, I'll call him Manuel, said that there is a moment after "the colors" when you need to concentrate on your goal. Fail to do so, he said, and you will lose yourself. The shaman's son told us the same thing: the transition point is fast, and if you do not focus, yopo will carry you off. Both learned this lesson as apprentices of shamans. It's simple advice in hindsight, yet it is one facet of a sophisticated understanding of yopo, its effects, and the role of expectations in the experience. More than simply using a psychedelic to feel otherworldly, Orinoco shamans are psychopharmacologists, attuned to the sensitive relationship between mind and drug.

Paralleling the discourse about proper psychedelic use, we discovered a unique brand of Amazonian mysticism. Shamans, as well as non-shamans who used psychoactive drugs for "*sabiduría*" (wisdom), tended to have a deep reverence for the world, especially nature. They felt they intimately knew divine forces. Manuel told us that, when he was twenty, he asked his grandfather, a shaman, to take him on as an apprentice. He consumed yopo and caapi, a vine famously known as an ingredient in ayahuasca, and worked with his grandfather to interpret the worlds that opened up. He came to realize that all humans are born like dogs, he said—spiritually blind and deaf. He recognized that the forest and its inhabitants speak yet that most people are incapable of listening. He told us that it was only through training with yopo and caapi that the world became interpretable. He came to know the anaconda deity that dwells in the river. He started to truly hear the rain forest. His sense of self schismed, dividing like a mitotic cell into what he called a spiritual self and a moral self.

Davi Kopenawa, the Yanomami shaman, has also described

the perceptual and mystical shifts that came with shamanic training. Through deprivation and the snuff *yãkoana*, he said, he slowly
began to discern the blissful songs of spirits resounding in the
world. "Ordinary people could not hear them, but for those who
had become ghosts [shamans], they were very sharp." Although
they may emerge to enhance the theater of shamanic ceremonies,
altered states can also create numinous experiences, making the
divine feel realer and more palpable.[21]

The reality of shamans' altered states is far from universally
accepted. In the mid-1700s, the German chemist and botanist
Johann Georg Gmelin published a four-volume account of his
decade-long journey throughout Siberia. He wrote about the
shamanic practices he encountered, using words like *Schaman*
and *Schamanka* as well as the German terms *Zauberin* (sorceress),
Hexe (witch), and *Schelm* (rascal). At one point, he described a
shaman "decked out with all kinds of iron instruments" who was
"running to and fro along the fire":

> At length, after a lot of hocus-pocus and sweating, [the
> shaman] would have had us believe that the devils were
> there. He asked us what we wanted to know. We put a
> question to him. He started his conjuring tricks, while two
> others were assisting him. In the end we were confirmed
> in our opinion that it was all humbug, and we wished in
> our hearts that we could take him and his companions to
> the Urgurian silver mine, so that there they might spend
> the rest of their days in perpetual labor.[22]

The language here is insensitive. The call to subject shamans
to forced labor reeks with colonial violence. Yet is there some truth
here? Throughout this chapter and the last, I have presented shamans as performers. I have recast the many facets of shamanism—
deprivation, initiations, non-ordinary states—as spectacles of
otherness. If we strip away the colonial disdain, was Gmelin's
basic point—that shamans are dishonest con men—correct?

Many people seem to think so. And I don't just mean missionaries and imperial explorers, but shamans' clients, too—even, in some cases, shamans themselves. In a story recorded by the German-American anthropologist Franz Boas, a Pacific Northwest shaman named Quesalid admitted to doubting shamans' powers early in his life. "I desired to learn about the shaman, whether it is true or whether it is made up and (whether) they pretend to be shamans," he said.[23]

Quesalid's story has since become a go-to example of Indigenous skepticism, propelled into stardom by the French celebrity ethnologist Claude Lévi-Strauss. Its fame might not be justified, however. The story comes across as the pristine account of an unacculturated medicine man, and that is how many writers, including Lévi-Strauss, have treated it. Yet Quesalid was probably Boas's longtime informant, George Hunt. The son of an Englishman and a Tlingit princess from Alaska, Hunt wrote somewhere between three thousand and five thousand pages on the Kwakwaka'wakw for Boas. More problematically, by the time Boas published Quesalid/Hunt's story, he had worked with Hunt for more than forty years. In that time, Hunt had also collected museum specimens, accompanied expeditions, arranged ethnographic collections at the American Museum of Natural History in New York, and had a major role, including as a writer, translator, recruiter, and totem-pole carver, in the production of the 1914 film *In the Land of Head Hunters*.[24]

These interactions meant that Hunt was well acquainted with Euro-American perspectives on Indigenous religion. "The Indian likes to appear rational and knows that shamanistic practices are disbelieved by whites," wrote Boas. It is very possible, then, that Quesalid's story is packaged for a dubious audience.[25]

Even if Quesalid's story has been misrepresented, however, the basic point holds: people who work with shamans sometimes suspect them of quackery. Recall the Japanese community who considered a certain shaman's behavior to be "weak and unconvincing." Peoples as diverse as the Okinawans, the Plains Ojibwe, and the Tanala of Madagascar have similarly voiced suspicions of shamans. Distrust was common enough among the Quinault of the Pacific Northwest that they told a story to unbelievers about a skeptic who was dragged through the trees by shamanic power, becoming a hairy, bearlike spirit that can still be heard in the forest. Davi Kopenawa even admitted to having doubts early on. "My father-in-law did not lie to me and he did not want to make a liar of me," he said. "He truly made me know the *xapiri*. At the beginning, when I did not know anything about them, sometimes I told myself: 'Maybe he is lying and deceiving us!'"[26]

Such skepticism seems warranted. In many societies, shamans claim to extract embodiments of illness. They might suck or rub a patient's body and then display an illness-causing object, such as a worm, arrow, or small quartz crystal.[27] Perhaps unsurprisingly, such extractions often involve sleight of hand. While living with the Azande in southern Sudan, the English anthropologist Edward Evans-Pritchard paid for his personal servant, Kamanga, to be initiated as a shaman. Kamanga passed along many of the tricks he learned to Evans-Pritchard, including one in which healers filled a decapitated spider's body with red tree sap and hid it in the patient's poultice. Kamanga explained,

> After massaging a patient for a time they remove the poultice, discover in it this spider, and show it to the people, saying: "Heu! Look at the sick man's blood in the belly of the spider." They press the belly of the spider between their fingers and with a pop squeeze out the juice of the *bakure* tree.[28]

Shamans are conjurors, then—masters of prestidigitation. Yet many still believe that they have powers. I have known many Mentawai *sikerei* who not only call one another when they are sick, but also treat their own sick children, sometimes desperately cycling through different rituals until something works. Some shamans apparently think that their stage tricks are necessary. A Selk'nam shaman in Tierra del Fuego once asked the Austrian priest Martin Gusinde why he thought aspirin alone could treat people: "If a Selk'nam *xon* [shaman] wants to remove the ailment, he must sing and afterwards draw it out of the body with his mouth. Why do you never sing when a patient comes to you? You only give him that 'white thing'!"[29]

Shamans both believe and do not believe. They lie. They use ruses and subterfuge. But they are humans, too. They experience the vivid super-reality of some non-ordinary states. And they notice that some patients recover after healing ceremonies. They see that rain falls after weather rituals, that those friendly neighbors indeed had a child after a fertility ceremony.

Shamanism is not an elaborate hoax put on by tricksy con artists. To the contrary, it is a dazzling institution that culturally evolves, assuring specialist and client alike of the practitioner's otherworldly powers.

CHAPTER 5

Behold the Birdhead

Glenn Treisman, a professor of psychiatry and medicine at Johns Hopkins, is a legendary healer. "When I walk on the ward," he told me, "the nurses and physical therapists and the nursing aides and the pharmacy techs and the residents and the nurse practitioners—they're all waiting for me to come and save the day. And they've been telling the patient, 'Dr. Treisman is coming. Everything is going to be okay.'"

The reputation is well deserved. Treisman has a knack for taking on impossible cases—the average patient in his service has already seen somewhere around twelve to fifteen doctors—and somehow making them better.

Consider a patient I'll call Jim. A veteran, Jim was injured in an accident that left him paralyzed. For years, he was confined to a wheelchair. He became depressed. He had given up. Yet within weeks of working with Treisman, he was walking again.

Or consider a patient I'll call Sarah. Treisman first saw her when she was seventeen. By that point, she had spent years in and out of some of the best pediatric hospitals in the world. She was confined to a wheelchair, got her nutrition through a tube, and defecated once every two weeks. Her leg muscles had atrophied. Yet less than two months after her first appointment with Treisman, she took her first steps in four years. Two months later, she was walking. As I write this, she is living a life that once seemed impossible. She got her GED, has a boyfriend, and is attending junior college. Treisman himself uses the word "miraculous" to describe her recovery, seemingly attributing it to a power beyond him.

How could he solve these impossible cases? How could he reinvigorate people against all expectations?

Simple, he told me. "I am a shaman."

If we are to understand shamanism and its timelessness, we need to confront a fundamental question: Does it work?

To many people, the answer is a resounding and obvious yes. For them, the ubiquity of shamanism is a testament to its efficacy. How could it last, they reason, unless it provided a benefit? This logic taps into what the former biology professors Heather Heying and Bret Weinstein call the Omega principle. As they write in *A Hunter-Gatherer's Guide to the 21st Century* (2021), "Any expensive and long-lasting cultural trait (such as traditions passed down within a lineage for thousands of years) should be presumed to be adaptive."[1]

But Heying and Weinstein are mistaken. Persistence does not imply adaptiveness. Big Macs, incest porn, and addictive opiate drugs are all notoriously hard to quash, yet few people maintain that they are good for individuals or societies. Bloodletting was used in medical settings around the world until someone bothered looking at the mortality statistics, which revealed it to be scientifically unsound and unhelpful for all but a few indications, most of them rare diseases. In his book *Sick Societies* (1992), the anthropologist Robert Edgerton listed myriad practices that are long-lasting and seem harmful, from witchcraft accusations to taboos on nutritious foodstuffs.[2]

Understanding why these and other traditions linger requires looking not at objective benefits but at subjective appeal. This is because culture relies on individual decisions. Bloodletting endures as long as people consider it useful. Big Macs and step-sibling porn are manufactured as long as people want to consume them. In short, it is our subjective evaluation of a practice's appeal—and less its real-world impact on our health, fertility, or strength—that often determines whether it sticks around and spreads. Of course, subjective appeal and objective benefits often converge. Hammers, matches, and spears produce material advantages, which is why we continue to use them. But plenty of practices circulate because they make us feel good or because people erroneously perceive them to be useful for everyday goals.[3]

Everything we have reviewed so far suggests that shamanism develops because of this kind of subjective appeal. People want to manage life's uncertainties, and shamanism emerges to provide a captivating feeling of this control. Yet this does not deny shamanism's potential payoffs. People may turn to shamanism in desperation yet nevertheless enjoy other benefits.

Which gets us back to our guiding question: Does shamanism work?

───────────

There are different ways that shamanism might "work." A friend of mine, the musician and somatic therapist Josh Elbaum, put forward one interpretation in an email after I defended my dissertation in 2020:

Dear Manvir,

I really enjoyed your dissertation defense! I thought of a potential hole in your argument but didn't want to embarrass you in front of your mom. The hole is as follows: what about the possibility of the existence of magic? That the shamans are indeed affected by nether spirits?

Best,
Josh

Many scientists would dismiss Josh's question. But I think it's an important one to address. Most of the traditions I review in this book assume that shamans are, one way or another, "affected by nether spirits," as Josh put it. It is only fair to explain why I find this unlikely.

To be clear, I am open to the idea that invisible agents exist. I take seriously the proposition that we know next to nothing about reality—that, for all we know, our universe is a tiny speck on the outer membrane of a cosmic, unfathomably complex, many-dimensional cephalopod-like being, or that we inhabit a simulation, or that it's turtles all the way down. Yet there are good reasons to conclude that shamans do not engage with invisible forces and provide services through that engagement. The most compelling, I think, is that no one has conclusively demonstrated those powers, even when there are huge monetary incentives.

An example is Abraham Kovoor's challenge. One of South Asia's most famous rationalists, Kovoor was born in 1898 in the Malabar region of southwestern India. The son of a priest in the Syrian Christian Church, he was skeptical even as a child. Once, when sick, he explained to his older sister why he refused to take medicine and pray to Jesus. "If I do both at the same time, I won't be knowing which of the two helped to remove the cough. So I will take the medicine now, and if there is no effect I can try prayer later."[4]

This skepticism blossomed in adulthood. After retiring from teaching in 1959, he devoted himself to empirically testing the claims of South Asia's most prominent "godmen." Starting in 1963, he offered between 1,000 and 25,000 Sri Lankan rupees to anyone who could tell him the number on a currency note rolled up in an envelope. The challenge evolved until, in 1969, he promised 100,000 Sri Lankan rupees—about $16,800 at the time—"to any one from any part of the world who can demonstrate supernatural or miraculous powers under fool-proof and fraud-proof conditions."[5]

Here's the list of miracles he pledged to reward, reproduced in full:

1. Read the serial number of a sealed up currency note.
2. Produce an exact replica of a currency note.
3. Stand stationary on burning cinders for half a minute without blistering the feet.

4. Materialise from nothing an object I ask.

5. Move or bend an object using psychokinetic power.

6. Read the thought of another person using telepathic power.

7. Make an amputated limb grow even one inch by prayer, spiritual or faith healing power, Lourdes water, sand, holy ash, etc.

8. Levitate in the air by yogic power.

9. Stop the heart beat for five minutes by yogic powers.

10. Stop breathing for thirty minutes by yogic powers.

11. Walk on water.

12. Leave the body in one place and reappear in another place.

13. Predict a future event.

14. Develop creative intelligence or get enlightened through transcendental or yogic meditation.

15. Speak or understand an unknown language as a result of rebirth or being possessed by a spirit holy or evil.

16. Produce a ghost to be photographed.

17. Disappear from the negative when photographed.

18. Get out of a locked room through spiritual powers.

19. Increase the quantity of weight of a substance by divine power.

20. Detect a hidden object.

21. Convert water into petrol or wine.

22. Convert wine into blood.

23. Palmists and astrologers, who hoodwink the gullibles by saying that palmistry and astrology are perfectly "scientific," can win my award if they can pick out correctly—within a 5 per cent margin of error—those of males, females, the living and the dead from a set of ten palm prints or astrological charts giving the times of birth correct to the minute, and places of birth with their latitudes and longitudes.[6]

No one completed Kovoor's challenge. A few people tried and failed. Many more publicly accepted the challenge but never turned up. A doctor in Bangalore paid a deposit of 1,000 rupees, convinced that his guru and a six-year-old child could produce miracles. He eventually asked for the deposit back, but, Kovoor wrote, "I had to decline his request as it was against the conditions of my challenge."[7]

Kovoor's was neither the first nor final cash prize for miracle workers. In 1922, *Scientific American* made two offers of $2,500, worth about $40,000 today. One, they said, would go to "the first person who produces a psychic photograph"; the second was for "the first person who produces a visible psychic manifestation." Superstar magician Harry Houdini was one of the judges. No one got the prize money, although the contest attracted a cavalcade of charlatans. The first medium tested, George Valiantine, claimed that, in darkness, he could summon spirits to touch onlookers and speak through a trumpet. He didn't realize, however, that his seat was wired with a light that went off in another room whenever he got up. As it turns out, the ghostly acts occurred whenever he was up and about.[8]

The most famous challenge was issued by the skeptic and stage magician James Randi. In 1964, he offered $1,000 of his own money to the first person who could present proof of the occult, paranormal, or supernatural. Donors enlarged the pot until, in 1996, it had reached $1 million. Over a thousand people applied. He invited prominent psychics like Sylvia Browne and Rosemary Altea to be tested. Yet when the prize finally closed in 2015, the money remained unclaimed.[9]

According to Wikipedia, there are twenty-five standing prizes for demonstrations of paranormal and supernatural abilities. They have been issued in nineteen countries and exceed $1 million in total prize money. Another dozen or so prizes, including Randi's, Kovoor's, and *Scientific American*'s, have been discontinued. None has ever been won. Mystics, psychics, and mediums charge steep sums to perform miracles. But as long as they refuse to perform their powers under controlled settings, it is hard to accept that they truly engage with the beyond.[10]

By Treisman's telling, his magic works less by communing with nether spirits and more through theatrics. He showed me a video of him evaluating Jim, the veteran consigned to a wheelchair. The encounter looked like a normal doctor-patient interaction, with the noticeable exception of Treisman's clothes. He went all out. He wore a bow tie, black slacks, and a black jacket. His navy-blue dress shirt was furnished with a white collar and white shirt cuffs, themselves studded with navy-blue cuff links. It was an almost comic level of formality.

"I'm really shamaning out here," he admitted. The look was intentional. "I don't dress beyond a tie and jacket most days," he said. "But if I'm going to try to pull a miracle off, I go up a notch."

The outfit is an example of what Treisman calls "putting on the birdhead." It's a concept he teaches to his medical residents, and it was the phrase that inspired me to get in touch with him.

"I want people to think of the medicine man," he said. "I want people to think of the shaman who puts the birdhead on and acquires magical powers from it. That's really what we do in medicine. We read all this science. We know all this stuff. And we acquire magical powers." Emphasizing these powers inspires faith, he says. And "the faith they have in you really provides power for your efforts on their behalf."

Treisman did not always put on the birdhead. When he arrived in Baltimore as a medical resident in 1987, he preferred to dress casually. His patients were inner-city Black people, he said. "I grew up in Detroit. I had a lot of friends in the inner city. I talked like them. I hung out like them." He felt that dressing formally created too much distance between him and them. It made him unrelatable.

But with time, he saw that his patients weren't looking for someone to hang out with. "They want you to wear a tie and a jacket and look like you're a professional," he said. He noticed that, once he dressed up a little, his patients told him details that they wouldn't share with a friend or neighbor.

Like what? I asked.

"That they have crab lice in their pubic hair. They didn't want to tell you that if you're wearing jeans and a T-shirt," he said. "They don't want to tell you about the fact that they were hitting their wife, or their husband was hitting them."

The birdhead is only part of Treisman's approach. Just as important is the narrative—the story he co-creates with patients to explain why they are feeling bad. Many of the people he sees have been told that there is nothing clearly wrong. Doctors have run tests and concluded that their pain or paralysis or difficulty digesting food has no basis in biology. But, says Stephanie Harper, a psychiatrist in Seattle who worked with Treisman during her residency at Johns Hopkins, "the patient is approaching it from a body perspective. Their body is causing them issues, and that is real."

Treisman respects the patient's viewpoint. He builds a story that resonates with that perspective while also creating opportunities for recovery. Consider again Sarah, the patient who wouldn't eat and couldn't walk. The doctors did a thorough workup and found no biological reason for her problems. But Treisman dug into her personal history until he learned that, as a toddler, she swallowed a toxic liquid that corroded her digestive tract. He also found evidence of an autoimmune condition that he treated with antibodies. "Yes, there was a very real event here," Harper remembered Treisman saying. "The good news is that we are no longer seeing that."

Treisman took a similar approach with Jim. He learned that Jim had suffered an accident. He accepted that there had probably been some spinal damage. But he insisted that the damage had healed. He recreated a conversation between him and Jim:

"Whatever happened to you then, I've examined you now and physically you are capable of learning to walk again."

"Well, the other doctors told me I couldn't walk."

"How'd they do with you?"

"Not very well."

"Okay." Birdhead time. "Do you think I got to be the Eugene Meyer Professor of Psychiatry and Medicine at Johns Hopkins by being wrong? I'm right. I did the neuro exam. I'm an expert. I got neurology to come and see. They agree with me."

For Treisman, working with the patient's narrative is crucial. It makes them receptive. It builds trust. "At the same time," he said, "I'm introducing the idea that when you have a biological illness, you don't do what your feelings tell you to do. You do what your doctor tells you to do."

The narrative and the birdhead interact to create faith. The patient sees their affliction as physical, as something that must be treated by a doctor. The birdhead, meanwhile, enhances the perception of the doctor's power and unique expertise. Just as shamans present themselves as superhuman in precisely the ways necessary to engage with invisible forces, Treisman cultivates the image of the super-doctor, someone who can once and for all deal with your medical ailment and make you better.

The narrative and birdhead sound reasonable. But how exactly do they heal?

One way is by changing the patient's understanding. People come to healers with stories about themselves. They may believe that they are paralyzed, that they are unlikable, that someone is attacking them with witchcraft. These stories create expectations of who the patients are and what they can do. If you believe you are paralyzed, you won't walk. If you suspect that witches are attacking you, you may stay home and avoid people you distrust.

These stories can be self-perpetuating. Stephanie Harper listed examples for me. If someone has trouble walking and sits in a wheelchair, their leg muscles can atrophy and make it harder to walk again. If they do not eat because it makes them nauseous, their digestion can slow down, making digestion even harder. Narratives about personality and mental health can be just as self-defeating. A person who believes they are disliked may pull away from social interactions, weakening their relationships and intensifying feelings of isolation. Harper said, "If you start to believe something is wrong, then physical things can happen that make it wrong."

The power of a specialist is that they can change the stories we tell ourselves. If you believe you are fatigued for a medical reason, a powerful doctor should be able to fix you. If you believe that vengeful ghosts haunt you at night, an effective medium should be able to chase them away. To the extent you consider a specialist powerful, you give them the power to rewrite stories about yourself.

Shamans seem to do this. I encountered a potential example while visiting Huottüja communities, known to outsiders as the Piaroa, near the border of Colombia and Venezuela. A friend described a time when his wife, let's call her María, was troubled. It was three months into her pregnancy, and her head hurt. She fainted sometimes and woke up screaming. It was clear to everyone that dark forces were involved: She dreamt of big, headless figures. At night, she felt that she was joined in bed by little black spirits.

María and my friend talked it over with her father. They decided to get María healed. They visited three shamans who, with their assistants, took yopo, along with a liquid made from *Banisteriopsis caapi*. As the shamans journeyed to learn why she was sick and how to treat her, my friend sprinkled a magic powder to protect them and María from evil spirits. After the journey finished, the shamans slept briefly, then rose at dawn to bathe María in a waterfall. Again, they took the snuff and the brew, this time singing and playing a maraca over her. María fainted during the cleansing.

After the ceremony, the shamans presented their visions. They learned that a man in love with María had used dark powers against her. But their procedure had worked, they said. Any evil residues were removed. Looking back, my friend agreed. Days after the ceremony, María started to recover slowly. Within three weeks, she had improved substantially.

As with Jim, María's understanding of herself may have changed. The healing power of the ceremony may have stemmed from rewriting her story—from assuring her that she was no longer haunted and thus free to return to her life. Granted, there are other reasons María might have recovered. Maybe she happened to get better for reasons unconnected to the ceremony. Or maybe the shamans really did identify and remove evil forces sent by a spurned lover.

Even so, there are good reasons to suspect that narrative shifts matter. Therapists have appreciated the power of rewriting patients' stories for more than fifty years, in large part because of another Johns Hopkins psychiatrist named Jerome Frank. In 1961, Frank published a now-legendary book called *Persuasion and Healing* that proposed, quite provocatively, that the brand of healing is unimportant. Psychoanalysis, behavioral therapy, ecstatic trance healing—all these, said Frank, have a similar capacity to cure. What's important, he said, are the simple building blocks of healing encounters. He stressed four factors specifically: a healing setting; an alliance with a trusted healer; a story that connects the patient's trouble to a solution; and a treatment that makes sense given the story.[11]

For Frank, these elements work together to combat what he called "demoralization." The way he saw it, patients suffer because they feel incompetent and helpless. They have concluded that they are broken. Therapy works by rewriting this understanding—by giving patients hope and assurance and freeing them from self-defeating narratives. Once you feel that a healer has cleansed you of evil energies or cured whichever injury is behind your paralysis, you are free to live your life again.[12]

When Frank proposed this "common factors" approach, there was little evidence to back it up. Yet in the decades since, hundreds of studies have been conducted probing the effects of different healing elements and techniques. When researchers run meta-analyses—analyses that incorporate the findings of many studies—the results support Frank's arguments. In 2015, the psychologist Bruce Wampold showed that, while some treatments might be better than others, these differences are small compared to the effects of contextual factors, like patient expectations, the relationship with the healer, and a shared understanding of the reason for suffering. Much of healing, whether by Colombian shamans or Johns Hopkins physicians, boils down to assuring someone they are being healed.[13]

Changing the stories people tell about themselves is certainly a powerful mechanism of healing. Yet in my journey to understand shamanism, I have come to suspect two other mechanisms, too.

I learned one from Ted Kaptchuk. In 1977, Kaptchuk opened a Chinese medicine clinic in Cambridge, Massachusetts. He had recently returned from Macao, where he spent years mastering the arts of herbalism and acupuncture. Once he started practicing, however, things didn't seem to add up.

"I would treat people, and they would get better before I even treated them," he told me. "I would write an herbal prescription, and as they walked out of the door, before taking the medicine, I could see they walked straighter and seemed a bit happier."

One incident stuck with him. He treated an Armenian woman. "And then two weeks later, her husband walks in with a beautiful rug and says, 'Thank you so much from preventing my wife from getting surgery.' And I don't fucking know what he's talking about. I thought I was treating her for bronchitis. I gave her expectorants and some cough suppressants."

Experiences like these "shook me up," Kaptchuk said. They inspired him to dig into the more enigmatic parts of healing, a pursuit that has come to define his career. Sometime in the 1990s, he transitioned from Chinese medicine to full-time research, eventually landing a professorship at Harvard Medical School. It has been an unconventional path. Writing for *The New Yorker* in 2011, Michael Specter observed that Kaptchuk is "the first prominent professor at Harvard Medical School since Erik Erikson with neither a medical degree nor a doctorate." (Erikson was the German psychologist who coined the term "identity crisis.")[14]

Kaptchuk—or Ted, as he likes to be called—is iconoclastic and avuncular. I first met him at his home office in 2016. I emailed him with questions about Mentawai healing ceremonies, so he invited me over. Books, many splayed open, were everywhere. I saw volumes on plants, Islam, Kabbalah, and computational models of the brain, not to mention hundreds of works in Chinese. The floor was lost under Oriental rugs, which was cozy, given that neither of us was wearing shoes. He prepared two cups of tea and brought a yellow notebook with him. He wore a yarmulke and cursed often.

I had heard about Ted because of his work on the placebo effect. Defining the placebo effect is a slippery task, so I will follow Ted and use it to mean the therapeutic effects of medical ritual. It's worth stating, however, that when most doctors say "placebo effect," they have in mind the effects of so-called inert treatments, like sugar pills or sham surgery. Swallow a sugar pill and feel less nauseous. Rub an innocuous ointment on your chest and see the ache melt away. Of course, saying that an inert substance has a therapeutic effect is an oxymoron, which is partly why I prefer Ted's definition.[15]

The placebo effect is like the vaginal orgasm: obvious to some; questioned by others. A reason that Ted is so respected is that he has designed elegant studies that demonstrate its reality. His most well-known study was published in 2008 in the *British Medical Journal.* He assigned 262 patients with irritable bowel syndrome to one of three conditions. One group was put on a waiting list and given no treatment. Another was given what Ted and his team called "limited placebo"—sham acupuncture with very little patient-practitioner interaction. (Sham acupuncture feels just like normal acupuncture but does not involve penetration of the skin.) The final group was given "augmented placebo"— sham acupuncture with an attentive, empathetic practitioner who spent forty-five minutes understanding each patient's situation.[16]

You can guess the results. Patients given placebos reported greater relief, less severe symptoms, and a higher quality of life. On top of that, patients in the augmented placebo group fared better than those who got the limited placebo. The effects were big. Sixty-two percent of the augmented group said that they felt "adequate relief" afterward, compared to 44 percent in the limited group. The average quality of life in the augmented group was 9.1 on a 12-point scale, compared to 4.3 in the limited group. The placebo effect is not just real, the results suggested. It can also be encouraged with compassion and connection.[17]

More than changing the stories we tell about ourselves, then, ritual healers also seem to reduce pain, curb fatigue, and dissipate nausea. But how exactly does that happen?

The standard explanation is expectation: a patient trusts that a treatment will make them feel better, and this expectation somehow produces therapeutic effects. Ted decided to put this idea to the test. At various points in the experiment involving patients with irritable bowel syndrome, he brought in an anthropologist to interview subjects who got the placebo.[18]

"It changed my life reading the transcripts of these patients," he wrote to me in an email. Contrary to what nearly every placebo researcher assumes, the patients had no expectations of recovery. Of twelve patients interviewed, ten were equivocal. When the interviewer asked a patient named Abigail what she anticipated, she said, "I guess it's a long shot. I don't know, I have no clue." Another, Kate, said, "I can't say that I'm expecting that much, but I think if something did happen, it'd be a pleasant surprise." A third, Fred, was most explicit: "I really have no expectations whatsoever." Nevertheless, they got better. Healing occurred in the absence of belief.[19]

Puzzled, Ted decided to push things further. Again, he located patients with IBS. Half got a placebo, in this case a pill. The other half got no treatment. But he did something few experimenters had dared: he was honest with the placebo group. They were given a bottle clearly marked "placebo pills" and told that the pills contained no medication. If expectations mattered less, Ted thought, then maybe you could get the placebo effect without deceiving patients.[20]

The results were staggering. After three weeks on the pills, the placebo group reported more relief and larger improvements in their symptoms. Anthony Lembo, another Harvard professor and one of Ted's co-authors, was quoted in *The Guardian* saying, "I didn't think it would work. I felt awkward asking patients to literally take a placebo. But to my surprise, it seemed to work for many of them."[21]

Skeptical scientists have since run more versions of Ted's study, testing whether placebos without deception, also called "open-label placebos," produce therapeutic effects. In 2021, a team from the University of Freiburg analyzed all the studies they could find—at that point, eleven. They computed what is called the "standardized mean difference," a statistic for determining effect sizes, and found that it was 0.72. This is a substantial effect. For context, it is larger than the non-placebo effects of using SSRIs to treat depression (0.5), certain antipsychotic drugs to treat schizophrenia (0.25), and antidepressants to treat generalized anxiety (0.39).[22]

This doesn't mean that the healing experience doesn't matter. To the contrary, the more vivid or tactile or invasive a procedure, the more people respond to it. Ted showed this when he found that empathetic practitioners provoke a stronger placebo effect, but other studies have examined further dimensions of the healing experience. We now know that acupuncture works better than oral placebos for reducing the pain of migraines. Something similar applies to treating osteoarthritic pain: sham surgery works better than fake needles or injections, which, in turn, work better than sugar pills. The more your body can feel itself being healed, the better you will feel.[23]

I bring up these results for two reasons. For one, they tell us that, in the case of the placebo effect, experience trumps belief. You can go to a shaman as a skeptic. You can come away a skeptic, too. Nevertheless, if the healing encounter is gripping—if it engulfs you in sound and touch and imagery, and implicitly signals that you are being healed—we should expect it to still be soothing.

This can be hard to grasp, especially for people ensconced in a Western intellectual tradition. Belief is supposed to be king. Look at how you respond to the world, however, and you will see that your mind often discounts the real/not-real distinction. The clearest domain is fiction. We read books and watch movies aware that characters are made-up, yet we still love them. We shout instructions at them. We cry when they die or succeed. Many people admit to missing characters after they finish reading a book. Viewers of soap operas in the United States have even physically attacked actors who play villains. Real or not, the world touches us.[24]

Another reason to pay attention to these results is that they underscore why shamanism should be a powerful healer. Shamanism is about creating a captivating, consuming reality—

a conflagration of light, touch, costumes, music, and theater that, in the case of healing, persuades a client they are being treated. Recall the healing ceremony that I observed in Siberut for the *sikerei* Mangga. Like many ceremonies, it started in the evening and ended at dawn the next day. The other *sikerei* fed him herbal remedies. They sprinkled his body with magical water to repair taboo violations. They sucked on his abdomen and removed an object said to cause pain. They clanged bells and sang haunting tunes and swept away bad spirits. After a pig was sacrificed, the *sikerei* danced around in a hypnotic ring, every so often becoming animals.

When I interviewed Mangga afterward, his skin looked unfazed, yet he said he felt better. And why shouldn't he? Compared to a sugar pill or even sham surgery, his experience had been a curative odyssey—exactly what someone like Ted would concoct to optimize the power of placebo.

———————

Mangga's healing ceremony brings me to the final mechanism of healing: social support. We've already seen the power of social support, like in Ted's work showing that compassion supercharges the placebo effect, but it is distinct and important enough to consider on its own.

I began to appreciate social support after talking to the anthropologist Polly Wiessner. For four decades, Wiessner has worked with the Ju/'hoansi of the Kalahari Desert as they have transitioned away from a hunting-and-gathering lifestyle. (Like other so-called Bushmen or San peoples of southern Africa, the Ju/'hoansi speak a language with clicks, denoted by symbols like "/" and "!".)

The Ju/'hoansi traditionally healed one another in all-night trance dances. Four times a month, the community assembled around a fire. As women clapped, a group of healers—including men and sometimes women—trotted in a circle with shakers on their legs. The dancing was understood to activate *n/um*, or energy, propelling healers into an altered state called *!kia*, when they were said to experience half death.[25]

Healers' descriptions of *!kia* evoke both its energetic vigor and transcendental nature. An experienced healer once said, "When I pick up *n/um,* it explodes and throws me up in the air and I enter heaven and then fall down."[26] K"au ≠Dau, a blind man who ranked among the most formidable healers, described it differently but no less powerfully:

> God keeps my eyeballs in a little cloth bag. When he first collected them, he got a little cloth bag and plucked my eyeballs out and put them into the bag and then he tied the eyeballs to his belt and went up to heaven. And now when I dance, on the nights when I dance and the singing rises up, he comes down from heaven swinging the bag with the eyeballs above my head and then he lowers the eyeballs to my eye level, and as the singing gets strong, he puts the eyeballs into my sockets and they stay there and I cure. And then when the women stop singing and separate out, he removes the eyeballs, puts them back in the cloth bag and takes them up to heaven.[27]

Wiessner told me about a time in which she was healed. She had just flown to Namibia from the United States, where she spent two months sitting with a family member in the hospital. "I was very anxious," she said. "I was out with the Ju/'hoansi one night just doing my work, and I woke up screaming. I don't think I've ever woken up screaming before."

The community responded at once. "They just got up out of their beds and started to clap and sing and dance, stoked up the fire, took all the firewood in the camp, made a big fire."

Then the healing began. The ten or so women in the camp began to clap, while the men got up and danced. Two of those men were *n/um k"ausi,* or healers. "They immediately went into trance healing and they worked on me for hours and hours and hours," she said, "rubbing their sweat and everything all over me and healing and rubbing my body." When it was over, she slept soundly.

The next morning, Wiessner was driving to get supplies when a black mamba, a highly venomous snake and the most feared in Africa, shot into her car. It just missed her, striking the door next to the passenger. "I just said, 'You bastard, you missed!'" she recalled. "I felt, after the healing, all my anxiety was gone. After that, I just felt so much better."

When I asked how trance ceremonies heal people, she mentioned how soothing physical touch can be. But most important for her was social support. "It gives [the patient] the feeling that they're loved," she said. "Everyone is uniting to fight for you, because we want you to live."

Her answer instantly clicked for me. Humans are a deeply interdependent species. During our evolution, we relied on one another for almost everything that was important—food, sex, information, protection. Dozens of studies, conducted in countries around the world, have found that people who perceive greater social support have greater mental health. Our social network even impacts our risk of dying. In 2010, a team of researchers looked across 148 studies covering more than three hundred thousand participants and reported that the effect of social isolation on mortality is similar to that of smoking and alcohol consumption and higher than risk factors like reduced physical activity and obesity.[28]

Feeling loved, wanted, and surrounded literally wards off death. It thus shouldn't surprise us that strengthening and being reminded of that support feel curative.

Given all the ways shamans are therapeutic, some researchers insist that shamans exist to heal people. Among them is the evolutionary sociologist James McClenon, who argues that humans genetically evolved to respond to shamanism because of its benefits. He envisions a kind of gene-culture coevolution, where shamanism and religious thinking developed in response to each other, ultimately producing a potent healing system.[29]

I am convinced that shamanic healing can make us feel better. But I still doubt that this explains why shamanism exists. The main reason is that shamans offer many more services than healing. They control weather. They attack enemies. They help businesses succeed and summon animals for hunting. Some Inuit shamans halted the cracking of ice. Haida shamans in the Pacific Northwest divined the location of beached whales. Some shamans, critically, do not heal at all.[30]

These are a problem for McClenon's story, because they mean we would need two explanations of shamanism, not one. Assume for a moment that McClenon is right: shamanism emerges and survives because of its curative properties. We still need to explain why some shamans use many of the same techniques but do not heal. And we need to explain why shamans deal not just with illness but with reams of other unpredictable domains, from rain magic to dead-whale divination. McClenon's explanation gets us only halfway.

We don't run into this problem with the account I've presented. The theory that shamanism is a compelling technology for dealing with uncertainty explains the spectrum of shamanic activities. Illness, weather, and beached whales are not scattered, unrelated events but members of a single class: big outcomes that we want control over and for which we are apt to suspect supernatural involvement. Shamans are not healers who happen to do other stuff. They are mystical intermediaries who offer security to the insecure. Granted, once people recognize that they feel better after visiting some shamans, it is perfectly plausible that shamans incorporate the most therapeutic techniques. But this drives the elaboration of shamanism—not its existence in the first place.

Another drawback of McClenon's theory is that it neglects the darker side of healing. Shamanism exists in a fraught interplay with witchcraft. The fear that illness is caused by other people's dark powers inspires sufferers to seek out shamans. As shamans name and cast off witches, they reify that fear, making it realer and more dreadful. The line between the shaman and the witch is not a clear one, however. Both figures are considered mystically powerful, and shamans familiar with the workings of witchcraft inhabit a precarious place. A healing gone wrong can turn a trusted doctor into a dreaded sorcerer.[31]

All this means that curing is socially charged—a restorative act, yes, but one that just as easily sows distrust and explodes into violence. Bringing a person back to health easily gives way to accusations and, in some cases, executions. The institution can even devour itself as competing shamans indict one another. Working with the Mundurukú in 1952–53, the anthropologist Robert Murphy observed that "one or two shamans are executed as sorcerers during an average year," with the result that "many villages are without shamans." Three decades later, another anthropologist, Steve Burkhalter, saw that Mundurukú shamans were fleeing to missions to practice safely. Even there, however, they were not secure; ten months into his fieldwork, a shaman was hacked to death by five assassins.[32]

Rather than thinking of shamanism as a healing apparatus, then, I think a more intellectually honest perspective is to see it foremost as a mind technology: a moving performance that assures people a practitioner can perform the extraordinary. This performance can have positive effects, like alleviating pain and freeing people from restrictive illness narratives. But it can also be manipulated, weaponized, and turned into a source of distress.

Having established the nature of shamanism, we are better equipped to track its innumerable resurrections, to behold the timelessness of humanity's oldest religious practice. Naturally, then, we return to a beginning.

Part Two

THE TIMELESS RELIGION

What I did here will spread everywhere. All the people around us, even those of different languages, will have their healers. Everyone!

—TAXÉS-PO, THE FIRST SHAMAN,
ACCORDING TO A MYTH TOLD BY THE CHOROTE OF BOLIVIA

CHAPTER 6

The First Religion

Finally, after years of anticipation, I was approaching the cave. Yet here, a mere hundred yards from the entrance, the thing I found most remarkable was how normal everything looked. There was no signpost, no announcement—just tall grass. Hundreds of French people probably drove on this small road every day, unaware that one of humanity's greatest treasures lay just beyond the fields. It was almost as if the Bégouën family, who owned the cave and the land directly above it, had hidden their jewel in as mundane a landscape as possible.

Robert Bégouën, who was in his mid-eighties but as lithe and energetic as a fifty-year-old, asked my friend François to get out of the car and open the fence using the rubber handle. François did as he was told, and Robert edged the car forward, off the road. We got out, and Robert fished kneepads out of the trunk. We put them on over our coveralls and followed him through the high grass. We approached another fence, which separated the grassy fields from a forest. Robert opened it using a spring-loaded hook, then led us a short distance farther until we arrived at the mouth of the cave.

Since three Bégouën brothers first explored the cave in 1914, their family has permitted only a few researchers to visit each year. After finishing my PhD, I got a position as a research fellow at the Institute for Advanced Study in Toulouse, France, barely a two-hour drive from the cave. When I started thinking about this book, I knew I had to go there. But I had no idea how to get invited. I emailed Marie-Brune Bégouën, the only family member whose email address I could find online, but got no response. I had started to give up, when I mentioned my wish to François-Xavier Ricaut, a biological anthropologist at the University of Toulouse. François, who has a goatee and a boyish eagerness, works in Papua New Guinea and has wide-ranging interests, including rock art, shamanism, and ancient human migrations. He had never been to the cave, but he is well acquainted with the archaeology scene in southwest France. Whereas I considered a trip to the cave to be near impossible, he described it as "easy." To start, he knew that the person to contact was not Marie-Brune but Robert Bégouën, the cave's primary guardian and a son of one of the discoverers.

So it was with François's help, and Robert's hospitality, that I found myself at the entrance to the Grotte des Trois-Frères, or the Cave of Three Brothers. We were joined by François's colleague from the University of Papua New Guinea, the physician Christopher Kinipi.

Robert opened two doors—one grated and rusty, the other solid and stainless—that his family had installed at the cave's entrance. We stepped into what looked like cauliflower world. I wanted to touch the white cave wall to make sure it was hard. Robert told us that this was a new entrance, not one prehistoric humans had used. He explained that we would be underground for three hours and that there would be no light source apart from our headlamps. We clambered on our knees and followed him down two sets of ladders to what he called "the archaeological level." He established the two most important rules: always stick to the path, which was delimited by string, and never touch the walls.

"We will move slowly," he added, "because we are in a virgin cave, and my father insisted that it never be modified."

Robert's father first entered the cave more than a century before us. On Thursday, July 16, 1914, Louis Bégouën, aged seventeen, went out in search of Paleolithic artifacts with his brothers Jacques (nineteen) and Max (twenty-one), and their father, Count Henri Bégouën. They knew what they were doing. Two years earlier, they had taken a homemade raft along a stretch of the Volp, a twenty-five-mile-long river in southwest France, following it as it ran underground through an ancient limestone cave. As Henri waited by the raft, the boys crept down a passage, eventually discovering the Tuc d'Audoubert, a cave filled with drawings, sculptures, and footprints left by ancient hunter-gatherers 17,000 years ago.[1]

Now, two years later, they were following the Volp again. Rather than riding it underground, however, they were charting it from the surface. While they scanned the terrain between where it submerged and came out again, a farmer pointed them to a sinkhole. He explained that fresh air issued from it but that it had been covered with rocks to prevent sheep from tumbling in.[2]

It took Louis, his brothers, his father, and their friend François a day to clear a passage. Once inside, they were stunned. "Max picked up a spear-thrower and a flint scraper from the ground," wrote Louis in his journal. "We return enchanted, and we put off the rest of the exploration until tomorrow."[3]

That was Friday evening. The next three days were exciting although lackluster compared to what they would eventually unearth. On Saturday, they found bones and more spear-throwers. On Sunday, they organized their discoveries. On Monday, they stayed home while it rained.[4]

On Tuesday, they set out again. "We go down—difficult descent," wrote Louis. They crawled through a corridor on all fours and descended into a chamber crowded with stalagmites. "At the bottom, François sees lines on the clay when suddenly I shout 'drawings' and in fact superb bisons, horses etc. were engraved, and a woman in black was drawn." That was just a subset. As they explored the cave, they eventually came across etched owls, a salon of stenciled hands, and enigmatic rows of dots and engravings.[5]

The boys had discovered one of the greatest sites of Paleo-lithic rock art. Named in their honor, the Cave of Three Broth-ers contains more than 1,300 engravings and paintings.

The most famous artwork is the one Louis called "a woman in black," known more commonly in French as "le Sorcier" (the Sorcerer) or "le Chamane" (the Shaman). Louis's brother Max sketched it the day they discovered it, although the image that appears on mugs, T-shirts, and Wikipedia was drawn years later by the French archaeologist Henri Breuil. If you're a shaman-ism enthusiast, you've almost certainly seen this version. Breuil depicted a strange, stalking figure with a long beard, the eyes of an owl, the ears and antlers of a stag, the forelimbs of a bear, the perched, unsure legs of a human, and a horse's tail that hangs over backward-facing male human genitalia. Reflecting on this and other cave art, the anthropologist Weston La Barre con-sidered the paintings evidence that "there were shamans before there were gods."[6]

The Sorcerer is the reason I had come to the Cave of Three Brothers. I had read skepticism about the accuracy of Breuil's drawing and wanted to see the figure myself. Nevertheless, it is just one of numerous finds said to indicate prehistoric shaman-ism. There are hallucinogenic cave paintings and scattered depic-tions of human-animal hybrids. There are 11,000-year-old red deer headdresses and the pre-agricultural burials of misshapen bodies with menageries of animal parts. There are enigmatic structures in the deepest recesses of caves—sites that are inexpli-cable beyond a ritual function. The more we dig into our past, the more it seems our Paleolithic ancestors brewed together the strange, natural, and otherworldly in enchanting amalgamations.[7]

This antiquity is what we would expect if shamanism were timeless. And yet deep history is hard to know. Stones and bones preserve, but ideas do not. In his blockbuster book *Sapiens* (2011), Yuval Noah Harari wrote that "we have only the haziest notions about the religions of ancient foragers." We can assume they believed the world was filled with spirits, he admitted, but that's hardly informative. "It's one of the biggest holes in our under-standing of human history."[8]

Harari's skepticism is fair. The history of anthropology is

replete with people projecting their expectations onto ambiguous finds, bending the complexity of reality into a bastardized corruption that gels with their limited worldview. We are like maggots born in broccoli who assume the world is all green and florets. Is Harari right, then? Are proponents of ancient shamanism falling into the same trap? Or is he wrong? Can we indeed discern shamanism in the oldest human religions?

We followed Robert through the chambers of the cave. Some were cramped, but others felt like expansive cathedrals. Everything was wet; tiny water droplets hung suspended on icicle-like stalactites. In places, stalactites and stalagmites had fused, producing rippling columns or waterfall-like cascades. In a predictably French fashion, François pointed to a structure hanging from the ceiling and called it a big meringue.

Walking through the cave, I felt the proximity of ancient worlds. We passed stenciled red-ochre handprints, the bones of extinct bison, and an etching of a lion's face. Robert pointed out the trinkets, including stone tools, a seashell, and animal teeth, that long-dead humans had inserted into cracks and crannies. After forty minutes, we entered a gallery some nine stories high. Before us lay a massive heap of bones and dust. Robert explained that an earthquake had opened up a hole connecting the cave to the outside world, and unwitting creatures—including horses, bison, reindeer, and hyenas—had fallen in. Another earthquake eventually closed the hole, but Ice Age humans seem never to have taken any bones. "Perhaps it was a shrine," mused Robert.

Unlike in neighboring caves, people did not live in the Cave of Three Brothers. There are no signs of long-term habitation. Instead, they visited it, trekking into its recesses with animal-fat lamps, scratching designs into the walls and tucking objects into the cave's crevices. This was during a period called the Upper Paleolithic, and the world then was very different from the one we know today. Glaciers stood like giant, lost ships in the high mountains. A cold, dry grassland stretched from Spain to Canada—the earth's largest biome at the time. Known as the mammoth steppe, the landscape was so cluttered with big animals that modern minds struggle to imagine it. Herds of horses, bison, and reindeer fed on nutritious grasses and herbs. Mammoths walked among them. Bears, wolves, lions, and hyenas crept in their wakes.[9]

Archaeologists organize the Upper Paleolithic into cultures, or clusters of art and artifacts that share stylistic similarities. For the most part, the artists who visited the Cave of Three Brothers were part of the Magdalenian, a western European culture dated to between 19,000 and 14,000 years ago. The people of the Magdalenian were hunter-gatherers. They subsisted on big herbivores, probably supplementing their diet with hare, grouse, fruits, roots, leaves, berries, and mushrooms. Although often depicted as pale cave dwellers, they probably were dark-skinned and preferred to live in valleys and plains or at the foots of cliffs.[10]

The Magdalenians were master artists, leaving dozens of sites across modern-day Spain, France, and Germany. The most famous is Lascaux. Situated 225 kilometers north of the Cave of Three Brothers, Lascaux houses the Hall of the Bulls, a spectacular chamber muraled with horses, stags, and wild bulls, one of which covers sixteen feet of cave wall. The artwork is bold and moving, evoking the experience of standing among truly alive behemoths. Upon leaving the cave, Pablo Picasso is rumored to have said, "Since Lascaux, we have invented nothing."[11]

The drawings in Lascaux and the Cave of Three Brothers have many similarities. Both caves are filled with stylized depictions of large beasts. Both intersperse the animals with geometric shapes, like dots, grids, and lines. And both have human-animal hybrids, known as "therianthropes." The Cave of Three Brothers has two well-known therianthropes: the Sorcerer and a man with a bison head, sometimes called the Small Sorcerer. Lascaux, meanwhile, is home to a birdman.[12] The mythologist Joseph Campbell described it in tawdry detail:

A large bison bull, eviscerated by a spear that has transfixed its anus and emerged through its sexual organ, stands before a prostrate man. The latter (the only crudely drawn figure, and the only human figure in the cave) is rapt in a shamanistic trance. He wears a bird mask; his phallus, erect, is pointing at the pierced bull; a throwing stick lies on the ground at his feet; and beside him stands a wand or staff, bearing on its tip the image of a bird. And then, behind this prostrate shaman, is a large rhinoceros, apparently defecating as it walks away.[13]

These three artistic themes—animal representations, geometric patterns, and hybrid figures—turn up far beyond these two caves. They appeared in designs in Australia and southern Africa, as well as in other Upper Paleolithic art. In 2019, an international team of scientists announced what was then the oldest known figurative art, discovered in a limestone cave in Sulawesi, Indonesia. It showed tiny animalish humans hunting buffalo and beefy pigs.[14]

There are as many theories of rock art as there are archaeologists who like to argue. The splashiest explanation, however, may be the shamanistic theory, developed by the South African archaeologist David Lewis-Williams. In a 1988 paper with his student Thomas Dowson, he put forward a three-stage model of altered states of consciousness and linked it to rock art. In stage 1, they argued, people in trance see dots, grids, zigzags, parallel lines, nested curves, and meandering grooves. These forms are "'wired' into the human nervous system," Lewis-Williams later wrote, "all people, no matter what their cultural background, have the potential to experience them."[15]

In stage 2, the altered mind purportedly tries to make sense of this imagery, massaging it into figurative forms that are familiar and relevant. Ask a shaman to divine the location of prey, and their hallucinating mind may coalesce wavy lines and curves into a chubby bison. Finally, in stage 3, the shaman is said to feel surrounded by a swirling vortex or rotating tunnel, creating the impression of traveling through worlds. In this phase, the geometric and the figurative churn into each other. The person in trance might merge with their imagery—a sensation of alien transformation.*

---

* Lewis-Williams and Dowson noted two subtleties. First, not all trance involves the three stages in sequence. You might start in stage 1 and never leave, or you

With these three stages in mind, Lewis-Williams and Dowson proposed that rock art is often produced by trancing shamans. Geometric shapes arise from stage 1. Animals and humans come from stage 2. Therianthropes are born in stage 3. More than beautiful paintings, they suggested, the beasts, swirls, and hybrids of Ice Age caves may have been the original psychedelic art.

The shamanistic theory is the blue cheese of archaeology—some love it; others can do without it. When it was first published, the scholar of Paleolithic art John Halverson wrote that it "offers an extremely interesting and persuasive explanation of those indeed 'intractable' figures traditionally called 'signs.' In fact, it is the first really credible explanation that I have seen."[16]

Others, however, pointed out cracks. One is the same issue we considered earlier—the fallacy of ecstatic equivalence. "We do not know if the trajectory of mental imagery is identical for all drugs and for non-drug-induced states," wrote Lewis-Williams and Dowson, "but we believe that a broad similarity can be accepted." This assumption might have been reasonable in the late 1980s, when there was less systematic work on non-ordinary states, but it is not justifiable today. Just look at entries on PsychonautWiki or descriptions on Erowid. People who take classic psychedelics like psilocin, mescaline, and DMT report seeing visual geometry, yes, but people who experiment with datura do not. In fact, the European team who reviewed the literature on altered states found that techniques like starvation and breathing dampen sensory experiences rather than encouraging hallucination.[17]

A second issue is that there are many alternative explanations for why people produce these designs. Take the animal-human hybrids. Sure, shamans may have drawn them in altered states. But the figures might also be gods, ancestors, tricksters, mytho-

----

might supersault straight into stage 3 without visiting its predecessors. Second, the stages are not discrete. Grids might coexist with bison, bison with shamanic hybrids.

logical heroes, masked dancers, or hunters in camouflage. When I asked Mentawai people to draw the water spirit Sikameinan, several non-shamans blended human and crocodile traits. Likewise, when my colleagues and I examined 770 myths, folktales, and legends from around the world, we found that nearly one in six included shape-shifters.[18]

I recognize, and partly share, the urge to project shamanism into the past. But to insist, as Lewis-Williams did with the archaeologist Jean Clottes in 1998, that "these images of transformation are clearly part of a shamanic belief system" is to overlook human inventiveness. For Paul Bahn, an archaeologist and one of Lewis-Williams's most vocal critics, the shamanistic theory is thus "an insult not only to the intelligence of readers, but also and above all to the intelligence, capabilities, imagination, and creativity of the prehistoric artists."[19]

A similar problem applies to geometric shapes. Do we really need to turn to shamanic trance to explain dots, lines, and zigzags? It doesn't seem so. A compelling counterpoint comes from work by the psychologist and preschool director Rhoda Kellogg. From 1948 through 1966, she collected five hundred thousand drawings by Californian children and another five thousand from kids in thirty additional countries. In her book *Analyzing Children's Art* (1969), she decomposed the illustrations into twenty building blocks, what she called "the basic scribbles." These included all but one of the shapes Lewis-Williams and Dowson claimed appeared in altered states. The exception, the grid, was also common in children's artwork; Kellogg just considered it more complex than a "basic" building block.[20]

The point is not that children could have produced Paleolithic rock art. Nor is it that our Ice Age ancestors had childlike minds. Rather, it is that these are aesthetic fundamentals. They are produced early in development, in the absence of altered states, and by people everywhere. Adults like them, too. A century ago, Franz Boas surveyed diverse peoples' art, from Inuit ivory carvings to West African metallurgy. He found universal preferences for circles, spirals, curved lines, and straight lines; the many figures in his book *Primitive Art* (1928) reveal that these designs are often combined to produce grids and zigzags.[21]

Rock art is not the only context in which prehistorians see shamanism. One day, 12,000 years ago near the Mediterranean coast of modern-day Israel, an elderly, misshapen woman died. According to the archaeologists who discovered her, her deformed spine and pelvis forced her to limp, giving her an "unnatural, asymmetrical appearance." Yet her community apparently saw something special in her. Within days of her death, they collected eighty-six tortoises, four newborn gazelles, and more than fifteen hundred snake vertebrae. They located the wing of an eagle, the pelvis of a leopard, the forelimb of a wild boar, and the skulls of weasel-like mammals called martens. They traveled to a small cave that looks out over the Mediterranean plain and gave her a consecrated burial atop blocks of limestone, filling the grave with the zoological curios before sealing her in with a massive stone slab. Struck by the ritual and respect afforded the disabled woman, the discovering archaeologists suggested this to be "the burial of a shaman, one of the earliest known from the archaeological record."[22]

Three millennia later, another hunter-gatherer woman died in the forests of what is now Germany. She was between twenty-five and thirty-five years old and was entombed with an infant. Her burial, too, was a bevy of riches—sixty-five fragments of tortoise shells, 120 pieces of mussel shell, a crane bone filled with microliths, pendants carved from the front teeth of cattle and deer. Archaeologists discovered two pieces of roe deer skull with attached antlers—headgear, perhaps?—along with twin boar canines, which may have been worn symmetrically. Based on abnormalities in her skull, a team of German researchers speculated that she experienced neurological symptoms, like a loss of control over body movements or a feeling of ants crawling over her skin. She was deemed a shaman and has been depicted as such in artistic reconstructions. In fact, a painting of her has become the model for archaic European shamans, inspiring everything from a Playmobil figure to a character in the German television show *Barbarians*.[23]

Despite enthusiasm about these findings, other scholars urge caution. The past is a foreign country, far wilder than anything we can imagine. When I brought up the burials with Paul Pettitt, an archaeologist at Durham University who specializes in Paleo-lithic burials, he urged intellectual humility. "There is nothing among the materials buried with them that shouts, 'I am a sha-man!'" he said. "So how do we know if most people looked the way they did but for whatever reason simply were never buried?"

———————

Determining the prehistory of shamanism requires looking beyond lavish burials and inscrutable cave art. One place to start is with modern analogs. Shamanism is near universal. It was observed in the vast majority of nonindustrial societies, includ-ing among nearly all hunter-gatherers. There are two possible reasons for this global distribution, both of which have implica-tions for deep history. The first is convergent cultural evolution: something about human minds or societies fates the practice to develop whenever we lanky primates get together. By this logic, shamanism should be as old as modern human cognition. It would have been practiced not only by Magdalenian hunters but throughout Paleolithic Africa and Asia as well. Convergent evolution also challenges the hubris of modernity. It implies that shamanism is not some arcane tradition limited to past and tribal societies but is something timeless with an enduring appeal for human minds.[24]

By now, you should know that I favor convergent cultural evolution. Yet many experts have rejected it. Mircea Eliade, for example, "gave this no time at all," according to Ronald Hutton, the English folklorist. Instead, Eliade favored the alternative: historical diffusion. He saw shamanism as an ancient practice that spread from a Eurasian homeland and that "still survives in the most distant parts of the world." This is why he focused on Siberia—not because that's where the word "shaman" comes from but because he believed that societies there had preserved "the prehistoric culture of the Siberian hunters."[25]

There is no doubt that shamanic practices diffuse. The French researcher Charles Stépanoff found that across thousands of miles, from western Siberia to eastern Canada, diverse peoples had a surprisingly similar ritual, known variously as the "dark

tent" or "shaking tent." A shaman was tied up in a tent without
a fire. An audience gathered around and soon heard the yelps of
bears, owls, and other spirit animals. The audience asked these
spirit beings about illness and the location of game. The spirits
came down one after another, their arrivals marked by the trembling of the tent, and gave answers. Not all peoples across Siberia
and North America practiced the ritual, but Stépanoff claims that
these features—especially the tent, darkness, and wild animal
cries—occurred together nowhere else in the world, suggesting
they spread as a package, possibly thousands of years ago with
migrations into the Americas.[26]

So yes: shamanic elements diffuse locally. But the dark tent
suggests only local diffusion, not that shamanism had a single
birthplace from which it conquered the world. The more convincing way to test between these hypotheses would be to rewind
time—to peer into the spiritual lives of primordial humans and
watch their religions emerge, evolve, and diversify. Barring that,
however, we can pursue something almost as thrilling: seeing
what happens when societies start anew.

———————

In 1978, the linguist Derek Bickerton submitted a proposal to
the National Science Foundation for what he called the "Island
Experiment." His plan was to populate a tropical island with
six couples and their two-year-old toddlers. The couples would
fish, dig wells, build housing, and raise their kids. But there was
a catch: each couple would speak a different language. To make
sure of this, and to ensure that they would thrive in simple conditions, he decided to solicit participants from the most remote
corners of the Pacific—places like Borneo, New Guinea, and an
outlying island in the Philippines.[27]

Bickerton wanted to learn about language. He guessed that
as people tried to talk, they would mash together their different languages, producing an unstructured pidgin. Then, as the
infants grew up, they would use their innate language capacities
to transform the pidgin into a language with highly structured
grammar. Because those capacities are universal, he expected, the

new language would share features with languages everywhere. Bickerton wanted, in other words, to grow an aspect of culture from scratch.

To his delight, a panel of experts arranged by the National Science Foundation approved the project. But months before the experiment was supposed to start, the NSF deemed it risky and unethical. Although it was shut down, the questions at the core of the Island Experiment continue to seduce us. What is the fate of a pristine society? How do structured practices emerge from cultureless minds? The Polish director Andrzej Żuławski wrestled with these questions while producing *On the Silver Globe* (1988), an epic, ethereal film that depicts the birth of a new society after three astronauts crash on a habitable planet. Surrounded by elaborate culture, we can't help but wonder where it comes from.[28]

After I returned from my long stay with the Mentawai, I searched for places where this might have happened. If shamanism indeed develops because of convergent evolution, I figured, then we should expect a new society to produce it. Of course, I didn't expect to find a truly pristine society. Humans are cultural organisms, heavily reliant on socially learned information. The idea that a babble of cultureless babies has, at some point, rebuilt society from scratch seems scientifically obtuse.

Instead, I was looking for a spot where populations have crashed, rebounded, and then remained culturally quarantined. The idea was to exploit what the Harvard anthropologist (and my PhD advisor) Joe Henrich calls the "Tasmania effect." When populations become small and isolated, they tend to lose cultural complexity. This happened with Indigenous Tasmanians. About 12,000 years ago, the land bridge separating Tasmania from mainland Australia was drowned by rising sea levels. Cut off from their neighbors, the Tasmanians lost the know-how to make bone tools, cold-weather clothing, and fishing technology. While aboriginal Australians across the strait used spear-throwers and boomerangs, Tasmanian men hunted using rocks, clubs, and one-piece spears. Like the back-to-nature survivors of a techno-apocalypse, the Tasmanians lived in the shadow of a much more technologically sophisticated past.[29]

These kinds of cultural contractions can destroy shamanism.

Take the Sirionó of Bolivia, one of the hunter-gatherer groups that, according to the research led by Hervey Peoples, did not have shamanism. Studied by Allan Holmberg between 1940 and 1942, they were among the most technologically simple populations ever studied. They lacked games, traps, and watercraft—even, presumably, the ability to make fire—leading the Cornell anthropologist Lauriston Sharp to refer to them as "a still-living Old Stone Age people." But the Sirionó were not prehistoric survivals; they were refugees. Decades before Holmberg arrived, epidemics reduced their population from 3,000 people to just 150. During the preceding centuries, the Sirionó may have split off from an agricultural tribe, the Chiriguanos, to escape war. The traumas took a toll. In 2012, the evolutionary anthropologist Robert Walker and his colleagues demonstrated that the Sirionó experienced a catastrophic cultural breakdown, losing complex social structure, much of their agricultural lifestyle, the ability to make canoes, and critically, for our purposes, shamanism.[30]

My aim, then, was to locate a place where populations have gotten to such dangerously low levels that they would have lost much of their culture, including shamanism. As their populations recovered, then, we would get a chance to see cultural complexity re-emerge, to study as close to a pristine efflorescence as possible. Finding shamanism there wouldn't prove that shamanism has independently evolved over and over—and thus would have developed among our Paleolithic ancestors—but it would increase our confidence in the hypothesis.

———————

Many populations have been reduced to meager numbers, undergoing what scientists call "bottlenecks." Yet it's devilishly hard to find any that remained isolated afterward. As I asked geneticists and anthropologists, however, I was directed to one place over and over: the Andaman Islands.

Controlled by India but closer to Myanmar, the Andaman Islands loom in the popular imagination as the quintessential remote archipelago: a necklace of tropical islands blanketed with jungle, fringed by a rainbow-rock reef, and home to hunter-gatherer peoples so technologically unsophisticated that the Indian writer F. A. M. Dass said they belonged to "the Bamboo Age." "Hill-clad and sea-girt," Dass wrote, "these islands appear to have been meant by Nature to be kept aloof from the rest of the world, untouched by the social, economic and political forces that stir humanity abroad."[31]

Fourteen tribes lived in the Andaman Islands in 1858. They spoke distinct tongues and sorted into at least two language families: the Great Andamanese, who covered the northern part of the archipelago, and the Ongans, who lived in the southern islands. (The language of one tribe, the Sentinelese, remains undocumented, so it's unclear to whom they are culturally related.) As happened with so many Indigenous peoples, pestilence and land grabs decimated Andamanese numbers. According to some estimates, their population fell from about 5,500 people in 1858 to about 400 people in the twenty-first century—a decline of more than 90 percent. At least nine of the original tribes have gone extinct.[32]

The Andaman Islanders inhabited a vibrant psychic world, much of it recorded by the British anthropologist A. R. Radcliffe-Brown, who spent ten months with the Great Andamanese starting in 1906. He was told that, following a person's death, they became a spirit, or *lau*. Spirits were invisible to most people but rumored to have small bodies with freakishly long arms and legs. They were responsible for all illness. Walk alone in the jungle at night, and you risk spirits striking you, crippling you with disease, and then devouring your lifeless corpse like hellish pigs.[33]

In his monograph, Radcliffe-Brown wrote about specialists called *oko-jumu* or *oko-paiad*, translated as "dreamers" or, more mythically, "those who speak from dreams." By the time he arrived, they teetered on extinction. "Most of the old *oko-jumu* and *oko-paiad* are now dead," he wrote. Nevertheless, everything he reported suggests they were shamans. They communed with spirits in dreams, using the ability for curing, harming, and averting storms. Many were said to acquire their powers after dying and coming back to life. At least one renowned *oko-jumu* had what appeared to be epilepsy. Another disappeared into the forest for hours or days at a time. When he returned, he wore a crown of palm-leaf fiber—a gift from spirits, he announced.[34]

Does Andamanese shamanism represent a pristine production? Answering this question requires gazing into their past. The ancestors of the Andamanese arrived a long time ago. Exactly when remains hazy. Some people argue that it was within the last 10,000 years; others, that it occurred long before. The size of the founding population is similarly fuzzy, although geneticists at the University of Tartu, who have analyzed Andamanese genomes to reconstruct their history, assured me that it was tiny—probably a couple hundred people. Notably, this is about how small populations are when they lose shamanism. Three of the four hunter-gatherer groups that Peoples and her colleagues said lacked shamans—the Tiwi, the Hadza, and the Sirionó—had populations around or under a thousand when anthropologists studied them.[35]

So the original Andamanese went through a bottleneck. Check. But did they stay isolated afterward? I asked geneticists this question, too. Mayukh Mondal, the lead author of a 2016 analysis of Andamanese genomes, said the current consensus is that they have indeed remained pure, at least genomically. "Neither the analysis using sex chromosomes nor the autosomal analysis shows anything otherwise," he wrote to me in an email. Check again.

The extreme bottleneck and ensuing seclusion suggest that Andamanese shamanism is as close to a pristine emergence as we might find. Yet we shouldn't get too excited. The Andaman Islands and their inhabitants were far from untouched when Radcliffe-Brown set up camp in 1906. The British had been running a penal colony for fifty years by then, and outsider contact goes much farther back. Arab travelers knew about the islands in the ninth century AD. Malay, Burmese, and European pirates long raided the islands for slaves. Around 1025 AD, the South Indian king Rajendra Chola Deva I annexed the archipelago; an inscription refers to it as Timai Thevu, "the islands of impurity," and a land of cannibals. The reputation of Andaman Islanders as ferocious savages was a common one; Marco Polo reported them to have "heads like dogs, and teeth and eyes likewise . . . they are a most cruel generation, and eat everybody that they can catch, if not of their own race."[36]

Despite the history of contact, these interactions likely did not transmit shamanism. Radcliffe-Brown noted that the British presence had the effect of corroding dream speaking, not buttressing it. And it is hard to imagine how centuries of slave raiding would have allowed most cultural innovations, let alone rituals of dream healing, to diffuse. Given current knowledge, Andamanese shamanism seems a local development.[37]

Andamanese religion is just one of many reasons to suspect that people independently invented shamanism around the world. We will see examples of its emergence and persistence in the coming chapters, so for now, let's focus on three other lines of evidence.

First, shamanisms are diverse. Like the evolution of flight in different vertebrates—in bats, birds, and pterosaurs—shamanic practices share broad similarities but play out differently in each setting. Andamanese *oko-jumu* consulted spirits in dreams. Mentawai *sikerei* invite spirits with songs and theatrical dances. Korean *mu* are possessed by gods and ancestors. This diversity implies less that the world's shamanisms derive from a single, ancestral practice and more that different societies play with a universal structure in ways that vibe with their varied worldviews.

Second, the cultural transmission supposed to underlie shamanism's pervasiveness is far from perfect. Humans adopt and pass on traditions, but rarely with 100 percent fidelity. Languages change so fast that many linguists consider it futile to reconstruct linguistic family trees beyond about 6,000 to 10,000 years. The French cognitive scientist Olivier Morin refers to this as the "Wear-and-Tear Problem" and points to the game of Telephone, also known as Chinese Whispers, as an example. Pass a message down a chain, and it takes only a couple links for it to become irremediably corrupted—for "My brother is a bachelor" to become "My mother is flatulent."[38]

The Wear-and-Tear Problem does not necessarily imply

that shamanism has evolved over and over. But it urges us to be skeptical of Eliade's alternative. We should not expect shamanism to have survived intact for tens of millennia solely through transmission and diffusion. Instead, it would need an appeal—an appeal so profound that it could have stabilized the practice as it multiplied across continents and ecologies, as it danced from ice worlds to grasslands to jungles, as its peoples underwent population expansions and contractions, as human history ticked forward—foragers to farmers, bands to states, backbreakers to overpaid chair sitters. Precisely the kind of appeal, in other words, that could have moved humans to recreate shamanism wherever they went.

The final reason to suspect independent evolution is everything we have reviewed thus far. The recurrent emergence of shamanism is not conjecture based on universality; it is informed by our understanding of human psychology and cultural evolution. Our desperation to control uncertainty, our suspicions that agents cause misfortune, our tendency to accept special powers when people move beyond humanness—all of them interact to produce a ripe psychic setting for shamanism to blossom.

The convergent evolution hypothesis suggests that shamanism should be as old as the psychological ingredients that compose it. In fact, each ingredient seems evolutionarily primitive. The psychologist B. F. Skinner famously demonstrated that pigeons use superstition-like behaviors when given food at random intervals. Even if that result turns out to be nonsense, there's little reason to suppose our reliance on magical rituals evolved recently. Our suspicions about agents causing misfortune have likely been useful for hundreds of thousands, if not millions, of years—that is, as long as we have been intensely social. And our tendency to accept special powers when people deviate from typical humans seems a reflection of more general-purpose cognitive machinery, probably involved in how we think about categories.[39]

Pinpointing the origins of shamanism thus requires thinking not about the psychology it taps into but about the broader social and cultural context. Shamanism requires sophisticated cultural learning. It requires being so cooperative that people turn to one another for specialized tasks. It requires linguistic skills at a level where clients can describe their problems and practitioners can explain solutions.

There still isn't agreement about when these abilities arose in their modern forms. One scholarly camp dates them to around 50,000 years ago. Another pushes them to at least 100,000 years back. Still others see analogs in our archaic relatives. Everything becomes more speculative the farther we go back. As we turn the clock back more and more, we increase our risk of becoming the maggots born in broccoli, of hallucinating our limited frame of reference onto an alien world. We must beware of seeing shamanism in line drawings.[40]

That being said, it's hard not to see curious signs in our relatives' remains. At another cave in southwestern France, nearly 200,000 years ago, Neanderthals constructed circles of broken stalagmites so far from the entrance that no daylight could have reached them. Even earlier, our diminutive, tiny-brained cousins *Homo naledi* crawled into underground chambers, where some anthropologists say they made fires, buried bodies, and drew on walls (although many doubt the claims). In both cases, archaic humans did not live in the caves, nor did they find food in them. Instead, they visited them because of another, perhaps spiritual, allure.[41]

Regardless of when we became socially and culturally modern, it is difficult to imagine a time when people had religion but not shamanism. This is because both require the same psychological foundations. As with shamanism, religion can develop only after a species is sufficiently skilled in cooperation, communication, and cultural transmission. Beliefs in supernatural beings need to be passed along. Rituals for engaging with them need to be shared and developed. Once we crossed this socially intelligent Rubicon—that is, once we became a floridly cultural species with a rich cosmological universe—not only would we have fought and pleaded with the invisible world; we would have sought out specialists to do so, as well.

After an hour and a half of exploring, Robert led us down a descent. We slid on our butts and landed in a large chamber. Robert stood up and gestured at the wall, which at first looked bare in the darkness. "It's all engraved." He pointed. "All of that. All of that. All of that." He said that we were surrounded by around a thousand paintings and engravings, constituting three-quarters of those discovered in the Cave of Three Brothers. Everything up to about four or five feet was supposedly covered in art. He called us toward the wall and aimed his light at an enormous engraved phallus pointing toward a vulva-shaped depression. Bison and horses crowded around it.

"Why did they choose this room?" I asked.

"We don't know with certainty," Robert replied. "But there is an acoustic." He whooped. "It resonates."

The chamber was special in other ways, too. It was the lowest point of the cave, lying some 130 feet underground. It felt protected and secluded, which is probably why it's been named the "Sanctuary." The massive walls were smoother than the ones we had seen earlier. But the most salient feature was its dryness. There were no stalactites or stalagmites, none of the alien mineralized structures that filled the rest of the cave. "It's a miracle," explained Robert, "because if there are stalactites, they eat the engravings."

Robert gave us a tour of the artwork, focusing on his favorites. A complete mammoth, the only such drawing in this part of Paleolithic France. A human head with a mask. A bison fleeced with arrows. Another bison. The penis again, which, Robert explained, was overlooked until his son, twenty years old at the time, pointed it out. A strange, childlike drawing of a face. ("It looks like it doesn't belong here," commented François.) That was just the beginning. Robert went on to show us countless other engravings, including more bison, an ibex with surreally long horns, an arrow-studded bear vomiting blood, and the Small Sorcerer. Unlike its larger counterpart, the Small Sorcerer has the head of a bison and seems to dance next to large herbivores. I was lucky to get very close, my face barely a foot or two away from the engraving, but it was still difficult to make out all its features. I saw the Small Sorcerer's bison head, the flute or bow suspended from its nose, its uppermost arm, the tail, the knee, and the top part of a leg. But I had trouble discerning its feet and some of the lines presumably connecting the upper body to the lower body.

Then Robert turned his light on the crown jewel of the Cave of Three Brothers, the Sorcerer. I had read up on it before the visit and knew about the debate. Henri Breuil famously drew it as an anthropomorphic figure with owl, stag, bear, and horse features. He was convinced it was a magician-priest and, along with Robert's grandfather Henri Bégouën, gave it its name. This interpretation gained popularity, and the Sorcerer became another indication of shamanism's deep antiquity, even as Breuil changed his mind and followed the British author Margaret Murray, who considered the figure to be an archaic European deity she called "the horned god."[42]

A few years after Breuil's death, in 1967, the archaeologists Peter Ucko and Andrée Rosenfeld published *Paleolithic Cave Art*, which included newer photographs. They wrote, politely, that "many of the details shown in Breuil's drawings are not visible." In the case of the Sorcerer, they didn't see many of its most notable traits, including its owl eyes, animal ears, front paws, and at least one of its antlers. Perhaps, they guessed, Breuil had misread "faint scratches on the rock." Or maybe the figure had been damaged. Later photographs reinforced the doubts; when Ronald Hutton wrote about the Sorcerer in 2003, he considered it an example of a "Bold Fact, a confident and striking piece of information produced by a pioneering scholar, which is accepted uncritically by successors for long after its appearance."[43]

Unlike the other engravings in the Sanctuary, the Sorcerer is easy to see, even in dim light. It is large, but more importantly, it is the only engraving that is also painted. It sits suspended above the other artwork, as if watching over the creatures below. Gazing at it, I understood Breuil's conviction that this figure, whatever it was, was special for Paleolithic humans.

Because the Sorcerer is so high, I could see it only from about ten feet away. I noted the engraved toes on its feet and the painted lines of its body and tail. Unlike Ucko and Rosenfeld, I thought I saw the etched front paws. But its head and facial features were indeed hard to make out. Jean Clottes has asserted that the ant-lers are engraved and easier to discern up close. He might be right. But if I had visited the cave clueless about the Sorcerer's history, I would come away thinking it had been important to its creators but ultimately unknowable—an enigma whose true nature has been lost with the melting glaciers.

CHAPTER 7

The Rebel and the Redeemer

In 1987, the East African country of Uganda was rocked by a religious civil war. An army of seven to ten thousand soldiers marched toward Kampala, the country's capital. Known as the Holy Spirit Movement, the force was first composed mostly of soldiers from the Acholi, an ethnic group mostly located in northern Uganda that had been affected by decades of political and military conflict. As it expanded beyond the Acholi homeland, however, it absorbed peasants, women, and schoolchildren, growing into a pan-ethnic crusade.[1]

At the army's helm was a surprising face: a thirty-year-old former fishmonger named Alice Auma. A photograph from around this time gives the impression of a humble, almost hesitant woman. Alice has short-cropped hair and is biting her bottom lip. She wears a modest white top with no jewelry other than a simple beaded necklace. Taken at a time when many African rebel leaders preferred moss-green military garb, Alice looks less like a bush commando and more like a pious parishioner headed to church.[2]

Little about her biography could have anticipated her ascent. Born in 1956 to a catechist father, she attended primary school for seven years and then married a man from a neighboring village. When she couldn't bear children, her husband left her. Her second marriage, too, fell apart after she failed to get pregnant. She joined a friend selling fish and flour and, following another failed love affair, became what one Ugandan writer called a "loose woman."[3]

Then, suddenly, she lost control. Her body was no longer her own. She looked crazy and became mute and deaf. Her father brought her to eleven healers, none of whom could cure her. Soon after, she disappeared for weeks into the wilderness. When she returned, she announced that she was a healer and diviner, possessed by the spirit of a Christian Italian army captain who spoke seventy-four languages and drowned in the Nile at the age of ninety-five. She called the spirit "Lakwena," which translates in Acholi to "messenger."[4]

This was in August 1985. A year later, Alice—then also known as Alice Lakwena—was commanding her first troops of soldiers. In an interview with the *Sunday Nation*, she would later declare that Lakwena's objective was to topple the Ugandan president, Yoweri Museveni, and unite the people of Uganda. Hers was a war against the internal enemies of society: witches, sorcerers, soldiers corrupted by sin. Although Lakwena remained Alice's chief spirit, he came to share her body with a cavalcade of other spirits, including an American named "Wrong Element" and an East Asian called "Ching Poh," each of whom led their own companies. She invented a ritual to purify warriors and established the 20 Holy Spirit Safety Precautions, a list of Ten Commandment–style decrees that included items like "Thou shalt not steal," "Thou shalt not kill snakes of any kind," and, the strangest, "Thou shalt have two testicles, neither more nor less."[5]

Alice Lakwena's followers were hard-core believers. When, in 1995, an anthropologist hesitated to express belief in her abilities, Alice Lakwena's former secretary, an intellectual, asked, "Do you believe that when bombs are falling and you believe and pray and I put up my hand against the sky the bombs stop falling? Do you believe that when you believe and bullets are coming straight towards you they start encircling you without hitting or injuring your body?" Probably the most prominent figure to join the movement was Professor Isaac Newton Ojok, a former minister of education. After he was captured, an interviewer asked him how the war might end. "It all depends on how the government can take care of Lakwena being a spirit," he replied. "It needs to find out where the spirit comes from and how to net it in."[6]

Alice Lakwena was a shaman. She entered altered states, interacted with unseen agents, and provided services. Yet she was also much more. She united and destabilized. She set forth commandments and created what looked like a new religion. She inspired self-sacrifice and amassed a following in the thousands. She was deified, an infertile woman turned savior fabled to have been joined by bees, snakes, rocks, and rivers to combat the evil coursing through Uganda. She was relied on to bring what the Acholi, and northern Ugandans more broadly, so desperately desired: peace.[7]

Alice Lakwena is not the kind of figure that comes to many people's minds when they think of a shaman. More than a ritual specialist in a band of hunter-gatherers, she was a leader who mobilized thousands of combatants in a war against the state. She healed and divined, yes, but also vowed social disruption.

Alice is far from the only shaman to inspire fervor like this. For decades starting in the late 1800s, New Guinea and the surrounding islands hosted messianic movements, also called "cargo cults," in which shamans prophesied social transformations, often involving boatloads of goods. It was a shaman, Smohalla, who founded the Dreamers religion that swept through the Pacific Northwest in the late nineteenth century, and a trance-stricken weather wizard, Wovoka, who led the Ghost Dance movement that followed. The Inuit prophets who emerged with the arrival of Christianity in northeastern Canada all began their careers as shamans. On the opposite side of the globe, in Japan, spiritual movements bloomed after General MacArthur permitted freedom of religion in 1945. According to Carmen Blacker, the large, successful ones were all started by shamans.[8]

These figures are all examples of messianic prophets. There is no line you can cross, no requirement you can fulfill, that suddenly qualifies you as a messianic prophet. Rather, it exists on a continuum. From the examples we've reviewed, we can pinpoint four common features of messianic prophets:

1. They claim special powers and engage with supernatural beings. Compared to run-of-the-mill shamans, however, their powers tend to be more impressive (they might claim immortality, for example) and their supernatural engagement more exceptional (it may be said that the Creator chose them to spread a message).
2. They prophesy social upheavals, which can include peace, prosperity, the return of ancestors, the dethroning of corrupt rulers, the land consumed in hellfire, and enclosures filled with delectable livestock.
3. They promise benefits. These include standard shamanic services, like healing and protection, as well as larger-scale blessings, often linked to the awaited social transformation.
4. They have lots of followers. More than mere clients, however, these followers often cooperate on a large scale. They might fight together, as Alice Lakwena's followers did, or seclude themselves somewhere and create a new society. As leaders, messianic prophets may enact edicts and establish missionizing enterprises that spread their doctrine. Bound by ritual and ideology, communities of followers can outlast their founders, evolving into new religious movements.

Not all messianic prophets are shamans. Various so-called cult leaders, even when not technically shamans, exhibit these traits. Jim Jones, the preacher behind the mass suicide of 909 followers in Guyana in 1978, checked all the boxes: he healed, claimed divine status, lectured about an apocalyptic coming, and led the Peoples Temple, which had more than three thousand members at its peak—all without entering trance.[9]

Still, shamanism positions a person well to become a messianic prophet. Through their altered states, initiations, and displays of special powers, shamans cultivate auras of divinity, setting themselves up as transformative figures in their societies. The intersection of shamanism and messianic prophecy exemplifies shamanism's timeless potency—not just as an appealing spiritual practice, but as a political tool that unifies, threatens social stability, and, in many cases, redirects history.

For the first year after her spiritual calling, Alice Lakwena barely stood out among other local mediums. Her infertility, the Christian syncretism, the crisis that kicked off her career, even the foreignness of her possessing spirit—all were common themes. But on August 6, 1986, the spirit Lakwena directed her to stop healing and start fighting. Barely three months later, she had assembled 150 soldiers and was training them in the Holy Spirit Tactics, her unique brand of war making.[10]

Alice Lakwena's early success was attributable to more than her charisma. Northern Uganda was then being ravaged. Acholi people were frightened. Museveni, of the Hima ethnic group, had seized power from the country's former president, an Acholi officer named Tito Okello. Museveni's army tortured and murdered demobilized Acholi soldiers, who, returning from years in the military, had become marauding strangers in their homelands. When the army demanded the Acholi hand over their weapons, many Acholi feared ethnic extermination, a panic supercharged by national radio broadcasts denouncing them as criminals and murderers. Death seemed inescapable. Alice Lakwena's followers later told missionaries, "The good Lord who had sent the Lakwena decided to change his work from that of a doctor to that of a military commander for one simple reason: it is useless to cure a man today only that he be killed the next day."[11]

The connection between violent upheaval and messianism is common. In every example I have mentioned—cargo cults, the Ghost Dance, the Holy Spirit movement, postwar Japan—shaman-prophets were born of anxiety. As people's worlds were overturned—as invaders usurped their land, as their lives became violent or confusing, as they became aware of obscene but unattainable riches—they sought out miracle workers. Just as everyday shamans appear to satisfy the need to tame local uncertainty, prophets emerge to feed a desperation for renewal.

Why do people gravitate to shamans? Like other leaders, shamans often have traits well suited to social coordination, like charismatic rhetoric or a knack for organizing. But their supernatural authority gives them an edge. Through a combination of myth and performance, shamans are believed to access divine powers. Leaders can seem supernatural in other ways, such as by studying texts considered ritually powerful. But these are less compelling, less experiential, less *real*. Shamans make great messiahs for the same reasons we seek them out as healers and diviners in the first place: they are well attuned to human minds to look, and feel, like miracle workers.

Even as Japanese, New Guinean, and Indigenous North American prophets are recognized as shamans, there is one class of religious leader that often escapes anthropological comparison: the Abrahamic prophets. Shrouded in a veil of Western exceptionalism, Abrahamic prophets have been studied more as theological figures than as expressions of a cross-cultural tendency. Yet there is little to justify this. If, as I have argued, shamanism suffuses society and history, then we should expect to find it everywhere, including at the spiritual foundations of Western civilization.

Say we traveled to the eastern Mediterranean during the classical period. We would have little difficulty finding shamans. If we stopped in Babylon from about 1500 BCE onward, we would hear about *maḫḫû* and *maḫḫûtu*. Translated as "prophet" and "prophetess" by modern scholars, these words derive from the verb *maḫû*, meaning "to become crazy" or "to go into a frenzy." They refer to figures who transmitted divine messages, or prophecies, in altered states of mind. A Neo-Assyrian prayer summed up their role and performance: "I have become affected like a prophet: what I do not know I bring forth."[12]

Shamanic forecasters weren't confined to Mesopotamia. If

we traveled northwest to Greece, we might encounter *manteis* (sing. *mantis*), a word meaning "diviners" and that, according to Plato, derived from *mania* (madness). In Plato's dialogues, the character of Socrates recognizes three important uses of *mania*: divination, curing sickness, and inspiring song and poetry. Other terms for diviners existed, among them *prophētēs*, which came from *pro-* (before) and *phēmi* (to say) and implied either speaking on behalf of a deity or speaking in front of people. Plato emphasized the importance of altered states for effective prophesying, arguing that "no man achieves true and inspired divination when in his rational mind, but only when the power of his intelligence is fettered in sleep or when it is distraught by disease or by reason of some divine inspiration."[13]

The most famous shaman in the Greek world was and still is the Oracle of Apollo at Delphi. Older scholarship reconstructed her as a virgin, cloaked in white, who entered a dark room. She was said to inhale vapors from a chasm in the ground, to become possessed by Apollo, and to spew frenzied, unintelligible cries, which priests translated into messages. Most of these details have been questioned. What is not doubted, however, is that she appeared to receive messages from Apollo, likely in an altered state, and shared them as prophecies. And she wasn't alone. The Minoan queen may have likewise been an ecstatic priestess. Other renowned female oracles foretold the future at the Temples of Apollo at Didyma and Zeus in Dodona.[14]

In other words, the ancient eastern Mediterranean was much like the rest of the world: shamanic. This was also the case for the Hebrews and Israelites. Hebrew prophets are referred to mainly as *nābî'* in the Hebrew Bible. The term pops up 325 times and is the root for the words *nibbā'* and *hitnabbē'*, which mean "to act as a *nābî'*."[15] As we'd expect, these verbs almost always describe someone delivering a message and at times involve non-ordinary behavior:

> He stripped off his garments, and he too prophesied in Samuel's presence. He lay naked all that day and all that night. This is why people say, "Is Saul also among the prophets?" (1 Samuel 19:24)

The Spirit of the Lord will come powerfully upon
you, and you will prophesy with them; and you will be
changed into a different person. (1 Samuel 10:6)

As in the last example, the divine spirit is sometimes said to
be "on" people. This phrasing often seems to entail a suite of
shamanic behavior—supernatural engagement, altered states,
and divination. See, for example, Joel 2:28:

And afterward, I will pour out my Spirit on all people.
Your sons and daughters will prophesy, your old men will
dream dreams, your young men will see visions.

Or 2 Kings 3:15–17, in which Elisha seems to enter music-
induced trance and divine:

While the harpist was playing, the hand of the Lord came
on Elisha and he said, "This is what the Lord says: I will
fill this valley with pools of water. For this is what the
Lord says: You will see neither wind nor rain, yet this valley will be filled with water, and you, your cattle and your
other animals will drink."

In parts of the Hebrew Bible, like Ezekiel 37:1, this phrasing
even appears to involve soul journeying, a non-ordinary experience common to many (but not all) shamanic traditions:

The hand of the Lord was on me, and he brought me out
by the Spirit of the Lord and set me in the middle of a
valley; it was full of bones.

The link between divine contact and altered states, at least
according to the timeline set out in the Hebrew Bible, seems
ancient. In Genesis 15:12, before God told him about the future
of the Jewish people, Abraham "fell into a deep sleep, and a thick
and dreadful darkness came over him." The original Hebrew for
"deep sleep" (המדרת, or *tardemah*) is also sometimes translated as

"trance." When Jews rendered the text into Greek in the third century BCE, they used the word *ekstasis*, meaning "ecstasy."[16]

Drawing on this and other evidence, a growing number of biblical scholars argue that many Hebrew prophets divined in altered states. This doesn't mean, of course, that ancient Jews were all shaman followers. According to the Finnish theologist Martti Nissinen, the "ecstatic element" of Hebrew prophecy became a problem by at least the Second Temple period (516 BCE–70 CE).[17] Scribes sought to replace shamanic diviners as intermediaries with God. Even with this professional tug-of-war, however, ecstatic prophecy lived on. Writing around the time of Jesus, the Hellenistic Jewish philosopher Philo of Alexandria commented:

> A prophet possessed by God will suddenly appear and give prophetic oracles. Nothing of what he says will be his own, for he that is truly under the control of divine inspiration has no power of apprehension when he speaks but serves as the channel for the insistent words of another's prompting. For prophets are the interpreters of God, who makes full use of their organs of speech to set forth what he wills.[18]

Which of the Hebrew prophets qualify as shamans? Obvious candidates are Samuel, Elisha, and possibly Elijah. There's also John the Baptist, who wore clothing "made of camel's hair, with a leather belt around his waist" (Mark 1:6), an outfit that indicated prophetic status from at least the time of Elijah. Mark (11:32), Matthew (21:26), and Luke (20:6) all refer to him as a prophet (*prophētēs* or *prophētēn* in the original Greek), which, as established, often entailed possessed divination. As the biblical scholar Stevan Davies put it, John the Baptist "looked like a prophet, he spoke like a prophet, people evidently thought of him as a prophet and so, by the logic of the duck, he was a prophet."[19]

The recognition that Hebrew prophets resemble similar figures elsewhere in the world took a long time to sink in, and it still faces resistance. It has a lot conspiring against it: a sense of biblical exceptionalism, a bias that places shamans into the realm of "magic" and prophets into the domain of "religion," and, for many years, a lack of documentation of other practices, both around the world and throughout the ancient Near East. "Perhaps it is only now that we have enough sources, open-mindedness, and theoretical tools to compare prophets and shamans in an appropriate manner," Nissinen wrote to me in an email.[20]

The resistance to cross-cultural comparisons has been just as intense, if not more so, in the study of early Christianity. The theologian Colleen Shantz suspects that people associate shamanism, possession, and ecstatic states with foreign, nonwhite, and seemingly primitive peoples. As a result, scholars avoid studying these among early Christians, often treated as forebears of Western civilization. Reflecting on the reluctance to consider the trance experiences of the Apostle Paul, she wrote, "The generalized cultural bias against religious ecstasy placed its practitioners almost irretrievably in the category of Other, while Paul was firmly the exemplar for Us."[21]

Paul, for anyone not familiar, is maybe the most important figure in early Christianity other than Jesus. Originally a persecutor of Christians, his vision of Christ on the road to Damascus turned him into a devoted missionary. He crisscrossed the Roman Empire, setting up churches, formulating doctrine, and composing many of the New Testament's letters. According to Shantz, many labels have been used to describe Paul, including "apostle, convert, Pharisee, apocalyptic, even tentmaker," yet "that of ecstatic is seldom used. In fact, it is often forcefully resisted."[22]

Shantz argues that this resistance is unjustified. In *Paul in Ecstasy: The Neurobiology of the Apostle's Life and Thought* (2009), she compiled evidence that Paul was an ecstatic, likely understood in his time to be spirit possessed. His writings burst with references to spirit-inspired powers and experiences, including revelations, rapturous prayer, a visionary journey to heaven, and "signs" and "wonders" that he performed. Among his most important behaviors was "speaking in tongues," or glossolalia. This refers to ecstatic vocalizations in which a person utters words normally unknown to them, often understood to be in a spirit language, an ancient tongue, or a language of foreign peoples. Although not strictly universal, glossolalia has characterized shamanic trance states throughout time and space, from ancient Greek divination to modern Haitian vodou.[23]

Paul's experiences represent a tile in a far richer spiritual mosaic. Much of what we know of the early church reveals it to have been an environment where people interacted with spirits, entered xenized states, and, in many cases, delivered services like healing and forecasting. A quintessential example is the day of Pentecost, recounted in Acts 2, when the followers of Jesus "were filled with the Holy Spirit" and began to speak in heavenly or foreign languages. Paul even described a division of spiritual labor. In 1 Corinthians 12:4–11, he said the Holy Spirit grants some people the power to prophecy, others the gift of healing, and still others the ability to speak in tongues, among other powers.

The New Testament tells us only so much. It shows early Christians entering ecstatic states and proffering miraculous services, but we don't know if they performed them at the same time, shaman-style. Turning to records from slightly later, however, we find evidence that early Christians linked non-ordinary behavior to divine services. The Greek philosopher Celsus, for example, wrote that Christians prophesied while speaking "strange, fanatical and quite unintelligible words, of which no rational person can find the meaning." As with shamans everywhere, early Christians seem to have accessed miraculous powers in inspired states distinct from everyday functioning.[24]

What about Jesus? The central figure of Christianity, he is known by many titles and epithets: Lord. Christ. Messiah. Lamb of God. Light of the World. King of the Jews. Should "shaman" be among them?

Most scholars agree that the best sources for studying Jesus's life are the four canonical gospels: Matthew, Mark, Luke, and John. Scholars also tend to subscribe to Markan priority, the hypothesis that the Gospel of Mark was written first, around 60–75 AD, followed by Matthew, Luke, and then John. Matthew and Luke share a lot of content with Mark, suggesting they both used it as a source. Matthew and Luke also share passages not in Mark, hinting at the influence of another source, now lost, commonly dubbed "Q."[25]

Prioritizing the canonical gospels, then, we can check whether Jesus exhibits the three criteria of a shaman: providing services like healing and divination, engaging with unseen realms, and entering non-ordinary states.

The first and second criteria are clearly met. To quote the priest and biblical scholar John Meier, "Nothing is more certain about Jesus than that he was viewed by his contemporaries as an exorcist and healer." Mark tells us that Jesus "healed many who had various diseases" and "drove out many demons" (Mark 1:34). Looking through the Gospels of Mark and Luke, we find Jesus treating deafness, muteness, blindness, fever, paralysis, a bent spine, a shriveled hand, abnormal swelling, excessive menstrual bleeding, and a skin condition, possibly psoriasis. Luke summarizes Jesus's life in Acts 10:38 as "doing good and healing all who were under the power of the devil." Importantly, Jesus's healing often revolves around the power of an invisible agent, like when he says that "it is by the Spirit of God that I drive out demons" (Matthew 12:28).[26]

What about the third criterion of shamanism? Did Jesus enter non-ordinary states? Answering this question is less straightforward, although scholars like Stevan Davies and Pieter Craffert have pointed to intriguing evidence.[27] Let's start with the following scene from the Gospel of Mark, when people flock to Jesus for healing:

> Then Jesus entered a house, and again a crowd gathered, so that he and his disciples were not even able to eat. When his family heard about this, they went to take charge of him, for they said, "He is out of his mind."
>
> And the teachers of the law who came down from Jerusalem said, "He is possessed by Beelzebul! By the prince of demons he is driving out demons." (Mark 3:20–22)

Here, and throughout this book, I have used the New International Version of the Bible. But as with all translations, this version is layered with interpretation, and scholars still debate over what each word means. For example, this translation talks about Jesus's "family," although the author may have meant his neighbors, followers, or associates. Likewise, where this version says that people "take charge of" Jesus, other translations say they "restrain him" (Christian Standard Bible) or "take custody of Him" (New American Standard Bible).

Especially interesting for our purposes is the phrase "out of his mind." For English speakers, this suggests craziness, although that may not have been the original gist. The phrase comes from the Greek base verb *existémi*. Going by the system established by the theologian James Strong, forms of this word are used throughout the New Testament, such as to describe how people felt seeing Jesus heal paralysis (Mark 2:12) and raise a girl from the dead (Mark 5:42). Paul uses it in 2 Corinthians 5:13, when he writes, "If we are 'out of our mind,' as some say, it is for God."[28]

Thus we have a scene where people approach Jesus to heal them. He is acting crazy, astonished, or religiously inspired. Someone close to him restrains or takes hold of him, while onlookers accuse him of being possessed by the devil.

Accusations that Jesus is possessed appear elsewhere in the New Testament. In the Gospel of John, Jews ask Jesus, "Aren't we right in saying that you are a Samaritan and demon-possessed?" (8:48). Two chapters later, they again suspect spiritual invasion: "He is demon-possessed and raving mad. Why listen to him?" (10:20).

Jesus himself uses intriguing language to describe his relationship with the Holy Spirit. In Luke 4:18, he borrowed a line from Isaiah: "The Spirit of the Lord is on me, because he has anointed me to proclaim good news to the poor." What does it mean for a spirit to be "on" someone? We saw in the Hebrew Bible that this phrasing often involved non-ordinary behavior; if we look elsewhere in the New Testament, we find similar implications. In Acts 19:6, for instance, Luke says that "when Paul had laid his hands on [twelve baptized men], the Holy Spirit came on them, and they spoke in tongues and prophesied."[29]

None of this evidence is conclusive, however. The accusations of demon possession might just be glorified mudslinging. The New Testament includes descriptions of people who are possessed, which are far more graphic and dramatic than anything ever reported for Jesus. A child seized by a spirit, for example, screamed, convulsed, and foamed at the mouth (Luke 9:39). And recall that, when the Holy Spirit descended on early Christians, they spoke in angelic and foreign languages. Jesus is never described in such ecstatic language.

We also need to remember that Jesus is notoriously malleable. It is easy to pick and choose quotes to construct a character to one's liking. Different writers have presented him as a zealot, a magician, a social radical, an antipatriarchal revolutionary, an end-times doomsayer, and a cynic. His ideology seems to shift with the times—a European progressive one day, an American conservative the next. "I am a mirror to thee who perceivest me," he says in the apocryphal Acts of John, almost warning us against these interpretive gymnastics.[30]

We are left with two options. The first is that Jesus was a shaman. I think this is more likely, at least going by historical and literary evidence. The ancient eastern Mediterranean was filled with shamans. His baptizer, John, seems to have been one, and his immediate followers were ecstatic healers and mystics. A Jewish prophet, he came from a lineage of shamanic diviners and compared himself to at least one. By interacting with a powerful spirit being, he cured, exorcised, and foretold the future. When people flocked to him for healing, others accused him of being demon possessed. If he lived in almost any other part of the world, and started almost any other religion, we would more readily entertain the possibility of his being a shaman.

The second option is that he wasn't. This may have been the case—but if so, why wasn't he? Trance states are powerful. They garner spiritual credibility while making supernatural contact all the realer for a messiah. From the earlier quote by Philo of Alexandria, we know that at least some first-century Jews thought of possession and altered states as necessary for genuine prophecy. It is true that some leaders get spiritual authority from their institutional position or familiarity with texts, but Jesus seemed to rely on neither, instead leveraging his "spiritual gifts." Whether we examine him as a classical, eastern Mediterranean prophet or in a larger cross-cultural perspective, the proposal that Jesus was a shaman is far less puzzling or surprising than the alternative that he was not.

On September 30, 1987, Alice Lakwena's Holy Spirit Movement faced off against the National Resistance Army (NRA), President Museveni's armed forces, in Tororo District. They had fought many times before. A couple of weeks earlier, they had skirmished in swamps to the north, with Lakwena's army scaring off Museveni's and securing a radio, AK-47s, and other arms. Now, however, Lakwena's army was getting dangerously close to Uganda's capital—a mere two hundred kilometers away—and the NRA had come to destroy them.[31]

A little before midnight, NRA soldiers surrounded Alice's camp and began lobbing artillery shells. The Holy Spirit soldiers maintained their position until dawn. Around noon, they broke through NRA lines, although at enormous costs. A third of the forces got cut off and separated. The civilian contingent fled into the swamps, where they wandered, lost. The battle, among the bloodiest in the Holy Spirit Movement's history, marked the beginning of the end.[32]

Alice had long served as a scapegoat for her movement's failures. Earlier that year, the spirit Lakwena—apparently speaking from her mouth—demanded that she receive six blows with a stick for failing to respect his rules. After an alliance with the Uganda People's Army fell through and five of its commanders were killed, Lakwena promised to punish Alice and told troops that they should never act without consulting him first.[33]

But the scapegoating worked only up to a point. According to the German anthropologist Heike Behrend, "Alice's power began to wane" following the defeat in Tororo. The movement hemorrhaged support as Alice increasingly contradicted her spirits. By November 2, Holy Spirit troops were within a hundred kilometers of Kampala, yet the army had become a shadow of its former strength. When Lakwena asked which soldiers would remain, only 360 stepped forward. Days later, this final force would crumble under the threat of NRA bombs. Along with a few loyal followers, Alice fled to a Kenyan refugee camp, where she lived until her death in 2007.[34]

Why did the Holy Spirit Movement fall apart? Ask different people, and you'll get different answers. Perhaps it was about resources. Museveni's forces were larger, after all, and better armed. Or perhaps it was because of local disloyalties; as they marched southward, Holy Spirit troops had more difficulty ingratiating themselves with local communities, some of whom betrayed them to the NRA.[35]

When Behrend asked former Holy Spirit soldiers, many provided alternative takes. Some said that Lakwena had punished the movement for not upholding the 20 Safety Precautions. Others blamed Alice, who they said strayed from Lakwena's commandments and thus lost his support. Another group said that Museveni had hired magicians who supplied his armies with mighty medicines, or that Alice was a witch, or an HIV-infected prostitute, who refused to die alone and so built a rebellion to follow her into the afterlife.[36]

According to another perspective, however, the Holy Spirit Movement did not fall apart in 1987; it transformed. Many of Alice's followers briefly joined her father, Severino Lukoya, who became possessed by Lakwena and, like Alice, mixed healing with end-times prophecies. Unfortunately for him, his movement was short-lived. After about a year, another shaman-prophet, Joseph Kony, proclaimed Severino a sinner and imprisoned him. Severino was told to stop any spirit-related activities and was beaten whenever he experienced spiritual takeover. He eventually escaped Kony's custody, only to be arrested by the Ugandan state.[37]

Joseph Kony was the most successful shaman-prophet to emerge from the rubble of Alice's movement. He claimed to be her cousin and vowed to destroy evil, witchcraft, and sorcery. Allegedly possessed by Juma Oris, a minister of the former Ugandan dictator Idi Amin, Kony cannibalized Alice's and Severino's organizations, establishing what he called the Lord's Resistance

Army. It would grow into a scourge. Throughout the 1990s and 2000s, the Lord's Resistance Army terrorized eastern and central Africa, eventually attracting the attention of the United States, which labeled it a terrorist organization and spent millions of dollars a month to combat it. By 2006, according to UNICEF, it had kidnapped an estimated twenty-five thousand children "for the purposes of forced conscription, labor, and sexual servitude."[38]

As I write this, at the end of 2023, Joseph Kony's whereabouts are unknown. He, like Alice Auma and her father, might be dead. Yet if history is any guide, his tactics will outlive him. Even if Kony's organization is not itself commandeered by a new prophet-medium, some shamans will always ascend to messianic status, unsettling the social order and carving new paths through history.

CHAPTER 8

Ouroboros

On March 9, 2014, a healer was visited by a desperate man. A machine had fallen on him, and now he had a steel plate in his neck. He felt numbness in his hands sometimes. He had trouble twisting his neck. He wanted to be free.

With a crowd watching, the healer held the man's head between his hands, massaging his neck and searching for the plate. Eyes closed, the healer called upon a supernatural being often associated with the sky.

"Woo! There it is," he said. A power seemed to surge through him. Staring into the distance, his words became uninterpretable. "BRRA RA RIBO KAI," he boomed. "REBO AHA. REBO SOMBROVONDO. NOW BRO AH HEE DEH OH SHAH AH MONDO." He returned to his senses and released the man, who fainted and was carried gently to the floor.

"Pick him up," commanded the healer. "What's happening? Look at me. What's happening?"

The man stumbled as if intoxicated. He stared at the healer with alarm, then relaxed into a smile.

"Look at me," the healer repeated. "What's happening?"

"My neck is—"

"Your neck is . . . Your neck is what? Move it around. Do what you couldn't do."

The man swiveled his head. "The steel is gone," he said.

"The steel is gone. I want you to turn as far as—" The healer cut himself off and turned to the crowd. "Look, I felt it go. I felt it go from hard, under my hand, to totally loose. I promise you. I felt the moment it happened. I felt the moment it happened. I felt the moment it happened. I felt the moment it happened." The crowd was cheering by now. "I felt it. I felt it. I felt it. I felt it."

The healer looked at the man, and they laughed.

I found a video of this session on YouTube, where it was titled "Steel Plate in Neck Healing Miracle and Testimony." It took place during a Sunday night service at the River at Tampa Bay Church in Florida and was performed by Rodney Howard-Browne, a South African–born evangelical pastor.[1]

Howard-Browne is a shaman. He calls upon a heavenly being, sometimes entering an inspired state marked by inscrutable speech—all in the service of healing. He isn't unique. The wild, glorious, unregulated marketplace of American Christianity teems with religious leaders who mix altered states with promised miracles, especially curing. An internet favorite is Kerney Thomas, who had an early morning ministry on the TV channel BET (Black Entertainment Television). People called in with problems like back pain or financial stress. He got himself into an excitable temper, urged on by screaming words like "God" and "now" in high-pitched screeches, and communed with God to help them. Sometimes, in mid-sentence, he shuddered or recoiled, as if a wave of electricity rippled through his body. His face looked like he was either in pain or in bliss, and he broke out into exotic babbling, often variants of "shalala bokosha."[2]

Figures like these aren't supposed to exist. Many writers treat shamanism like the primitive ape in Rudolph Zallinger's famous *March of Progress* illustration: the earliest phase in a progressive evolution. "The shaman is the first step toward an archbishop or an ayatollah," wrote the journalist Robert Wright in his book *The Evolution of God* (2009). He regarded shamans as icons of "primordial religion" and "pre-agricultural societies," existing either in hunter-gatherer bands, which tend to "have almost no structure in the modern sense of the word," or in "societies that are a shade more technologically advanced." With the transition to agriculture and social hierarchy, he envisioned a "transformation in social structure that carried religion beyond the age of shamans."[3]

This is what I call the Pokémon theory of religious history. Just as Pikachu and Charmander level up and transmute into new forms, shamans are thought to metamorphose into new specialists. The Pokémon theory seeps into scholarship. The Swedish shamanism expert Åke Hultkrantz wrote that, wherever agriculture supplanted foraging, "priests and cult servants replaced shamans." Other researchers, among them the Oxford anthropologist Robin Dunbar, have asserted that "shamanic" or "primitive" religions gave way to "doctrinal" ones, the latter characterized by priests, big gods, temples, and moral codes.[4]

To be clear, Wright, Hultkrantz, and Dunbar are pointing to real differences. Silent prayer is not shamanic trance. The Catholic Church is far more centralized and bureaucratic than any religious institution in a hunter-gatherer community. And yet the Pokémon theory falls short. Shamans persist, often prominently and in the traditions said to have replaced them. They lead megachurches. They get television deals. Howard-Browne was even invited to pray over Donald Trump in the White House. These ecstatic pastor-healers are not quirky survivals of an obsolete practice. They are testaments to shamanism's durability, incarnations of a timeless tradition, and their existence forces us to revisit our assumptions about the arc of history.

―――――――

For more than 3,000 years, people have reproduced the image of Ouroboros, or the serpent eating its own tail. It appeared in the tomb of the boy pharaoh Tutankhamen and in the texts of Gnostics and Greek alchemists. Although, at first, it might seem a symbol of self-annihilation, it probably meant the opposite. According to the Egyptologist Jan Assmann, ancient Egyptians used it to refer to regeneration and cyclical events, like the annual flooding of the Nile. Greek thinkers likely also considered it a symbol of infinite time, of perpetuity.[5]

This confusion—seeing destruction instead of eternal return—is at the heart of historical stories about shamanism's decline. It's reasonable to look at history and conclude that shamanism died with the rise of doctrinal authorities. In the decades after Jesus's death, for example, expressions of ecstasy started to decline. From 70 to 140 AD, a church hierarchy crystallized. Power was wrested from prophets and consolidated in the bishop, while ecstatic behavior was, in some instances, purged from the historical record. Around 96 AD, the bishop of Rome, Clement, asserted that the Old Testament prophets were not loud but reserved. Even Moses "never indulged in high-flown speeches," he wrote. And when it came to the gifts of the Holy Spirit—which, according to Paul, included healing, prophecy, and speaking in tongues—Clement opted for boring abstractions: humility, chastity, mutual respect. The new church was targeting its unruly parts, a snake pursuing itself as prey.[6]

The changes boiled down to power. Allow prophecy and spirit possession and other direct contacts with God, and you risk a litany of competing doctrines. Anyone's grandma can act frenzied, predict an apocalypse, and rewrite scripture. Shamans in the landscape meant competing intermediaries with the divine—something the church fought to snuff out.

A conflict between shamanism and the early church erupted at the end of the second century when three prophets—a man named Montanus and two women, Priscilla and Maximilla—started to amass a following. Little is known about their backgrounds other than that they were based in Phrygia, now in Asian Turkey. Montanus worked wonders and may have been a priest for the pagan mother goddess Cybele before converting to Christianity. The trio rejected the authority of bishops and the church. They endorsed a creed, later called Montanism, in which the Holy Spirit possessed people and acted through them. In trance, the shaman-prophets foretold the second coming of Christ. The prediction failed—Christ did not return—but the

Montanist doctrine, with its raw spiritual allure, found believers across North Africa, Asia Minor, and Mediterranean Europe—even in Rome itself.[7]

The church, no surprise, was not happy. The incident spurred some of the earliest regional councils or synods. Theologians emphasized that doctrine came from texts, not fiery-tongued upstarts. They also defended a legitimate line of authority that ran from Jesus to the apostles to the bishops—and particularly to the bishop and church in Rome. Yet the Montanists endured. They (or movements inspired by them) developed their own ecclesiastical systems and theological writings, including seven books on ecstatic prophecy. Nearly all their texts have been lost, however, partly because they were deliberately destroyed. History remembers the power-holding hierarchs, not the spirit-infused punks they crushed.[8]

Sequences like this have replayed over and over. Trancing rebels appear, attract followers, and annoy people in power. This is how groups like the Cathars, Anabaptists, Quakers, and Shakers got started. The Catholic intellectual Ronald Knox condemned these movements as sources of schism. Nevertheless, writing in *Enthusiasm: A Chapter in the History of Religion* (1950), he admitted their ageless appeal: "The pattern is always repeating itself, not in outline merely but in detail. Almost always the enthusiastic movement is denounced as an innovation, yet claims to be preserving, or to be restoring, the primitive discipline of the Church."[9]

Tensions between ecstatics and authority figures occurred outside Christian history. Polynesian shamans, for example, were spirit-possessed men or women who treated illness and answered questions about war, peace, feast times, and other pressing affairs. Their altered states ranged from the extreme—characterized by convulsions—to the passive, in which gods were said to inhabit or "eat" their innards. Strangely, however, their existence was "more or less sporadic" throughout the Pacific, to use Eliade's words. In some places, shamans had obscene levels of power; in others, they barely hung on.[10]

The distribution of Polynesian shamanism makes sense if we consider its main competitor: chiefly power. Like shamans,

Polynesian chiefs claimed divine connection, and the two seemed locked in constant rivalry. If an island or region had strong chiefs, it tended to have weak shamans, and vice versa. In the Hawaiian archipelago, female shamans prospered most in places far away from chiefly centers, like the small western island of Ni'ihau. In the Marquesas Islands, in contrast, where chiefs had little mystical power, the oldest and most powerful shamans were considered living gods. One of them, Tamapuameine, lived in seclusion and even received human sacrifices, displaying the bodies of victims from rafters and trees. Free from chiefly interference, Marquesan shamans were elevated to celestial royalty.[11]

Polynesian shamanism and the early church both demonstrate that shamans do not evolve Pokémon-like into bishops or ayatollahs. Rather, they are tangled together in a cycle reminiscent of Ouroboros—a dance between freedom and control, desire and dominion, anarchic spirit and organized might. Shamans are mirrors of their community's fears and cravings. Compared to big-time clergy, their credibility depends more on charisma and raw experience. Bishops, ayatollahs, and divine chiefs, meanwhile, garner authority from rules and doctrine, from their place in a formal institution. As they expand and solidify power, they use their platform to stifle shamans who threaten their authority and potentially siphon followers away.

What is most striking about this cycle is the way in which ecstatic religions turn on themselves. As religious movements institutionalize, they attack trance performances, replaying the conditions of their early oppression. This occurred at the dawn of Christianity, but it is common elsewhere. The Australian scholar Kirsten Bell, for example, observed such a cycle while working with followers of Cheondoism, a Korean religion that started in 1860 when a revolutionary fell into a trembling trance and spoke to God. By the late 1990s and early 2000s, the religion had developed a fully fledged organizational structure, and members of its governing body denounced inspired states. Bell saw a woman in trance be physically restrained; another was condemned twice in an afternoon and said to suffer from a fever, not authentic divine contact. When Bell asked an adherent, Mr. Lee, about the repression, he told her that "the center" doesn't like religious ecstasy because "they don't control the man."[12]

A similar evolution occurred in that Great American Institution, Mormonism. Its founder and prophet, Joseph Smith, started out as a magician. Imaginative and ambitious, he had a knack for leadership and a penchant for ritual, which he channeled into finding treasure. In 1826, when he was twenty years old, a New York court found him guilty of being a "disorderly person and an impostor." His neighbors rattled off accusations. Smith promised a person that he could see a far-off chest by looking into a hat. He led someone to an underground trunk but then refused to dig it up, suggesting that doing so might upset nearby Native people. One man, William Stafford, later swore that Smith and his family urged him to sacrifice a black sheep to coax an evil spirit into releasing buried treasure. He gave them the sheep to kill, but they told him something went wrong. The treasure stayed submerged.[13]

In 1827, magic gave way to revelation. Smith claimed to unearth golden plates covered in a strange script. He kept them hidden, however, wrapping them in a tablecloth and forbidding even his wife from looking. Using a seer stone and special spectacles, he translated the plates, producing what would become the Book of Mormon, published in 1830.[14]

For modern Mormons, the Book of Mormon is scripture. For non-Mormon historians, it's speculative fiction authored by Smith himself—an epic but very inaccurate chronicle of precolonial American history blended with musings on topics that nineteenth-century American Christians cared about. Penned in the style of the King James Bible, it's organized into smaller books, most of them named after prophets said to have lived in the Americas between 600 BCE and 421 AD.[15]

However you interpret it, the Book of Mormon celebrates miracles, including ecstatic performance. In 2 Nephi 31:13, the ancient prophet Nephi promised that believers who received the Holy Ghost would speak "with the tongue of angels." The angel Moroni proclaimed in Mormon 9 that healing, prophecies, exorcism, and speaking in tongues disappear only with unbelief. Doctrine translated into practice, and, from the beginning, the Mormon Church was filled with trance. Smith later wrote that, at a meeting in New York two months after the church was legally established, "the Holy Ghost was poured out upon the whole community." People "spoke with new tongues" and conveyed messages from God.[16] Brigham Young, who went on to become the second president of the Mormon Church, saw in ecstatic performance, and especially glossolalia, a throwback to Christianity's earliest days:

> A few weeks after my baptism I was at brother Kimball's house one morning, and while family prayer was being offered up, brother Alpheus Gifford commenced speaking in tongues. Soon the Spirit come on me, and I spoke in tongues, and we thought only of the day of Pentecost, when the Apostles were clothed upon with cloven tongues of fire.[17]

The parallels with Christianity's early days went beyond tongue speaking, however. Like the early church, the Mormon Church's attitude toward trance soon shifted. As its authority crystallized, officials stopped tolerating charismatic behavior. By 1864, Brigham Young's views on ecstasy had become unrecognizable. "Were I to permit it now," he said, "hundreds of Elders and the sisters would rise up in this congregation and speak in new tongues, and interpret as well as the learned of the age." To permit trance, in other words, meant disruption and the muddying of doctrine. Thus, he added, "I do not permit it."

Today, more than a century and a half later, Mormons understand the "gift of tongues" not to mean rapturous angel-speak but the God-given talent for learning languages to missionize. Spiritual experience has been replaced with institutional expansion.[18]

Fights against shamanism can be draining and prolonged. The church's campaign against Montanists, for example, started by the late second century AD. More than two centuries later, around the turn of the fifth century, the emperor Honorius was still passing laws against them and ordering their books burned. The movement died out eventually, but other trance-centered Christian heresies soon took its place.[19]

Some authorities, faced with the tricky task of destroying shamanism, have tried to domesticate it. They have weakened it, or built it into their rituals, or condoned only some trance practitioners, thus defusing threats while beefing themselves up with spiritual appeal. The Japanese state tried to do this with *miko*, or shaman-mediums. As far back as 645 AD, Japanese officials made practicing as a *miko* illegal among commoners. Records show that *miko* were exiled in the late 700s, while a series of codes sought to cripple the institution. The Japanese state first established a system of official shrines. Then they permitted only female *miko* to practice at them. Then they cut away at their privileges, attempting to turn religious authorities into domestic servants. Banished from official courts, the *miko* lost political sway.[20]

Finally, Buddhists came for them. As agents of gods, *miko* filled a similar role to Buddhist priests, plus they introduced a raucous element that some Buddhists found undesirable. Yet the shaman-mediums were so popular among everyday people that destroying the institution was impossible—a fact nicely demonstrated in the story of Rinkai.[21]

Rinkai was a Buddhist priest and scholar living in Japan in the eleventh century. According to a widely recorded tale, he had gone to the Kasuga Shrine, which you can still visit today in Nara, and was about to make an offering when he heard a crowd of *miko* chanting and performing with bells and drums. Frustrated, he vowed to end the song and dance if appointed administrator. Years passed, and he eventually got the job. But when he fulfilled his promise and banned performances, the shrine became quiet. It felt lonely. People feared the god was upset. The pushback was apparently strong enough that a later writer said Rinkai was divinely punished.

So, after weeks of prayer, Rinkai reported that the Kasuga deity actually wanted the mediums' music. Their drums resonated with the sound of true reality, he said, while the jingling of bells aroused the mind state of enlightenment. The mediums' performances were not distractions, in other words; they were expressions of Buddhist ideals.

This story was recorded after Rinkai's death. It could have been fabricated. Nevertheless, the historian Lori Meeks has uncovered reams of evidence showing that Japanese Buddhist clerics tolerated and even incorporated *miko*. They were hired by Buddhist monasteries to serve as curers, diviners, and necromancers. They were enlisted to entertain and dance for gods. For centuries, there was a blurry distinction between *miko* and Buddhist nuns. Even the circulation of Rinkai's story suggests that temples were committed to proving the compatibility of Buddhist doctrine with the *miko*'s performances. What better way to attract pilgrims and potential patrons, many shrine officials seemed to think, than to hire the shamans they normally consulted.[22]

––––––––––––

If doctrinal religions rallied against ecstatic religion for so long, why are pastor-shamans suddenly so popular? How does someone like Rodney Howard-Browne get invited to pray for the U.S. president? How did Kerney Thomas, not to mention other tongue-speaking healers like Nancy Harmon and Robert Tilton, get hours and hours of television airtime?

These questions gesture at a larger puzzle: the explosive success of charismatic and Pentecostal Christianity. Though distinct, both started in the United States in the twentieth century. Both value intense mystical experience, and both emphasize gifts like healing, prophecy, and glossolalia. Their growth in the last century is mind-blowing. As of 2020, their combined followers approached 650 million people, translating to roughly one in every twelve humans alive. Not only do they represent the most rapidly expanding segment of Christianity, but Pentecostalism stands out, according to theologian Allan Anderson, as "arguably the fastest growing religious movement in the contemporary world." Many charismatic and Pentecostal congregations feature shamanism, although it's worth pointing out that not all of them do. Indeed, it's common to see a shamanic inversion, with pastors staying levelheaded while their healing touch flings church members into celestial bliss.[23]

To understand the spread of these movements, it helps to look at times and places when they faltered. One of the best studied is Italy in the mid-twentieth century. If, around 1935, you questioned the minister of the interior, Guido Buffarini-Guidi, he would tell you that the country was without Pentecostals. And if, a couple years later, you traveled around Italy and asked people themselves, few would admit to following the new faith.[24]

But the silence masked a deeper commitment. Pentecostalism was carried to Italy in 1908 by Italian Americans. By 1929, nearly 150 centers had sprung up across the country. Most of the activity was in rustic and rugged areas, especially Sicily and the continental south, and it quickly attracted attention. Catholic leadership was already irritated by Protestant missionaries, and Pentecostals came to be considered the worst of the bunch. Like countless ecstatic cults before them, they were strange and unruly and threatened the church's traditional hold. In 1927, the chief of the police under Benito Mussolini, Arturo Bocchini, asked the Italian Embassy in Washington, D.C., about a link between Pentecostalism and communism. He was told that no such link had been established but warned that the cult had an obsessive, neurotic nature.[25]

The church and fascist state collaborated to snuff out Pentecostalism. In 1934, a Catholic high-up, Carlo Costantini, wrote a report on what another clergyman called "the Antichrists of our day." It burst with alarmist misinformation. Claiming to have infiltrated meetings, Costantini wrote that Pentecostals planned "to strip from the heart of Italians the glorious Faith of their fathers, to sow discord in families, and to compromise seriously the physical health that comes to those attracted to their pathological propaganda." He declared that the movement was founded by a homosexual, that at least one Pentecostal pastor was caught sodomizing a young Catholic man, and that the cult celebrated "free love, immorality, spiritism, hypnotism, false healings, and madness." In a later report, he accused Pentecostals of such unholy acts as murder, pacifism, desertion, Bolshevism, antifascism, hatred of the pope, and being ugly. Antichrists, indeed![26]

Smear campaigns like this were nothing new. Montanists were accused of using the blood of one-year-olds to make bread. The Cathars were said to be incestuous, devil-worshiping, infant-killing cannibals. The Quakers were deemed blasphemous anti-Christians "more dangerous than Atheism," while the Shakers were portrayed as traitors undermining the American cause during the Revolutionary War. The charges leveled at Italian Pentecostals were just the newest in a long line of attacks on spirit-trembling heretics. In a predictable replay of history, a centralized authority sought to demonize and destroy an ecstatic movement.[27]

On April 9, 1935, Mussolini's undersecretary criminalized Pentecostalism. "The cult" could no longer "be allowed in the Kingdom," he wrote, accusing it of being "contrary to social order and dangerous to the physical and psychic integrity of the race." The power of the fascist state was funneled into repressing Pentecostals, who continued practicing but in underground spaces and under generic names like "Protestants" and "evangelicals."[28]

The anti-Pentecostal decree lasted until 1955, eventually fracturing under the weight of a liberal world order. With the fall of Mussolini's fascist regime and the subsequent liberation from Nazi occupation, Italy established itself as a republic. In 1948, it ratified a constitution guaranteeing religious freedom. The conditions of Pentecostals improved compared to their time under Mussolini, due both to the new constitution and to the government's desire to maintain good relationships abroad, especially with the United States. In 1955, the anti-Pentecostal decree was finally repealed. Even in the capital of Catholicism, religious liberty prevailed, and Pentecostals were free to practice largely unmolested.[29]

This stretch of Italian history is a microcosm of a global shift. Since the eighteenth century, liberal democracy has spread worldwide. A core principle of the ideology is religious freedom. "Congress shall make no law respecting an establishment of religion, or prohibiting the free exercise thereof," reads the beginning of the First Amendment to the United States, alongside freedom of speech and before provisos on property rights and the rights of criminal defendants. The United Nations has reiterated the inalienability of freedom of religion in many documents, most notably in the Universal Declaration of Human Rights. A state that claims to respect the rights of its citizens while prohibiting some religious creed risks drawing international censure, as happened to Italy after 1948. As a result, religious officials, even ones as powerful as the pope, struggle to squeeze out rivals.[30]

Pentecostalism partly owes its success to this freedom. Not only do Pentecostal strongholds like Brazil, Ghana, Uganda, and the United States all protect religious expression, but a 2009 analysis by a senior researcher at the Pew Center, Brian Grim, showed that, across 143 countries, the level of religious freedom predicts the proportion of Pentecostals. You can see this clearly if you peruse the nearly thirty countries rated by the Pew Center as having "high" or "very high" government restrictions on religion; virtually none have substantial Pentecostal populations.[31]

In the *Encyclopédie*, that sanctuary of Enlightenment thought published between 1751 and 1772, the French writer and philosopher Denis Diderot referred to shamans as "impostors" who serve as "priests, jugglers, sorcerers, and medicine men." Adopting a stance popular among missionaries, he wrote that they "purport to have influence over the Devil, whom they consult to predict the future, to heal illnesses, and to do tricks that seem supernatural to an ignorant and superstitious people."[32]

The irony is that Enlightenment principles have set shamans free. By insisting on autonomy, tolerance, and a separation of church and state, Enlightenment thinkers have protected ecstatic religions from subjugation while creating open markets for religious services. And just as happens when shamans compete for clients, those markets have driven the evolution of practices that appeal to our instincts to gratify our needs. People in modern industrialized societies are like people everywhere. They want to be healed. They want to tame uncertainty. And they are pre-disposed to see supernatural contact as a potent way of achieving these goals. The rise of trance, spirit possession, and pastor-shamans is not a fluke in a shamanless end of history. It is a pre-dictable outcome of an unfettered race to provide spiritual relief.

CHAPTER 9

Meet the Shamanistas

Aaj guided me to the healing hut, which resembled a miniature domed amphitheater. Although large shade structures protected the entire camp from the brutal desert sun, the metal-frame hut was covered in its own camouflage-pattern shade cloth. A couple of pillows were strewn over ground tarp. Dust was everywhere.

I removed my boots, sat down, and got a better look at Aaj. He had marble-white skin and a beard the color of straw. I guessed that he was in his mid-twenties. His heavy-lidded eyes maintained their gaze, giving him the impression of being both detached and engaged. He wore two necklaces, one of red and white beads, the other of cowry shells, and a red sash, which he said the camp had provided. Like me, he was shirtless.

He asked why I had come to get a healing. Because I was curious, I said. That didn't satisfy him. He continued probing until I confessed that I was overly defensive sometimes, which I wanted to overcome. That pleased him, and he brought out a deck of cards. I saw "Mystical Shaman Oracle" written on the box. He fanned the cards out and asked me to take one while focusing on an intention. I pulled "The Drum," number 15, which showed a pale shaman preparing to hit an animal-hide drum. The shaman wore an eagle headdress and had feathers running down their arms. They stood in front of what looked like a solar eclipse, the rest of the sky concealed behind a hazy golden fog.

Aaj asked me what I saw. I listed features: the colors, the eagle, the shaman's face. He asked what the eagle was doing. It helps the shaman, I said. It provides the shaman with special abilities. Which abilities? Courage, I said. Wait, probably more like flight. And visual acuity.

He summarized my response and then asked me to lie down next to him. Our arms touched. He began to drum. I heard the drumming of nearby healing sessions, as well as a garbled jungle of electronic dance music in the far-off distance. A jaguar's face formed in the hazy darkness of my mind. It dissolved, and I felt like I was on the tip of an inverted cyclone, the drum's rhythm whirling me upward, away from the world.

He finished. We sat up, and he explained that he had entered an altered state. He called upon his power animal, a dragon, and journeyed with it to retrieve fragments of my soul. He saw me blindfolded and wearing shackles, and placed a flaming sword in my heart for me to use. He then switched to the language of psychotherapy. He speculated that I had been socialized, perhaps through parenting, to question myself and my opinions. He fused the shamanic discourse with the psychoanalytic. I had the sword now. I could destroy my reticence. I could become a leader.

Along with some seventy-five thousand other people, Aaj and I had come to a dry, lifeless wasteland in Nevada to build and enjoy a city. It was a loud, beautiful, effervescent city—a weeklong paroxysm of dust and heat, art and sex, radicalism and riches. It was called Black Rock City, and it was the home of Burning Man.

Burning Man is whatever people want it to be. The organizers provide a structure, including laying out the plan of the city, selling ice and coffee, distributing grants for art, and constructing an effigy, usually between sixty and one hundred feet tall, known as "the Man." Yet much of what makes Burning Man so surreal—a roller disco; a human car wash; bicycle repair stations; acro-yoga workshops; meditation parlors; a Friday night Shabbat dinner for a thousand people; modded-out animatronic cars, some the size of small houses; something called "the Orgy Dome"; something called "Barbie Death Camp"; grilled cheese sandwiches at three a.m.; ramen in a back alley; stationary and mobile music venues featuring schmancy-face DJs; saunas; gargantuan monoliths that invite you to climb on them; lonely sculptures in Tatooine-like expanses, all of it *free*—yes, all that exists because someone thought it would be fun and then decided to make it happen. Burning Man is an experimental playground where people try to bring joy and astonishment to one another. It is a kaleidoscope of human delight, a prism that reflects the tastes and tickles of the bohemian and well-off.

Most people attending Burning Man are members of camps. These are more than physical locations; they are self-organized, collaborative entities. Members of the same camp share public goods, like shade structures and communal kitchens, while working together to design, build, and maintain a "gift" for the wider community, which can range from passing out s'mores to running a fully equipped healing center.

When we met, Aaj was a healer at a camp called Shamandome, which describes itself as "an inclusive, collaborative, co-operative collective of diversely skilled and compassionate healers, shamans, shamanistas, spiritual practitioners, body workers and mediums honoring all spiritual traditions and coming together in a ceremony-centered community to learn, grow, heal and serve." Aside from one-on-one healings, the camp offers a medley of workshops, from Find Your Power Animal circles to the annual Death & Rebirth Ritual.

I wasn't surprised to find shamanism at Burning Man. In rich, industrialized societies like the United States, organized religion is waning. Between 2012 and 2023, the Pew Research Center reported that the share of Americans who considered themselves "religious and spiritual" slumped from 59 percent to 48 percent. Although some were replaced by nonbelievers, the decline was partly compensated for by a rise in people identifying as "spiritual but not religious." Waving the banners of reiki, yoga, mindfulness, higher powers, and crystal healing, the SBNRs, as they are called, hover at around a quarter of the U.S. population. Across the pond, a 2017 Pew survey found that more than a tenth of western Europeans similarly mixed a rejection of religion with an embrace of the spiritual. In fact, some of the least religious countries in western Europe, like Belgium, Sweden, and the Netherlands, have the highest proportions of SBNRs. "Religion is belief in someone else's experience," tweeted New Age superstar Deepak Chopra, summarizing the new zeitgeist. "Spirituality is having your own experience."[1]

The rise in creedless spirituality has been paralleled by an explosion of interest in shamanism. In the 2011 UK census, 650 people wrote that their religion was shamanism. A decade later, that number surged to 8,000, exceeding the number of self-identifying Rastafarians and Zoroastrians. These numbers vastly underestimate the craze. Many Westerners dabble in shamanism without identifying as such. In London, shamanic healers have become so popular that, during the COVID-19 pandemic, the *Evening Standard* published a "directory of the best shamans in town." The offerings ranged from the "purse-friendly" Aisha Amarfio, who predominantly treats people of color, to Shaman Durek, who worked as Gwyneth Paltrow's spiritual guide and is married to Princess Märtha Louise of Norway. Recent data on shamanic activity are hard to locate for the United States, but the 2007 National Health Interview Survey found that 186,000 Americans reported visiting a shaman in the previous twelve months; another 626,000 visited another kind of traditional healer. In 2013, a Pew survey concluded that one in seven Hispanic Americans—an estimated 7.7 million people—sought help from shamans, *curanderos,* or other mystically gifted healers.[2]

Many of these figures are known as "neo-shamans." The term covers a riot of specialists, from the collection of healers at Shamandome to the British bee shaman, Simon Buxton, to Viking-style mediums in northern Europe. They represent a medley of traditions and communities, drawing inspiration from inventive gurus, anthropological texts, other cultural traditions, and, most importantly, one another.[3]

Neo-shamans have been lightning rods for criticism. Some

are charged with cultural appropriation; others with falsely claiming Indigenous ancestry or peddling rituals like sweat lodges without any training. Some of the harshest rebukes are reserved for "plastic" or "Shake and Bake" shamans—mystical fraudsters who cash in on, and typically distort, traditions to which they have no connection. According to the Native American studies scholar Lisa Aldred, offensive incidents by plastic shamans have included "Sun Dances held on Astroturf, sweats held on cruise ships with wine and cheese served, and sex orgies advertised as part of 'traditional Cherokee ceremonies.' "[4]

As their name implies, neo-shamans presumably contrast with "traditional" shamans. While neo-shamanism is artificial and modern, the idea goes, traditional shamanism is ancient, enduring, and thus more authentic. Commentators, including neo-shamans themselves, like to point to all the ways in which neo-shamanism differs from its traditional counterparts. Neo-shamans elect themselves, while traditional shamans are chosen. Neo-shamans work for individuals, while traditional shamans serve communities. Neo-shamans try to embody the archetype of the wounded healer (the tendency is for many shamans to start out as patients), yet unlike traditional shamans, who are healed by spirits, neo-shamans heal themselves.[5]

These comparisons are often counterproductive. They affirm a separation between people in rich, industrialized nations, who are presented as dynamic and inventive, and the rest of humanity, which is portrayed as inheriting unchanging traditions. But of course, that is nowhere the case. Shamanic practices, regardless of where they are, change and adapt. I have seen this with Mentawai *sikerei*. Features of the institution might be old, yet a *sikerei* today would look shockingly strange to a Mentawai person from several generations ago. Many of the objects and symbols that have come to define *sikerei*, including bells, beaded necklaces, and dancing skirts, streamed in from trade with Malays and the Dutch and now from stores in Sumatra. In parts of southern Siberut, the *sikerei* present themselves as traditional while using new props, like wigs, to achieve that image. The most charismatic *sikerei* set up arrangements with tour guides, guaranteeing a stream of cash that can be used to build longhouses, get more tattoos, and enhance their prestige. Although *sikerei* embody a sense of tradition to build credibility among other Mentawai people, they are as modern as the high-speed ferries arriving in Siberut's southern port.

The *sikerei* similarly demonstrate just how inaccurate the stereotypes of "traditional" shamanism are. Most people become *sikerei* not because a community chooses them, but because they elect to pursue the path. *Sikerei* usually work for patients and their families, not for entire communities. It is true that some *sikerei* start out by recovering from a crippling illness. Yet the prevailing understanding is less that they or spirits heal them and more that the initiation does.

There's no question that neo-shamanism has its quirks—yet what about the industrialized world doesn't? The visual art, justice, and family structures of wealthy large-scale societies look nothing like they did in the past, but that doesn't make them any less legitimate. Is it meaningful to search for authenticity in neo-shamanic spaces?

Shamandome first appeared as an independent camp at Burning Man in 2007. Its roots go farther back, however, to an elevator at New York University in 2002. Anne-Katrin Spiess, one of Shamandome's founders, had just begun a master's program at the university. She was planning to combine art and anthropology, but a new dean changed the regulations.

"It was impossible for me to get into the anthropology courses," she told me. "I decided that this wasn't working for me." She got into the elevator to tell her advisor that she was leaving, when a stranger read her frazzled energy and asked her what was going on. After she explained her situation, he told her to stay.

"I was like, 'Yeah, but I can't get into the classes I want to get.' He's like, 'Don't worry. Come and talk to me in my office.'"

The man, Barnaby Ruhe, was a faculty member at Gallatin. He had graduated with a PhD from NYU more than a decade earlier and shared her passion for melding art with anthropology.

"It was clearly the universe putting us in this elevator together at the perfect time," she said.

Among their many shared passions was an enthusiasm for shamanism. Spiess traces her interest to a deep connection to nature, which she developed growing up in the wild mountains of Switzerland with a landscape-designer father. In her early twenties, she bought an Airstream trailer and traveled to empty parts of North America, making art and living alone for weeks at a time. It was on those trips, she said, that "I started getting a very strong sense that there are other beings around me. But I didn't know how to tap into that or how to connect or communicate with them."

That is, until one day she saw a flyer advertising a power animal workshop put on by Michael Harner's Foundation for Shamanic Studies. "That just opened up a whole new world," she said.

"I was extremely self-conscious about the fact that I have blond hair and white skin," she remembered. "I thought, 'I'm not even allowed to get connected with tribal culture, with Indigenous culture, because it's so removed.'" Yet she came away from that first event with a very different attitude. "We all have a shamanic background. All of our ancestors were worshiping the sun and the moon and the river and the trees. And we find during that first workshop that we can reconnect with it so easily."

From then on, shamanism became a part of her life. She took more courses with the foundation. She went on trips to the Amazon to learn from Indigenous shamans. She studied with Sandra Ingerman, a well-known neo-shamanic teacher. By the time she met Ruhe, she had spent three years in the world of shamanism.

Spiess and Ruhe started an academic, then a romantic, relationship. Spiess had an adventurous streak, Ruhe told me. She proposed they learn tango, that they travel to India and Nepal, and that they take Michael Harner's two-week course—all of which he agreed to. And then she suggested they go to Burning Man. In 2004, they went for the first time, staying with a camp called Aromatherapy. They liked it, but it didn't take them long to wonder, as Ruhe put it, "Well, why don't we form our own damn camp?"

The brand of shamanism that Spiess and Ruhe brought to Burning Man was called "Core Shamanism." It had been developed and disseminated by the anthropologist Michael Harner, first in his book *The Way of the Shaman* (1980) and then through workshops like the ones Spiess and Ruhe attended.

Harner is one of the most prominent figures in neo-shamanism. According to the *Encyclopedia of Religion and Nature* (2005), it is Harner's influence that "has led to a standardization of shamanic practices in the modern world." His interest began around 1961, and as with so many other neo-shamanic bigwigs, it started with anthropology. He was a PhD student at the University of California, Berkeley, and was deep into fieldwork with the Konibo people in the Peruvian Amazon. His research was coming along, but he had trouble getting people to talk about supernatural beliefs. "Finally," he later wrote, "they told me that if I really wished to learn, I must take the shamans' sacred drink made from *ayahuasca*, the 'soul vine.' "[6]

He didn't know what to expect. People said the drink induced frightening visions; they even called it "the little death." But the Konibo shamans he knew used it every night, so he assumed it was "not that big a deal."[7]

At twilight one night, with a small crowd watching, Harner's friend Tomás handed him a bowlful of the beverage. Harner drank it and lay down on a bamboo platform in the communal house. The chirps of insects and calls of howler monkeys filled the heavy silence. And then lines appeared. They grew clearer and erupted into a carnival of colors. He heard the sound of rushing water. His face became numb.[8]

Over the coming hours, he was hurled into a wondrous world. He visited a fun house of demons presided over by an enormous crocodile head. An atheist at the time, he saw people with the heads of blue jays and was convinced they were going to take his soul away in a vast ship with hundreds of oars. He encountered "the most beautiful singing I have ever heard in my life" and expected to die. And then he met reptilian ancestors— giant hulking dragons who showed him that they had arrived on

Earth eons ago, fleeing their enemies, and had created life on our planet, churning its evolution and dwelling within everything, including humans, whom they considered their servants.

Harner thought he recognized something evil in the reptilians and asked aloud for medicine. His Konibo companions poured an antidote down his throat, which relaxed him but didn't stop his vivid and fabulous journeys.

"I was completely in awe of the fact that a whole other reality had opened up," he later told an interviewer. "This was a reality that could not be fantasy." He came to believe that he had encountered divine beings that are mentioned in countless religious traditions. He spoke to American missionaries, who compared the dragon-like creatures to the Devil and his kin. A blind Konibo shaman told him that they were the Masters of Outer Darkness. The shaman also told Harner that he was impressed with his ayahuasca visions and that Harner could become a "master shaman." Harner took the comment seriously. In 1964, he went to the Ecuadorian jungle to stay with Shuar communities, with whom he had already spent time in the 1950s, and trained to become a shaman, ingesting datura, a powerful deliriant. He also took more ayahuasca.[9]

Harner's experiences convinced him that hallucinogens were key to shamanism. He studied medicinal plants used by Australian aboriginal healers, expecting to discover psychotropic effects. He assumed he'd find similar substances among the Inuit. But the searches failed.[10]

"I came to many dead ends," he later admitted. By the 1970s, his views had shifted. He appreciated that shamans around the world were seasoned psychonauts, equipped with a medley of tools for inducing non-ordinary states. In his introduction to the 1973 volume *Hallucinogens and Shamanism*, he conceded that "psychedelic agents" are just "one of the ways of achieving the trance-like states conducive to a sense of seeing and contacting the supernatural. In many cultures other methods are used: fasting (water and food); flagellation and self-torture; sensory deprivation; breathing exercises and yogic meditation; and ritual dancing and drumming."[11]

Harner's writings in the 1960s and early 1970s express a

nuanced understanding of shamanism. He was engrossed by its local richness and warned against studying the practice with too many preconceptions. He also avoided the impulse to view shamanism through a moralistic or rosy lens, recognizing instead that many shamans dwell in a moral gray zone. In a 1968 article for *Natural History* magazine, he stressed the blurry line between curer and sorcerer. Shuar shamans were often suspected of causing illness, he wrote; some were even blamed for ailments they were summoned to treat. On top of that, shamans were spiritual competitors. They drank ayahuasca, claimed to create magical rainbows that led them to their rivals, and then fired magical darts along the rainbows. Stunned by the attacks, the rivals left their own darts unattended, allowing the attacking shamans to siphon them up over the rainbow.[12]

By the time Harner published *The Way of the Shaman* in 1980, however, he had expunged much of the nuance. Shamanism became a homogenized tradition—a bite-size bundle amenable to Western consumption. Shamans, he stated, went on soul journeys, usually to Upper or Lower Worlds. They had "power animals" or "guardian spirits." They entered what he called the "shamanic state of consciousness," usually through drumming. (He recommended a monotonous rhythm of 205 to 220 beats per minute.)[13]

He also whitewashed shamanism. He turned shamans into paradigms of tolerant Western liberalism, asserting that "the shaman is an empiricist" yet "does not challenge the validity of anybody else's experiences" and "never says that what you experienced is a fantasy."[14] He also neutered and defanged shamanic practices, stripping them of terror and violence. Here's how he described the shamanic state of consciousness, for example:

> The shaman typically experiences an ineffable joy in what he sees, an awe of the beautiful and mysterious worlds that open before him. His experiences are like dreams, but waking ones that feel real and in which he can control his actions and direct his adventures. While in the SSC, he is often amazed by the reality of that which is presented.[15]

That might accurately describe some trance states. Yet just as many are scary, horrific, or violent. Especially common are battles between shamans and evil forces suspected of spreading illness. A Huottüja shaman in Venezuela, José-Luis, described his face-off with a sorcerer named Najaré and his spiritual minions (*märi*), which took place after José-Luis snorted yopo:

> I saw a hole open up in the ground in front of me. [Najaré] wanted to kill me. I flew to the mountains where there were five other shamans [including me]. I saw Najaré there. He shot a crystal at me but it missed. I have never fought this sorcerer before, but I know of him. He wanted to kill me, but I was too powerful for him. There were two thousand *märi*, one of which was sent to kill me. I killed it instead, and Najaré left.[16]

In fact, Harner himself had a disturbing experience ingesting datura during his initiation with the Shuar. As he described:

> Suddenly, about two hundred feet away amidst the tree trunks, I could see a luminous form floating slowly towards me. I watched, terrified, as it grew larger and larger, resolving itself into a twisting form. The gigantic, writhing reptilian form floated directly towards me . . . I turned to run . . . It separated into two overlapping creatures. They were now both facing me. The dragons had come to take me away! They coalesced back into one. I saw before me a stick about a foot long. I grabbed it, and desperately charged the monster with my stick outstretched before me. An ear-splitting scream filled the air, and abruptly the forest was empty. The monster was gone. There was only silence and serenity.
> I lost consciousness.[17]

Hard to call that "ineffable joy."

Harner turned his shamanic paradigm into a movement. In 1979, he cofounded the Center for Shamanic Studies, later renamed the Foundation for Shamanic Studies. In 1987, he resigned from a professorship at the New School in New York City to devote himself full-time to shamanism.[18]

Harner's foundation had three stated aims: to study shamanism, to preserve it, and to disseminate it. He seemed to pursue the last goal most intensively. According to the foundation's website in 2001, "more than 5,000 people each year" took its "rigorous training in core shamanism," with opportunities on every inhabited continent except Africa. Even after Harner's death in 2018, the foundation has continued to flourish. When I checked the foundation's website in August 2023, there were nearly fifty in-person workshops slated for the next three and a half months, taking place everywhere from Winnipeg to Santa Cruz to Buenos Aires and ranging in length from two days to two weeks.[19]

In *Shamans/Neo-Shamans* (2003), the archaeologist Robert Wallis wrote that Harner's Core Shamanism techniques were "probably the most widely known and practised in the West." Yet today, more than two decades later, Harner's influence seems to have declined. The workshops are still going strong, yet a smaller proportion of people seem to identify as practitioners of Core Shamanism. In its place has sprouted a myriad of new traditions, some of which are shared across communities, others of which are idiosyncratic blends customized to fit individuals' personal needs. Aaj, for example, said that he was formally trained in a paradigm called "Hypno-Journey" but that he also incorporates Ifá, a West African religion that has spread to Brazil and the Caribbean.[20]

Yet this apparent decline obscures a deeper trend. As Wallis told me in 2023, Harner's influence is "much more implicit now." The tenets of Core Shamanism—working with helper spirits, using drumming to induce altered states, going on soul journeys—have seeped into the marrow of neo-shamanism. Core Shamanism is like an old song that becomes so ingrained that, even while newer tracks overtake it on the *Billboard* charts, its essence is still discernible. A neo-shaman may see their healing as a blend of Inuit and Amazonian practices with a Siberian flair, yet, more often than not, their most important ancestor is Harner.

Or is it? Harner's goal, he once said, was "to find the basic principles that are common to most shamanic practitioners in most societies, and teach those basic principles without all these elaborations and specialisations that make them a product of each cultural context." This is why he called it "core" shamanism; he felt he was reducing the world's wisdom to its central tenets.[21]

Harner's approach is open to criticisms that it ignores local variation or that it appropriates knowledge without compensating communities. Yet even these miss an important point. Harner did not carve out the strumming heart of shamanism. Rather, he relied on Mircea Eliade.

"Through Harner," Wallis told me, "Eliade is the main thinking that people recognize when they talk about shamanism." Although Harner downplayed Eliade's emphasis on symbols like fire and the world tree, the version of shamanism that he advertised was overwhelmingly rooted in the scheme Eliade pushed in the 1950s and 1960s. Unfortunately for Harner, we know now that Eliade was mistaken, that even the basic premise that shamans go on soul journeys doesn't capture the trance healing of the Tungusic-speaking peoples from whom the word "shaman" derives, let alone the practices of Siberians or humanity more broadly.[22]

One of the strangest things about Harner's shamanic archetype is that it looks so little like the practices he himself reported among the Shuar. His book *The Jívaro: People of the Sacred Waterfalls* (1973) included some fifty paragraphs about Shuar shamanism, yet nowhere did he mention soul journeying, drumming, or a cosmology divided into three realms.[23]

Instead, he described spiritual combat centered mostly on *tsentsak*, or magical darts that doubled as spiritual helpers. People fell ill when shamans fired darts into them; they were cured when other shamans used their helpers to remove the harmful darts. *Tsentsak* were visible only while under the influence of ayahuasca; initiates received them by swallowing a substance vomited by a practicing shaman and then refraining from sex for several months. Harner described shamanic racketeering, where teams of curers and bewitchers would supposedly make people sick to charge them for healing services. He wrote of legendary shamans in neighboring groups said to become possessed by souls of dead people and to act as mediums while also sending demons into others, controlling their behavior. Reading *The Jívaro*, it is hard to fathom that the same author would, seven years later, push an image of shamanism that was not just more wholesome but nearly unrecognizable.[24]

Core Shamanism is thus less an example of appropriated wisdom and more a reflection of its unique cultural environment. Sure, there is genuine cross-cultural inspiration there, but that was warped and mangled—first through the biases of a Romanian historian, then through the marketing acumen of an enchanted American anthropologist.

None of this makes Core Shamanism any less legitimate, at least as a form of shamanism. Core Shamanists and their off-shoots may not tap into ancient or universal forms of shamanism, as they allege. But many shamanic traditions are similarly anchored in myths that give them legitimacy. Pentecostal pastors claim to channel the power of the One God, just as Jesus and his followers did thousands of years ago. Mentawai *sikerei* say they use techniques established by a culture hero, Pagetasabbau, who some say was also the ancestor of all living humans. The Yakut of Siberia said that shamans learned their skills from demons that descend from vermin that spilled out of the body of the first shaman when the sky god tried to destroy him for insolence. The assertion by Core Shamanists that they practice ancient, powerful techniques is, if anything, fittingly shamanic.[25]

Spiess and Ruhe brought shamanism to Burning Man in 2005. They practiced alongside bodyworkers, massage therapists, and other alternative healers at a camp called HeeBeeGeeBee Healers. The drumming was disruptive, however, so in 2007, they split off and formed their own camp.[26]

Ruhe told me about Shamandome's first day as an independent camp. It was a Tuesday. He had ten healers ready for the first batch of clients. "And I'm getting my coffee and walking over to the dome. It's ten in the morning. We're just starting work on the first day of our job at Burning Man. And there's this huge commotion, this dust in the street. It's like piling up in front of our welcome tent. There's like this wild dust rising up, and I look, and there's two hundred people dancing and shouting and happy and running into Shamandome. Two hundred. I got ten healers, and there's two hundred people ready for this release, for this next day of the rest of their lives, for this freedom, for this finally getting this yoke off their back, finally releasing their growth, finally being free from whatever guilt they have, and they're like ready to go, and they think, 'Shamandome! They're gonna do the job! They're gonna fix us!' And they're running in, and there's two hundred of them. And I'm looking at it, going, 'We're fucked.' "

He compared the camp to a field hospital. "We're at the war zone, which is Burning Man, and people come in." He estimated it would take two hours just to sage everyone, referring to the ritualistic burning of herbs for purification. Then, because all the healings were one-on-one, most people would have to wait several more hours until their turns. "I thought, 'This is horrifying. The math is terrible.' "

So he scrapped the original plan. Instead, he decided to teach everyone the basic techniques of Core Shamanism and have them treat one another. Each healer went to a separate location with ten to twenty patients. They drummed for them and led them in their encounters with their power animals or spirit guides. Afterward, the attendees paired up and gazed into each other's eyes for two minutes.

"You guys are the wounded healer," Ruhe remembered telling the attendees. "You're going to work on each other, and we're just going to guide you through this thing."

Ruhe remembers that moment as a paradigm shift. Within half an hour, he and the other healers had given the attendees everything they needed to cure themselves and one another. Rather than dividing curers from patients, everyone was capable of treating everyone else. "We don't even do any work," he said. "We just become this middleman."

Since that first year, Shamandome has refined this process. These days, the camp hosts a variety of two-hour sessions during which visitors can learn and practice different Core Shamanism techniques. It still has specialists, though. There is still a sense, both within Shamandome and from the outside, that someone like Aaj or Spiess or Ruhe can heal you more effectively than a newbie with zero credentials. "Yes, we want to encourage people to do the work," said Spiess. But, she went on, "I also don't appreciate when people have gone to the Amazon once and done an ayahuasca journey, and then, all of a sudden, they declare themselves a shaman."

I first visited Shamandome for a Find Your Power Animal workshop in 2015. It was my first time at Burning Man. I had just returned from my second summer in Siberut and was curious what exactly neo-shamanism looked like. So, with a couple dozen dusty Burners, I lay down in a circle in a large, airy dome. At our center was a small table covered in wispy colored shawls and assorted mystical curios, including several wads of half-burnt sage.

The instructions were simple. Once the drumming began, we were to close our eyes and visualize an opening into the Lower World. It could be anything: a cave, a pond, an animal's burrow, an interdimensional warp tunnel. We should follow it until we ended up at a landscape. There we should ask for our power animal. (You can try this for yourself by searching "shamanic journey solo drumming" on YouTube or a similar platform, lying down with your eyes closed, and then following the same instructions.)

I was surprised by how well it worked. The world I entered seemed more imaginative than something I would've devised during ordinary consciousness, yet I also saw myself directing the experience. I climbed through a ribbed tunnel and arrived on a rocky shore that reminded me of coastal British Columbia. The sky was wet and gloomy. Mountains loomed in the far-off distance. A seagull landed in front of me wearing a cartoonishly lost expression.

As per our instructions, I asked, "Are you my power animal?"

It squawked. Tens and then hundreds of similar-looking clueless seagulls congregated around me. "Are any of you my power animal?" I asked. I got no answer aside from more incessant squawking. Yet I also felt like I was inviting the squawking. I wanted squawking.

I squeezed through the seagulls and continued along the shoreline until I ended in a sun-dappled glade. It felt like a place where nymphs and fairies congregate. A chubby pink unicorn stood in front of me. It had an overbite and heavy, tired eyelids and looked to be in the style of the animated TV show *Adventure Time*. It was familiar; I had doodled something similar several years before. But it wasn't my power animal, either.

I kept walking and got to a section of shoreline that was quieter and more peaceful. The mountains were no longer visible. The beach had patches of green and wheat-colored sand. I came across a large cob house built into the earth, not unlike a hobbit home. I started to open the door, although I already knew what I would find.

An enormous walrus filled the house, sprawling luxuriously over the furniture. It had a walrus mustache and wore a top hat, a monocle, and a fancy suit.

"Hello, there!" it yelped, tipping its hat.

"You're my power animal?" I asked.

"Why, of course!" replied Walrus.

I enjoyed journeying, but it was hard for me to see it as anything other than guided daydreaming. On several occasions, I asked Walrus to show or teach me something, and at most, he urged me to reflect on concepts or values like compassion or sincerity, but never in a way that made his presence feel supernatural. Nevertheless, I found it intriguing—a time for dramatized, vivid self-reflection—and, in 2016, started attending the Cambridge Shamanic Circle near Harvard's campus. Unfortunately, I had to stop to prepare for my extended stay in Siberut. By the time I returned to Shamandome, in 2022, it had been some six years since I had been in a neo-shamanic space.

I witnessed different elements of neo-shamanism that week in 2022. It began with my one-on-one session with Aaj, after which I participated in another circle to find my power animal (Walrus, again). Nina and I returned the next day, this time to participate in a shamanic extraction workshop. The man leading it, whom I will call Sunglasses Joe, explained that our spirit bodies can become contaminated. Others' negative emotions can inject themselves into us, or our traumas can leave fragments that cause physical and psychological pain. He said that our attachments—to money, people, status, whatever—can have spiritual manifestations, some of them toxic. He had us pair up and, as he drummed, told us to work with our power animals to extract intrusions from our partner's spirit bodies.

"Sometimes the temptation is to remove everything," cautioned Sunglasses Joe. But we should be judicious. "All attachments are not bad. Without attachments, we would go insane."

Like Aaj, Sunglasses Joe combined the enchanted and the psychodynamic. Psychological trauma can become embedded in us, he suggested. Our attachments can be spiritually noxious, leading to further pain. Early life experiences can force us into suffocating narratives, which can be observed in the spiritual plane. The mind, he assured us, is both a source of pain and something to be healed.

This focus on emotion and mental states makes neo-shamanism exceptional in a cross-cultural perspective. Few, if any, shamanic practices throughout history have emphasized the mind as much as Western neo-shamans. Trauma and harmful patterns of thinking have usurped the position often filled by witchcraft, taboo violations, and resentful spirits. More than seeing shamans as healers of physical ailments, Western patients tend to seek them out for psychological remedies. When I interviewed Mentawai people about why they had summoned *sikerei* for healing ceremonies, they reported symptoms like fever and sore body parts; not a single person mentioned an emotional or cognitive issue. In contrast, when the medical anthropologist Shelly Beth Braun interviewed patients of neo-shamans in Salt Lake City, she found that 82 percent cited psychological reasons, like depression or "feeling stuck."[27]

Of course, the fixation with thoughts and feelings isn't unique to neo-shamanism. Rather, this seems to be another reflection of a broader cultural obsession. Western literature discusses the mind more than non-Western folktales and mythologies. Contemporary pop lyrics talk more about feelings, emotions, and inner mental states than do the song lyrics of nonindustrialized societies. Meanwhile, the proliferation of psychotherapeutic approaches over the last century, from psychoanalysis to cognitive behavioral therapy, has paralleled a growing focus on mental health. Like healers everywhere, neo-shamans have adapted their methods to fit the problems and interpretive frameworks of their clients. For Western patients, this means the mind.

Neo-shamanism is shamanism. Yes, it encompasses a jungle of evolving traditions. And sure, it's weird compared to many other shamanic traditions, partly because it is practiced by individualist Westerners and partly because it originated in the academic study of shamanism. Yet it is still clearly shamanic. Practitioners enter altered states; they commune with other realities and deliver pragmatic services. Clients go to specialists for recovery and control. Like anything cultural, neo-shamanic practices express their intellectual environments and particular histories, but this in no way invalidates them. Debating over their authenticity is like debating whether a shirt inspired by the academic study of shirts is still a shirt. Obviously, it is—just a peculiar one.

CHAPTER 10

Hedge Wizards

In 2015, one of Rustam's cousins took me around Mentawai villages near the southern port town, Muara Siberut. It was a new world, culturally. The local dialect was distinct from the tongue spoken upriver and, to my untrained ears, tricky to parse. The tattoos and taboos were unique, too. I was looking for *sikerei* who had grown up near Muara Siberut, but they were surprisingly scarce. In the island's forested interior, I encountered *sikerei* everywhere; I would later count ninety across four villages. After spending days touring the villages near Muara Siberut, in contrast, I met fewer than five, all of them elderly.

The shortage of shamans around the port town wasn't due to a lack of demand. People invited *sikerei* from the interior to heal them, and at least one, Rustam's father, had moved near the port town from a jungle community upriver.

Instead, it came down to geography. The villages around Muara Siberut were less protected from outsiders. Christian missionaries had been stationed there since 1932. In 1954, the West Sumatran government prohibited Mentawai spiritual beliefs, known as Arat Sabulungan, and gave locals three months to choose between Islam and Protestantism. For the next three decades, the government enacted vicious acculturation policies. People were moved to settlement villages. Anything tied to traditional Mentawai culture was forbidden. Ritual objects were burned, and even long hair was prohibited.[1]

"These new things are not of our world," a nominally Christian man told a documentarian in the early 1970s after an official discovered he and two others trying to initiate a new *sikerei.* "If we had the choice and were not afraid, most people in Mentawai follow old ways."[2]

The coercive policies lasted until 1987. Even before then, however, communities in the interior enjoyed greater freedom. The government struggled to keep officials in the malarial forests, and families like Rustam's could always escape to increasingly remote locales. "The only people coming to us then were police officers who burned our things and beat up people that wore loincloths," recalled a Mentawai man in 1996. So "as soon as we heard a speedboat coming on the river, we ran into the jungle."[3]

Intolerance silenced the *sikerei.* But in many parts of the world, shamanism is declining for another reason—what the German sociologist Max Weber called "the disenchantment of the world." This is the idea, closely linked to the Enlightenment and Scientific Revolution, that the supernatural and mystical have been purged from reality, replaced with a hard materialism. Eclipses are no longer divine disruptions but predictable oddities. Comets are not portents of doom but space chunks of rock, ice, and dust. Storms, earthquakes, and even dreams reflect the clockwork mechanics of our universe, not the whims of animated forces. Deities are dissolving into data.[4]

"One need no longer have recourse to magical means in order to master or implore the spirits, as did the savage, for whom such mysterious powers existed," Weber told an audience at the University of Munich in 1917. "Technical means and calculations perform the service."[5]

Some scholars argue that Weber spoke too soon. Enchantment still rules. Even in a country like the Czech Republic, one of the least religious in the world, most people believe in fortune tellers, according to a 2006 survey. A Pew survey conducted in the United States in 2023 found that almost 40 percent of U.S. adults feel that a spirit of the dead has communicated with them.[6]

Even accepting Weber's premise, though, the fixation on

logic and rationality is misleading. Many people, including many readers of this book, may not rely on literal shamans. They may have abandoned beliefs in spirits and may distrust trance as a sign of divine contact. Yet elements of shamanism persist. Whether in New York or highland New Guinea, we are all equipped with the same basic psychology, all susceptible to assurances that gifted seers can navigate the uncertain. Beneath the veneer of enlightened empiricism is a world of wizardry and showmanship—of people who convince themselves and others of miraculous powers. Say what you will about disenchantment, magicians live on.

Few people have thought more about analogs of shamanism than J. P. Millsap. A shade under six feet tall, with rounded cheeks and a slight stubble, he's quick to smile and likes to talk about his children and human psychology. We met at a Starbucks near his house in Walnut Creek, an affluent suburb in the San Francisco Bay Area.

Growing up in Southern California, Millsap had little sense of what it would be like to be rich. When he was in his teens, his parents declared bankruptcy. Yet his father, who worked as a crane operator and radio DJ before landing a job in marketing, was determined that his kids go to college. He demanded that Millsap take the SAT, an exam required for many college applications. Millsap obeyed, did well, and ended up at Texas Christian University.

In college, he gravitated toward finance. "There's an allure," he said. "Some people can do this. Some people can't. And it's hard. It's really hard." He considered finance to be a pursuit that required skill, one where the rewards are hard-earned but potentially lucrative.

"I started investing in college, even helped run the endowment," he told me. After graduating, he got a job in an investment firm, leaving a few years later to pursue an MBA at the University of Chicago. He remembered a moment from business school. "There were three of us who were going to be money managers, all sitting in the quad area. And our friend walks up and he goes, 'Did you know that two out of three of you are going to underperform?'

"We laugh, because we know this," he said. "We know that, in the field, we will be random."

This randomness is one of the open secrets of money management. People are treated like experts. Some pay hefty sums to attend world-class business schools and go on to collect fat-cat salaries. Yet there's little evidence that they can do what they claim. In a given year, roughly half of financial managers do better than the market. The other half do worse. Not only do they fail to consistently beat the market—they don't even reliably beat one another.[7]

Investing with a money manager seems a lot like playing roulette, then. In 2012, in fact, the British news outlet *The Observer* pitted a team of professional money managers against a cat named Orlando. While professionals used industry know-how and their best stock-picking strategies to build their portfolios, Orlando's stocks were chosen by throwing a mouse toy on a grid of numbers that corresponded with different companies. The competitors each started off with £5,000. By the end of the competition, the professionals had grown their portfolio to £5,176. Orlando, meanwhile, had £5,542.[8]

Examples like these abound. In 2009, a Russian circus chimp built a portfolio by choosing cubes representing stocks and beat 94 percent of Russian mutual funds. According to Guinness World Records, another chimpanzee, Raven, became the twenty-second most successful money manager in the United States when, in 1999, she threw darts at a list of 133 internet companies, creating an index that delivered a 213 percent gain.[9]

Gimmicks aside—and there are many, involving, among other characters, a porn star, a camel, and *Wall Street Journal* reporters with their eyes covered—the inability of investors to outperform the market is well established. Burton Malkiel, a Princeton economist and former director at the investment management company Vanguard, has made a career demonstrating this point. "I suggested, largely in jest, that a blindfolded chimpanzee throwing darts at the stock pages could select a portfolio that would do as well as the experts," he wrote in a 2005 article that reviewed three decades of empirical studies. "In fact, the correct analogy is to throw a towel over the stock pages and simply buy an index fund, which buys and holds all the stocks making up a broad stock-market index."[10]

Surely, you might point out, there are exceptions. A firm might figure out a way to get a technical advantage—they may move their computers closer to exchanges to get a microsecond edge, for example. But advantages are self-defeating. The nature of competition means that others learn quickly, eroding any lead. And even if there are moments, or firms, or individuals, that can guarantee outperformance, the difficulty is in discriminating those exceptional needles from the haystack of random wins and losses.

What about someone like Warren Buffett? Nicknamed "the Oracle of Omaha," Buffett has amassed an incomprehensible amount of wealth—$121 billion, as of December 2023—through investing. Yet even Buffett doesn't trust other money managers. In 2006, he issued a million-dollar bet that an S&P 500 index fund, a fund that tracks the biggest companies on the U.S. stock market, could beat any professionally managed hedge fund over a ten-year period. It was an invitation for professionals to put their money where their promises were, but only one, a specialized asset manager, stepped up. Buffett won and donated the money to charity.[11]

Buffett's distrust is more than just a gambling trick. He has told his heirs that, following his death, nearly all his wealth should be invested not with money managers but in an S&P 500 index fund. As he warned shareholders in 2016, "There's been far, far, far more money made by people in Wall Street through salesmanship abilities than through investment abilities."[12]

———

Millsap knew about all this going in, but it didn't bother him. "I'm aware that other people don't outperform, but that's because they suck," he said, recalling his reasoning. "And see, I don't suck. I'm gonna work harder. I'm gonna do things better."

After graduating from business school, he was hired at an

investment firm in downtown San Francisco. He had a nice life. He and his wife went on to have four children. Although his starting salary was around $100,000, it grew until his annual compensation, including bonuses, was in the low millions.

But time also brought dissatisfaction. The work started to feel hollow, even exploitative. One of his coworkers studied the firm's data and confirmed that, despite different pay levels, no one systematically outperformed anyone else. Millsap remembered imagining the next thirty years. "At the end of my life, I'm going to say, 'Yeah, I rode the elevator. I talked with these people about what companies were doing. It made no difference whatsoever. I have a bunch of money. My life's over.'"

The realization was disturbing. Everything felt like it was "crashing down," he said. He was as good as Malkiel's blindfolded chimps. "It was devastating, because it's like, 'Holy shit—I knew this. I knew it. And I did it.'"

Millsap retired in 2018, at the age of thirty-eight. He began taking his daughter to kindergarten every day, after which he would drive to Starbucks and write. "It was just processing," he said, "like 'What the fuck was that?'" Within a couple of weeks, he wrote a "rant" that ran for tens of thousands of words. He spent a year massaging it into a book, which he self-published as *The Shamans of Wall Street* (2020). The introduction begins, "The goal of this book is to explain, convincingly, to the layperson that no investment manager or pundit can predict the future; therefore, these prognosticators should not be paid so much for their non-existent clairvoyance."[13]

Millsap isn't the first person to compare money managers to shamans. Robert Wright drew a similar parallel in *The Evolution of God*, as did the cognitive scientist Samuel Johnson in a commentary published in 2018. Millsap's treatment, however, is the only one I've found that comes from a former money manager.[14]

To be clear, money managers are not shamans, and it dilutes the term to insist that they are. For one, they don't enter trance. But as Millsap and the other writers demonstrate, they fill similar niches. People want control and sense an order underlying the chaos. Financial experts compete to capitalize on that desperation, developing elaborate performances to convince people of their unique abilities.

Money managers aren't the only such pseudo-experts. Sports analysts, political pundits, economic forecasters—society is filled with performers who dress in credible and compelling costumes to convince an anxious public that they can decode the future. When Sandeep, my good friend, told his brother Sanjeev about the similarity, Sanjeev jokingly called them "hedge wizards," a term that combines the mystical and mundane and captures the bet-hedging decision-making at the core of so much superstition. So that's what I'll call them: hedge wizards.

———————

Money managers might be the most successful hedge wizards around. Tasked with overseeing pension funds, university endowments, and countless other gargantuan pots of money, they skim fees off the top, amassing incredible sums in the process. Why do people trust them?

One factor is what Millsap calls "customs that feed the illusion of skill." The work of investors is less about making accurate predictions, he argues, and more about deluding themselves and their customers. Financial analysts spend their time flying to industry conferences, where they meet with executives. They later produce reports about these trips and name-drop CEOs to clients. Whether these conferences give money managers any insight into future trends has yet to be demonstrated. And even if the meetings did improve forecasting ability, selectively sharing information is illegal, so anything an executive tells one investor has likely been shared with many others, erasing possible advantages. "Is it any wonder Warren Buffett stays in Omaha and reads alone quietly?" asks Millsap.[15]

On top of this ritualized work, he suggests, is the confounding prestige of wealth. According to *Forbes*, finance has produced more billionaires than any other industry. Clients reasonably use this wealth as a cue to competence: "You made a lot; you must do your work well." But, Millsap says, the inference is fallacious.[16]

It turns out that even investors who underperform on average can make a shocking amount of money. It's simple math. If a big investment firm manages $100 billion of other people's money and charges an industry standard of 0.7 percent of those assets as its fees, it collects a revenue of $700 million. Assume 250 employees, of whom half are low-status workers like secretaries. Subtract expenses for rent, insurance, taxes, and low-status salaries, and that leaves $320 million for 125 employees. Add in some standard hierarchy, and the top ten employees are plausibly splitting $270 million. If the owner of a money management firm owns a sports team and has a building named after them at an Ivy League university, presumably they're doing something right—or so people mistakenly infer.[17]

Samuel Johnson, a professor at the University of Bath School of Management, believes that something more is at play: otherness. His argument is similar to the one developed in this book. Just as trance, initiations, and eel taboos all xenize shamans, so does the mythology about money managers. They exude extreme charisma. They are intensely greedy (as in Oliver Stone's *Wall Street*) and lustfully hedonic (as in Martin Scorsese's *The Wolf of Wall Street*). They endure punishing schedules, working upward of seventy and even one hundred hours a week. (A *Harvard Business Review* article once mentioned a twenty-three-year-old Indian-born New York financial analyst for whom a ninety-hour work week was "light" season.) They don't technically enter altered states, but their personalities and brutal routines amplify views of their exceptional minds and abilities.[18]

––––––––––

Money managers aren't the only professionals who subject themselves to deprivation and severity. The tycoon class suffers from what the sleep researcher David Dinges calls "sleep braggadocio." At six hours a night, Elon Musk looks like a slacker. Donald Trump, Martha Stewart, and former PepsiCo CEO Indra Nooyi have all claimed to sleep four hours per night. Luxury fashion designer Tom Ford says he gets just three.[19]

Paralleling the sleeplessness is a wave of extreme dieting. Steve Jobs, that god-pharaoh of innovation, went stretches eating only fruit. Twitter cofounder Jack Dorsey has said he eats a single meal each day. Tech execs from Phil Libin (former CEO of Evernote) to Daniel Gross (former partner at Y Combinator) prostrated themselves at the shrine of intermittent fasting. Zappos founder Tony Hsieh practiced a twenty-six-day "alphabet diet," eating only foods that started with a different letter each day.[20]

Then there's Elizabeth Holmes. In late 2014, journalist Ken Auletta profiled Holmes and her company Theranos for *The New Yorker.* This was before her epic downfall—before there was a book, documentary, and miniseries recounting how the Stanford dropout had duped some of the loftiest names in government and venture capital. There are hints of the dodgy tactics that would eventually topple her, yet the overwhelming impression is of her extraordinary nature. Auletta paints her as beyond human, more like a humanoid alien or the offspring of a human-ghost mating. She is "unnervingly serene." She speaks in a "near-whisper." She designed a time machine at the age of seven and read *Moby-Dick* at nine. She can quote Jane Austen by heart and completed three years of college Mandarin by the end of high school. She has, according to Henry Kissinger, "a sort of ethereal quality."[21]

Especially striking is her diet. Her fridge is practically empty, we are told. Instead she sips a spartan brew of kale, celery, spinach, parsley, cucumber, and romaine lettuce. For years, this was one of the most popular talking points about Holmes, attracting write-ups in *HuffPost, Women's Health*, and Refinery29, many of them questioning how anyone could stay healthy on such nutritionally impoverished fare.[22]

Holmes may have fallen, yet Silicon Valley asceticism seems to grow more austere. By 2020 intermittent fasting was no longer enough, and dopamine fasting—an abstention not just from food but from any form of stimulation, including video games, music, and even eye contact—had taken off. These self-denial fads are often touted as biohacking innovations. While that's plausible for some, like intermittent fasting, others like Holmes's supposed regime are almost certainly dangerous. Moreover, dieting is just one facet of a trend that has grown to include meditation, psychedelic drugs, silent retreats, infrared heat lamps, DIY surgeons, and every other ancient or posthuman widget that CEOs and founders subject themselves to on the path to becoming, as one *Vanity Fair* writer put it, "some sort of doctrinal beings: saints with iPhones."[23]

I like that wording. It's apt. It captures the almost paranormal status that some tech figures have attained. And it reminds us that the recent wave of asceticism is not some newfangled innovation. Rather, it is familiar: a timeless tradition fashioned into funny new clothes. CEOs, it seems, are xenizing themselves.

***

Few people are better equipped to explain the shamanification of CEOs than Rakesh Khurana, a sociologist at Harvard.

"There's a sort of cultural archetype against which leaders are both evaluating themselves and being evaluated," he told me in 2022. Khurana has spent years studying how archetypes of CEOs change, both by analyzing historical datasets and by interviewing industry insiders. His research helps clarify the current moment.

For decades, he has shown, the archetypal CEO was "the organization man" (they were overwhelmingly men). A typical example was Lew Platt of Hewlett-Packard, who, in the words of Wikipedia, "was not considered media-savvy due to his thick glasses and hulking frame." The organization man was a conformer. He was a loyal subordinate who worked his way up in the company. A career bureaucrat, he rarely appeared on TV and never thought to hire ghostwriters to concoct a mythology. Many people in his company didn't recognize him.[24]

Organization men started to disappear in the 1980s, replaced by a new, shinier breed of executive. This was the era of Apple's Steve Jobs, Microsoft's Bill Gates, and IBM's Lou Gerstner. Showmanship became key. In 1999, Hewlett-Packard forced Lew Platt to resign. When Khurana asked the search committee what they wanted, they described something more elusive than Platt's white-bread managerial skills: "tremendous leadership ability" and "the power to bring urgency to an organization."[25]

Why the shift from dependable gray suits to charisma? Khurana, in his book *Searching for a Corporate Savior* (2002), argued that ownership was a major factor. From the 1970s onward, institutional investors like mutual funds and insurance companies started buying up major chunks of companies. At the same time, trading stocks became the new American pastime.[26]

"CEOs could afford to be bland and colorless when they were less visible in society," he wrote. But with the public owning their firms and monitoring their leaders, blandness was less of an option. CEOs had to start appealing to the populace at large, not just to other organization bureaucrats.[27]

A crucial insight of Khurana's research is that charismatic CEOs are most popular during times of uncertainty, like organizational crises. "Boards of directors bent on finding a corporate messiah are not much interested in ordinary qualifications," he wrote. Instead, they look for candidates who have an aura of noteworthiness, something distinctive that might redirect the company's fortune. Just as people in need of miraculous cures have long been drawn to xenized specialists, shareholders and their representatives seek out special-sauce CEOs to save their investments from collapse.[28]

If shifts in ownership selected for charisma, recent developments have intensified the pressure. In the years after 2008, the tech industry experienced a revolution. Digital platforms allowed companies to reach global markets without any physical presence, while network effects enhanced the value of services as more users joined. These changes created opportunities for fast, astronomical growth. The market values of companies like Airbnb and Uber skyrocketed, introducing terms like "unicorn" (a start-up valued at over $1 billion) and "decacorn" (valued at over $10 billion) into everyday parlance.[29]

These new market dynamics have cranked up the uncertainty of the investment ecosystem. The number of new start-ups has surged. In any given period, most are expected to flop, but some will mature into fat, dripping cash cows. Investors can expect life-changing payoffs, although identifying the winners is far from easy.

"There's no revenue," Khurana explained. "There are no

profits. There's an idea, which I don't want to discount, but that leaves you very little to evaluate, other than what school did the person go to, who do they know, where did they work."

As with magical specialists everywhere, then, founders and executives fall back on performances of otherness to convince investors that they can achieve, and sustain, the near miraculous. When I spoke to CEOs, some were transparent about the payoffs of performance. "There's some rationality" to playing the "charismatic messiah," one told me, "because, as a CEO, your job is to see to all sorts of different people. First and foremost, you need to convince people to join the company and buy the mission. You also need to sell to customers. And you need to sell to investors."

I heard something similar from a founder-CEO in San Francisco. "To do the role well, you do have to build a bit of a persona," he said. "Investors are often attracted to founders that have some sort of unique charisma or personality—*special*, I think, is the word they would use."

Are CEOs putting on a show? People the world over intuit that self-denial and similar behaviors cultivate power. Being human, tech executives presumably draw the same inferences. At least part of their decision to engage in shamanic practices, then, might stem from a sincere pursuit to be exceptional and achieve the extraordinary.

At the same time, humans are skillful performers. We pay close attention to which selves are esteemed and then craft ourselves to conform.[30] Sam Bankman-Fried, the crypto exchange cofounder convicted of defrauding customers of billions of dollars, was a media favorite, in part because of his stereotype-busting appearance. He was a vegan, resented flashy consumption, and seemed unconcerned with acting professionally. He wore shorts everywhere and failed to correctly tie his shoes during testimony before the House Financial Services Committee. Reporters were especially enamored with the untamed bramble that had colonized his head. "He might now be a billionaire but Samuel Bankman-Fried still has that wild puff of hair," began a CoinDesk article in April 2022. "It's hair that screams 'just rolled out of bed.'"[31]

Much of this, it turns out, was deliberate. One of his former colleagues told *The New York Times* that he urged Bankman-Fried to clean himself up. "And he said, 'I honestly think it's negative EV [expected value] for me to cut my hair. I think it's important for people to think I look crazy." Caroline Ellison, the former CEO of Bankman-Fried's hedge fund, as well as his on-again, off-again girlfriend, admitted that the sloppiness was a put-on. "He said he thought his hair had been very valuable," she testified, adding that ever since he started working on Wall Street, "he had gotten higher bonuses because of his hair and that it was an important part of FTX's narrative and image."[32]

Not everyone is as consciously performative. More often than not, we are guided by selfish, automatic psychological processes and delude ourselves and others with noble justifications. "The idea that some people would do this for the social benefits is sickening," a former CEO told me, despite speaking about his deprivation regimen publicly and even featuring it on his LinkedIn page. If tech executives are anything like the rest of us, many of their identities are tweaked for acclaim and then rationalized afterward.

Our survey of shaman analogs seems to leave shamanism in a precarious place. Hedge wizards exploit psychological vulnerabilities. They promise extraordinary outcomes and use shamanic techniques to convince us of their powers, amassing grotesque sums and often harming others in the process. Millions of people lost money, in some cases their life savings, because of Bankman-Fried's antics, leading to a backlash against what one critic called his "schlubby mystique." It is easy to thus conclude that hedge wizards—and by implication, the shamans they resemble—deserve moral condemnation.[33]

The question of their morality is more complicated, however. To say that shamanism is morally reprehensible is to conflate its nature with its abuses, like reasoning that planes are bad because hijackers have flown them into buildings. The most extractive hedge wizards exist alongside economic and political institutions that allow them to accrue unimaginable assets and deploy them in service of personal enrichment. Shamans, being human, have done the same when they could get away with it, although never on the scale of modern financial managers. Moreover, it's critical to appreciate that most shamans, like many hedge wizards, see their work as useful. Both evolve as generations of specialists discover services that best appeal to clients. They engage in some deception, sure, but also inhabit the reality they help conjure up. Just as sick shamans go to other shamans, many hedge wizards stay in on weekends to draft up reports that they believe will make them better diviners.

Another reason for moral complexity is that the interaction between specialist and client is not one way. Magical specialists do not force themselves onto us; they exist because we want them to exist. We should recognize their harms and ensure that they are minimized. But we should also appreciate that we are partly their architects—that, in our efforts to manage a chaotic world, we create the magicians who dazzle us.

A final factor to consider when weighing the morality of shamanism, particularly in contrast to hedge wizardry, is that people value their shamanic traditions. We covered the therapeutic benefits of healing rituals, but the defense of shamanism goes beyond efficacy. Shamanic traditions are spiritual traditions. They are sources of mystical insight, communal affirmation, and otherworldly experience. They are sites where myth, belief, ritual, and cultural heritage intersect, and they serve as loci of identity, especially for communities experiencing cultural onslaughts.

"Our ancestors couldn't make iron, and we don't know either," a Mentawai man told documentarians. "Making cloth? We don't know. In this, we are ignorant. Making machetes? We don't know. Making all these machines? We don't know. But our ancestors' ways—the ceremonies, *sikerei*, medicine—these things we know."[34]

CHAPTER 11

Archaic Revival

Beginning in 2001, the Austrian anthropologist Bernd Brabec de Mori spent six years living in the western Amazon. He first arrived as a backpacker, returned to do a master's thesis on ayahuasca songs, and eventually did a PhD on the music of eight Indigenous peoples in the region. Along the way, he married a woman of the local Shipibo tribe and settled down.

"I did not have a lot of money," he told me, "so I had to make my living there." He became a teacher. He built a house. He and his wife had children. That rare experience of joining the community, he said, forced him to realize that many of the assumptions he had picked up as an anthropologist were wrong.

Like most outsiders, Brabec de Mori arrived in Peru thinking that ayahuasca had been used in the western Amazon for thousands of years. This is the standard narrative; look up resources on ayahuasca, and you're bound to run into it. The website of the Ayahuasca Foundation, an organization founded by a U.S. citizen that offers ayahuasca retreats, states, "Ayahuasca has been used in the Peruvian Amazon for millennia, long before the Spanish came to Peru, before the Incan Empire was formed, before history."[1]

Yet with time, Brabec de Mori came to see just how flimsy this narrative was. He discovered "a double discourse, which happens in all societies where there is tourism," he said. "People start to tell the tourists—and I found that most Shipibo people did not distinguish tourists from researchers—the stories they think are interesting for them and not what they really live with."

His research showed just how large the discrepancy was. He discovered that, in their traditional stories about ayahuasca's origins, many Shipibo-Konibo people said the brew came from the Kukama, one of the first peoples to be missionized and resettled during the Spanish conquest. Other peoples from the region remembered adopting it in the last fifty years. When he examined old reports of travelers, Brabec de Mori found that he could connect the historic diffusion of ayahuasca to the movements of missionaries and the spread of the rubber industry through the western Amazon.[2]

Then there was the linguistic evidence. Peoples in the Peruvian Amazon speak a dazzling diversity of languages, but their words for ayahuasca and related activities are almost identical. The same goes for their music: lullabies, love songs, and festive songs are astonishingly varied, yet ayahuasca songs are very similar and often sung in non-Amazonian languages, like Quechua or Spanish. These patterns led him to conclude that ayahuasca hasn't been in the western Amazon for millennia. Rather, it seems to have arrived and spread much more recently.[3]

Based on this and other evidence, Brabec de Mori argues that ayahuasca diffused through the Peruvian Amazon in the last three hundred years. It may be older in the highlands and in regions farther north and to the east, yet it seems a relative novelty in the place most frequented by tourists. He isn't the first to make the argument—the anthropologist Peter Gow proposed something similar in 1994—but he, more than anyone else, has found the anthropological data to support it.[4]

Brabec de Mori's findings represent one of many cracks in the stories we tell about the history of psychedelics. As these substances skyrocket into the mainstream, so do narratives about their role in human societies, narratives that often bind them to shamanism. Just look at the media coverage. In 2020, a journalist for *The Washington Post* wrote that consciousness-altering substances "have been used by Indigenous cultures for physical and psychological healing for thousands of years." A year earlier, a writer for *Vox* asserted, "Cultures around the world . . . have been taking psychedelics for thousands of years, and each one developed rituals for them, led by experienced guides." Michael Pollan endorsed a similar narrative throughout his *New York Times* bestseller *How to Change Your Mind* (2018), like when he wrote that shamanism has "a role to play in psychedelic therapy—as indeed it has probably done for several thousand years."[5]

These quotes all subscribe to what I'll call the global archaic psychedelic shamanism (GAPS) hypothesis. It consists of three claims:

1. Psychedelics were widespread.
2. Psychedelics were ancient.
3. Psychedelics were used by shamans for therapeutic healing.

Like so many of the stories we tell about human history, GAPS is rooted in glimmers of truth, although these get wildly misrepresented. In fact, much of what passes as psychedelic history has been distorted by a seductive mixture of flimsy archaeological evidence, outdated anthropological approaches, and economically expedient ideology. Throughout this book, we have witnessed evidence of shamanism's timeless recurrence, yet we should also be wary of market-friendly perversions.

"It's a romantic image that Indigenous people have been using everything they do for thousands of years," Brabec de Mori said. "If we change the picture, it's kind of unromantic, and it seems that people like romanticism."

In June 1955, the vice president of public relations at J.P. Morgan arrived in a remote village in the Mexican highlands. He was accompanied by Allan Richardson, a photographer and teacher at an elite girls' school in Manhattan. They had come to eat fungus.

The banker, Robert Gordon Wasson, was a mycophile. For decades, he and his wife Valentina Pavlovna had studied humanity's relationship with mushrooms; Mexico would be the most promising place to explore it. Four centuries earlier, Spanish chroniclers had recorded how the Aztecs consumed a powerful psychoactive substance called *teonanacatl*, or "flesh of the gods." Some writers described it as a mushroom; one even noted where you could find it and how to visually distinguish it. Yet botanists and anthropologists bickered over its identity until the 1920s and 1930s, when they discovered that communities in the Oaxacan mountains swallowed psychotropic mushrooms in nighttime ceremonies.[6]

Wasson learned about the ceremonies in 1952. The next year, he and Valentina traveled to the town of Huautla de Jiménez, where they observed, but did not participate in, a mushroom ritual. He returned to Mexico again in 1954 and collected ethnographic data. In 1955, he traveled down a third time, this time with his photographer friend, and was lucky enough to meet a Mazatec *curandera* named María Sabina. Valentina and their daughter joined a day or two later.[7]

María Sabina "had presence," Wasson later wrote. He and Valentina considered her "a woman of rare moral and spiritual power, dedicated in her vocation, an artist in the mastery of the techniques of her office." He met her through a local town official under the pretense of determining the health of his son Peter. It was the ideal introduction. Not only had she spent her life exploring the psychic worlds accessed through mushrooms, but she was willing to let the foreigners try them, too.[8]

Wasson wrote up his experience for *Life* magazine in an article headlined "Seeking the Magic Mushroom." Over two nights, he ate mushrooms under María Sabina's guidance. When Valentina and their eighteen-year-old daughter joined them a couple days later, he gave them batches to enjoy as well. Published in the May 13, 1957, issue, the article popularized the term "magic mushrooms" and introduced millions of Westerners to the fungi's mind-melding effects. Six days later, Valentina told her story in *The Week*, a magazine included in thirty-seven newspapers and circulated to some 14 million readers.[9]

The impacts of the accounts were immediate and far-reaching. They sparked a surge of interest in Indigenous practices and the spiritual and therapeutic applications of hallucinogens. For many readers, the tales of otherworldly visions—of camel caravans, resplendent palaces, a mythological beast in a chariot, and the eighteenth-century court of Louis XV, to name a few—promised gateways to new realms. Writers, academics, and everyday adventurers started to make pilgrimages to Mexico, eager to taste the "flesh of the gods."[10]

The Wassons helped establish two tenets of the GAPS hypothesis: the ancientness of psychedelic use and its ubiquity. After decades spent studying mushrooms, Wasson wrote, he and Valentina found that peoples everywhere, from "the Arabs of the desert" to "the Maoris of New Zealand," regarded mushrooms as supernaturally powerful. This discovery led them to "hazard a bold surmise: Was it not probable that, long ago, long before the beginnings of written history, our ancestors had worshiped a divine mushroom?"[11]

Like a fungal mycelium colonizing new terrain, the threads of the GAPS hypothesis had taken root.

In the decades since the Wassons' articles, assertions of widespread archaic psychedelic use have diversified. They've inspired theories that religion broadly and Christianity, in particular, began with psychedelics or other hallucinogens. The American mystic and psychonaut Terence McKenna proposed that human cognitive evolution was catalyzed by a prehistoric psychedelic and that some of our modern issues, including myopia, might reflect our alienation from regular psychedelic use. With the rise of two industries, psychedelic tourism and clinical medicinal use, these stories have become commonplace mantras, often twinged with a therapeutic flair.[12]

It makes sense why these claims are so popular. As psychedelics prove effective for treating disorders like addiction and anxiety, scientists and enthusiasts push for their broader societal acceptance. Connecting psychedelics—and particularly, psychedelic therapy—to ancient worldwide traditions makes them, according to historian Erika Dyck, "more natural, more wholesome, perhaps more spiritual."

"I think there's some feelings of calm that come with linking it to these deeper traditions," she told me. Stories about early and universal use help "soften some of the edges of what we might think is a riskier or maybe profit-driven motive."

But is there any truth to these stories? In 2018, I met a man who set out to answer that question. I was visiting the École Normale Supérieure in Paris for two months and was urged to get in touch with a PhD student named Martin Fortier. Martin, I was told, had the air of an old-world intellectual. He wore three-piece linen suits with vibrant printed neckties. Although born and raised in France, he spoke French with a "barely discernible British accent," in the words of one of his friends. He was passionate about what he studied and had an avidly communitarian take on research. For him, insight came from conversation and cross-fertilization. He was the kind of person with whom you would have an embroiling intellectual conversation and who would then send three new books to your door. In 2016, he cofounded ALIUS, an interdisciplinary group dedicated to understanding the diversity of non-ordinary states of consciousness. The week I was scheduled to arrive, he was hosting a workshop on comparative mythology, population genetics, and linguistics in Paris.

I joined the workshop but didn't see Martin. He had a herniated disc, he said, and was resting at his parents' house in southwestern France. We continued corresponding, but by the end of my two months in France, we still hadn't had a chance to meet. His herniated disc had turned out to be caused by a cancerous tumor. He was just twenty-eight.

Martin began chemotherapy immediately. We finally video-called ten days after his second treatment. Martin was an anthropologist, philosopher, and cognitive scientist. Like Brabec de Mori, he worked with Shipibo-Konibo communities in the Peruvian Amazon. His interests were wide-ranging, covering essentialism, ethnobiology, supernatural thinking, and color categorization, although the project I found most exciting was a database he called HUTHAC, or "Hallucinogenic Use Through History and Across Cultures."

HUTHAC was, in his words, "the first academic source exhaustively documenting hallucinogenic use through history and across cultures." It was gloriously ambitious, meant to include more than a thousand cultures. To build it, Martin scoured hundreds of sources, including academic books, historical chronicles, and the diaries of explorers. For every mention of hallucinogens, he noted who used them, how they were used, whether they were used in hallucinogenic doses, and how reliable the evidence was.

HUTHAC promised to be the largest, most systematic survey of drug use across human societies. Unfortunately, it was never finished. In April 2020, at the age of thirty, Martin died.

Before his death, Martin published his preliminary findings in a series of posts on his Facebook page, sparking a small academic firestorm. He found that reliable evidence for early psychedelic usage was limited to the Rio Grande area (the modern-day border between the United States and Mexico) and southward. And even in those regions, usage was rare. In pre-Columbian times, he estimated, 5 percent of Indigenous American groups used psychedelics—and this, he wrote, "is probably a very liberal estimate." By these counts, 1 percent or less of the world's cultures consumed psychedelics at this time.[13]

Martin's tally was limited to classic, or serotonergic, psychedelics: substances like DMT, mescaline, psilocybin, and anything else whose effects mostly come from activating serotonin 2A receptors. But even if we expand to a broader usage—including drugs like ibogaine, deliriants, and dissociatives—hallucinogenic use remains marginal by his count. "These findings deeply challenge the view that hallucinogenic use is very ancient and belongs to an ancestral shamanic tradition that would have migrated from Siberia to the New World," he wrote on his website. "More broadly, they also challenge the view that most archaic cultures used hallucinogens."

Other research has echoed Martin's findings. In his book *Shroom* (2006), the ecologist Andy Letcher investigated every presumed case of traditional hallucinogenic mushroom consumption in history. He confirmed only two: the use of psilocybin mushrooms in pre-Columbian Mexico and the use of *Amanita muscaria* mushrooms—whose effects come mostly from acting on $GABA_A$ receptors, thus excluding them from the list of classic psychedelics—by scattered groups in northern Eurasia.*[14]

According to Fortier's and Letcher's research, psychedelics have been the exception in the history of humanity, not the rule. Yes, some peoples used them before a couple hundred years ago, but they aren't nearly as common as we've come to believe, and various popular examples seem relatively recent.

Still, some scholars disagree. Of the holdouts, most point to art and literature. They cite shroomy figures in cave paintings and descriptions of lost rituals involving mind-altering substances.[15]

To be fair, symbolic evidence like this sometimes corroborates botanical and observational reports. Pre-Hispanic manuscripts, for example, depicted mythological figures holding and even eating mushrooms. The *Codex Vindobonensis*, a fifty-two-page document made of tanned deer hide in the early 1500s, has one such scene. Near the bottom right, we find the solar deity Piltzintecuhtli, the "prince of flowers," holding a pair of mushrooms and crying, which some scholars take as a sign of trance. Nearby, seven gods are shown sitting and holding mushrooms, possibly representing a nighttime mushroom ceremony.[16]

Along with other codices, the *Codex Vindobonensis* suggests that mushroom use was ritualized, mythologized, and ensconced into Mesoamerican societies when the Spanish arrived. A sepa-

---

* While this book was being copyedited, a mostly South African team of researchers published a paper in *Mycologia* describing two new *Psilocybe* mushroom species (Van der Merwe et al. 2024). The article included a passage suggesting that Basotho healers in Lesotho add psilocybin mushrooms to psychoactive brews that are fed to patients. As of this writing, ethnographic research has yet to be conducted, but, if confirmed, this would represent the first, direct evidence of the hallucinogenic use of serotonergic psychedelics in traditional contexts outside the Americas.

rate set of discoveries, however, raises the possibility that mushroom consumption extends much earlier. Throughout Central America, hundreds of stone and pottery sculptures have been discovered that seem to feature mushrooms. A collection of nine miniatures from the Guatemalan highlands has been dated to somewhere between 2,500 and 3,000 years old. It's impossible to reconstruct what mushroom use would have looked like in its earliest days, but—in this part of the world, at least—it may indeed go back millennia.[17]

Is there similar evidence elsewhere? Many enthusiasts, including Michael Winkelman, the shamanism expert, insist there is. In 2019, Winkelman published "Evidence for entheogen use in prehistory and world religions" in the *Journal of Psychedelic Studies*. The article is a smorgasbord of supposed artistic and literary indications of ancient hallucinogens, listing sculptures, cave art, and passages of mythology. Yet, as Letcher warned more than a decade earlier, "none of these inferences is unequivocal, and each is open to a range of alternative explanations."[18]

Let's review a couple of examples. Winkelman presents what he calls "the mushroom stones of Chucuito," large sculptures with domed caps and elongated stems discovered in highland Peru. It's certainly possible that these were made to resemble mushrooms. Yet Winkelman fails to acknowledge the leading interpretation of these statues—that they're penises. "Although no definitive answer will ever be discovered," explains the travel website Atlas Obscura, "the rocks' resemblance to male genitalia remains uncanny." In fact, the site's local name—Inka Uyo—might come from the Quechua word for penis. Winkelman includes a picture of some "mushroom stones" yet does not present the most prominent statue, which towers above the others and has a large groove resembling the external opening of the urethra.[19]

Or take what might be the best-known example of ancient psychedelic iconography: the mushroom shaman, first popularized in Terence McKenna's book *Food of the Gods* (1992). McKenna's image is of Algerian rock art dated to between 7,000 and 9,000 years ago. It shows a bee-faced figure in a sumo squat, feathers poking out of its head and a checkerboard of dots covering its body and spilling out from its legs. Most notably, it holds batches of mushrooms, another fifty or so sprouting from its limbs and torso.[20]

The mushroom shaman is an icon of the psychedelic community. You can find it printed on shirts, mugs, paintings, and face masks. But as Letcher discovered, the popular image "is not a photo of the original, but a copy" made by McKenna's wife at the time, Kat Harrison. In fact, Harrison never saw the original painting, but instead deciphered a photograph in a book. And rather than copying the photo, she filled in features she thought were damaged or incomplete. Harrison's drawing clearly shows a supernatural figure blossoming with mushrooms, but "whether that was the intention of the original artist(s) is far from settled," wrote Letcher. An earlier archaeologist thought it was a sheepman.[21]

"The role of psilocybin mushrooms in the ancient evolution of human religions is attested to [in] fungiform petroglyphs, rock artifacts, and mythologies from all major regions of the world," asserts Winkelman. We've seen that at least some of the petroglyphs and artifacts are open to alternative interpretations. But what do we make of mushrooms starring in the world's mythologies? The Wassons, remember, had made a similar claim. Does it hold up?[22]

I conducted a simple test using the electronic Human Relations Area Files, or eHRAF. This is one of the gems of the internet, a repository based at Yale that contains nearly seven thousand digitized books and articles covering hundreds of human societies. Most documents were written by anthropologists, although it also includes reports by missionaries, explorers, and whoever else bothered to publish serious observations of human societies. If you want to learn something about humanity, from the structure of the Aztec priesthood to theories of illness among Palestinians, this is the place to look.[23]

Luckily for us, the topics of each paragraph in the eHRAF have been manually tagged. As of August 2023, 51,025 paragraphs, covering 325 cultural groups, were about mythology. How many of those include the words "mushroom" or "mushrooms"? Twenty-two. Those appeared in nineteen cultures, yielding a paragraph-to-culture ratio of roughly 1.2. For the most part, these mentions do not ascribe mushrooms any supernatural power, with fungi instead appearing as asides or scenery. In a myth told by the Yuki people of California, for example, Coyote transforms into a harmless old man picking mushrooms to escape people chasing him. In a myth from Tierra del Fuego, we read that some children "were so terrorized that they fled into the woods and became lost, surviving only by feeding on mushrooms, roots and berries."

In the table below, I've compared mentions of mushrooms to those of other psychoactive substances in passages about mythology. The takeaway is simple. Mushrooms appear very little in this collection of mythology, even compared to culturally important psychoactive plants with far smaller ranges, like peyote and kava. Mushrooms also have far fewer mentions per culture. Even when mushrooms feature in mythology, they are marginal.

	Total paragraphs	Cultures	Paragraphs per culture
Mushroom(s)	22	19	1.2
Beer	166	43	3.9
Kava	155	9	17.2
Peyote	308	10	30.8
Tobacco	465	85	5.5
Wine	94	36	2.6

This was a preliminary search. I invite others to do larger and more careful versions. But it is an attempt to probe the world's mythology using methods that are both systematic and unbiased. Rather than cherry-picking a couple of ambiguous examples and forcing a once-universal fungus cult onto them, I searched for mushrooms in possibly the most comprehensive resource on the world's mythology. And I found squat.

———

People don't just claim that psychedelics are old and widespread; they also believe that the modern therapeutic use echoes ancient shamanic traditions. As UCLA psychiatry professor Charles Grob explained in a Q&A published on Goop, "The shaman would administer these compounds only for very clear circumscribed reasons, such as an initiation rite or a healing ceremony to address individuals with severe medical or psychological problems."[24]

Reasonable, right? A patient comes to the shaman with a psychological problem, like depression or existential angst. The shaman administers the psychedelic, and the patient is healed. It's like visiting a psychiatrist, except with more ritual.

But this is a misleading characterization of how shamans have traditionally used psychedelics. The best way to appreciate this is to simply watch them taking the substances.

An easily accessible depiction of shamans using psychedelics is anthropologist Napoleon Chagnon's 1973 short documentary *Magical Death*, which portrays shamanism among the Yanomami of Venezuela. The film's beginning shows the shaman Dedeheiwa healing illness. He snorts a psychedelic snuff powder and calls spirits, which he experiences as entering his feet and climbing through his body. He draws on their power to remove illness and battle evil spirits. No patients consume psychedelics, and there's no mention of treating mental disorders.[25]

If the beginning represents a slight divergence from the popular story, the next part of the film is a total overhaul. Intent on killing babies in an enemy village, a squad of shamans snorts the snuff. Some shamans act like helpless babies. Others bend over the ashes and imitate murderous spirits devouring the babies' souls. As proof of their success, Dedeheiwa and another shaman act like dying babies, writhing "in agony in the ashes."[26]

Psychedelic shamanism here is nothing like the view endorsed on Goop. Anthropological research conducted since the mid-twentieth century shows that, among the Yanomami and many other groups, shamans use psychedelics to tap into the supernatural and provide services like weather change, divination, physical healing, and aggressive sorcery. They might confront heinous sorcerers. They might purge patients of treacherous ghosts. They might become supernatural beings themselves. Psychedelics—like dancing, drumming, darkness, and other psychotropic drugs—push shamans into a state where they and their communities believe them to access otherworldly powers. This contrasts with the Western clinical application, where psychedelics are administered like medicine and used to break down patients' harmful patterns of thought.[27]

This misconception seems to stem partly from biased interpretations of anthropological data. When I asked Charles Grob for sources describing the psychotherapeutic use of psychedelics, he pointed me to Marlene Dobkin de Rios, who conducted research on ayahuasca use among Peruvian mestizos in the 1960s and 1970s—groups that have been subjected to Christian missionaries for the last four centuries. There are obvious limitations with making inferences about "typical" psychedelic shamanism using religious and medicinal practices so profoundly shaped by European colonialism. As Dobkin de Rios herself has written, throughout the Peruvian Amazon, "influences of Roman Catholic proselytization, mixed with medieval metaphysical beliefs, and influenced by evangelical Protestantism, are widespread."[28]

Putting those issues aside, Dobkin de Rios's work is still much less a confirmation of the Goop view than a demonstration of its Euro-American flair. Consider her book *A Hallucinogenic Tea, Laced with Controversy* (2008), co-authored with the Peruvian journalist Roger Rumrrill. She and Rumrrill compared Amazonian shamans who treat Western tourists with those who work with locals. The tourist healers charge sums usually impossible for locals to pay. And they embody the Goop view: they treat psychological distress by administering ayahuasca to patients.[29]

"These tourists come to try to resolve personal problems," said healer Guillermo Arrévalo in an interview published in the book. According to the authors, Arrévalo had a university degree in pharmacology and was the owner of Espíritu de Anaconda, a healing center that charged foreigners forty to fifty dollars per day at the time of the interview. "They suffer a type of psychosis and psychological upheaval. They suffer from fear, paranoia, and other problems. These patients are ones that I treat with ayahuasca."[30]

The authors contrasted these tourist shamans with those who treated locals. "Ayahuasca played an important role in this world view where evil men and women would be able to bewitch their enemies and cause them illness, bad luck, and even death," they wrote. Shamans used ayahuasca to contact supernatural realms and identify and battle witches causing misfortune. Insofar as ayahuasca was used to treat distress, this meant combating evil. "What a difference," they wrote, "from the psychodynamic world view of Freud and contemporary Western psychology."[31]

"Of course, there's no single narrative," said Erika Dyck, "and yet it has been convenient as a way of selling psychoactivity."

For Dyck, who has studied the history of attitudes about psychedelics, stories about traditional psychedelic use are rooted in monetary and ideological goals. "A lot of the enthusiasm for investing in psychedelic drugs," she said, stems from an expectation that they will bring "a paradigm shift in the way we think about mental disorders." Our stories reflect that goal. We portray shamans around the world as psychotherapists and psychopharmacologists. We imagine how we want to use psychedelics and then project those imaginings onto peoples we know little about.

In 2022, Nina and I visited an ayahuasca retreat in the Peruvian Andes. It was run by a couple, a Quechua man named Jhon and his Dutch wife Janneke. Over two cool December nights, Jhon and an older Quechua maestro held nighttime ceremonies. They started by asking us to share our intentions. They gave us a mantra for dealing with the darkness that might arise during the sessions and invited us to pray to our higher power for safety, protection, and guidance.

I arrived with a scientist's agnosticism yet, after imbibing ayahuasca, felt a greater intelligence, something dark and stirring, cosmic yet subterranean, ancient and without comprehensible form. I saw myself, along with armies of alien acolytes, undergoing physical terrors to ask questions of this being that was at once earthy and celestial. My body spasmed uncontrollably. I moaned and felt possessed. Whenever I vomited, a protective, shadowy figure appeared, and I heard a spritz and the beating of wings. I thought about how the cultural descendants of colonizers suffered and sought refuge in the shadows of the colonized. Concepts melted. Movements had sounds were emotions; a flutter of an iridescent butterfly wing split open timelessness. I felt fear and compassion and saw myself with new clarity. I was convinced that I shat myself, and I accepted it.

The morning after the second ceremony, Jhon gave me the rundown. I mentioned the power of the different elements of the ceremony—the beating of feathers, the shrill of a flute—and asked about their history. He admitted to having little idea. He was confident that Quechua speakers consumed ayahuasca before the Spanish arrived, but he didn't know whether anything he and the maestro did had precolonial parallels. For all he knew, what we experienced was a postcolonial invention.

Jhon's honesty surprised me, especially because other guides and therapists take the opposite approach, dressing ceremonies with the trappings of ancient, Indigenous wisdom. This is the case with Françoise Bourzat, a well-known therapist based in San Francisco. Bourzat has spent years of her life training with Mazatec healers—people of the same ethnic group as Gordon Wasson's *curandera*, María Sabina. Bourzat's life work, she says, is "to introduce the healing ways of Indigenous rituals to people living in industrialized societies." The antiquity of these methods is key for her, and something she insists on. As she and Kristina Hunter wrote in their book *Consciousness Medicine* (2019), "We can receive much more by relying on the knowledge that indigenous cultures have maintained and passed down for thousands of years of how we can best approach and incorporate these experiences into our lives."[32]

Whatever her lofty claims, Bourzat's "consciousness medicine" looks a lot like psychedelic-assisted psychotherapy. A client, or "journeyer," works with a therapist, or "guide." The experience is interpreted through the lens of psychology, not the supernatural. The client uses the altered state of consciousness for inner exploration under the guide's supervision. They might loosen fears, liberate memories, or reclaim their inner child. Afterward, they work with the guide to integrate their experience, using newfound insights to move in a direction that feels healthy and satisfying.[33]

Consciousness medicine may be effective for psychological healing. Yet it looks nothing like the earliest reports of Mazatec mushroom ceremonies, which describe shamans consuming mushrooms and invoking saints, virgins, and nature spirits before treating illness or locating lost objects. Bourzat may have learned features of consciousness medicine from Mazatec healers, but Mazatec people themselves admit that streams of foreigners have demanded new takes on mushroom consumption. A healer told the Mexican researcher Diego Hannon Ovies that "those false medics working with outsiders do not care about respecting the sacred tradition." Others agree that the practice is transforming but see the modifications as necessary. "We have to adapt to survive, and we have to help those who need the medicine," said a healer who works with tourists. "They might not know it, but a person who feels the need to take the mushrooms needs spiritual healing, and it is our duty to help them."[34]

The healers' comments expose a common pressure in the world of so-called Indigenous medicine. Tourists arrive in remote communities with a sense of what an authentic ceremony looks like. But local cosmologies are often strange, scary, or confusing. Guests want to consume psychedelics themselves, not visit mushroom-chomping doctors. They want to be psychologically healed, not protected from sorcery. So they're buffered from local realities. Working in the heart of ayahuasca tourism, the Australian anthropologist Alex Gearin saw that "many ayahuasca retreats minimize interactions between guests and indigenous healers," likely because healers' talk about evil magic scares off potential clients. Maintaining an image of authenticity requires keeping out native interference.[35]

Cross-cultural comparison, much like psychedelics, is perilous. Just as snorting a blast of yopo can open your mind to insights or fill it with hellish delusions, searching for patterns across societies can lead to deeper understanding or gross misinterpretation. Both require care. They benefit from preparation. They demand a respect for the unknown and an awareness of one's biases and limitations. Without the proper caution, a traveler, whether journeying across human cultures or into mind-melding realms, can lose their way, misread the signs, and return with a warped perception that causes more trouble than good.

These perils are especially clear when studying shamanism. Long entangled with images of the exotic and the primitive, shamanism has become a stand-in for modernity's relationship with the Other. For those seeking to critique the alienation and environmental destruction of industrialized economies, the shaman embodies harmony, spirituality, and community. For those hoping to commend the achievements of Western liberalism, the shaman is an expression of pre-Enlightenment superstition. Psychedelic enthusiasts are simply playing the same game. The global, archaic, psychedelic shaman is yet another attempt to domesticate the primitive to prop up an ideology—a repackaging of history and diversity in service of the widespread acceptance of hallucinogenic drugs.

The danger, of course, is that useful portrayals are rarely accurate ones. They deny Indigenous peoples history. They place them, as Brabec de Mori explained, "into the role of reproducing ancient knowledge but not being allowed to develop new things." In their campaigns to make psychedelics palatable, enthusiasts end up misshaping humanity's spiritual traditions into exotified daydreams, thus stifling the insights that come from careful comparison. Distracted by convenient bastardizations, we blind ourselves to the structure humming within the infinite variety of human cultures.

Afterword

Rustam woke me up. I could make out drumming in the distance, along with a vague hubbub. Opa's house was evidently crowded. I pulled my watch close to my face and looked at the time: 10:20 p.m. I was told that the night's events wouldn't start until midnight, but clearly that was wrong. I put on my glasses, tied my hair into a topknot, and slipped on my waist pack and flip-flops. I had been sleeping at the house next to Opa's, so lost little time walking over.

During a *sikerei*'s initiation, nights are spent dancing and summoning spirits. This was no different when Opa became a shaman. As I approached, I noticed a small crowd buzzing around his veranda. Rustam pulled me through, and I saw the *sikerei* seated on the floor, a plate of magical green mush at their center. Around them, the veranda's benches were packed. Although Opa had a generator and several lightbulbs, the village's walkways were unlit, and many people were still wearing headlamps.

I had just missed the first performance, a hypnotic circle dance believed to lure good spirits. There would be many more, but the effects were already visible. A wailing issued from inside the house. I looked through the doorway and saw a group of women in trance. They had their eyes closed and seemed to move to a hidden metronome. Two were singing ghostly, shamanic chants while bounding back and forth. The older of the two was grabbed by a third woman, and the pair began lifting and lowering their arms in a birdlike ballroom glide. The younger one was supported by two men, each clutching one of her arms. A fourth woman sat cross-legged, her legs bouncing and her upper body swaying. A man pointed at her and told someone to look after her. Spiritual ecstasy requires supervision.

The drummers emerged from deeper in the house. Animal-skin drums absorb moisture from the air, which causes them to slacken and the sound to dull. Drummers thus heat them next to fires between songs, creating natural rest times.

The drummers sat on the veranda and began playing. The women in trance matched their chants to the drums' rhythms. The *sikerei* stood and adjusted their beads and leaves in preparation. Teu Rami, Opa's main teacher, held the plate of mystical pulp. He bent down and looked forward when, suddenly and in unison, the *sikerei* began stomping their feet on the floorboards. As they trotted in a circle, Teu Rami swept the plate, seemingly wafting the magical plants for onlooking spirits. At first, he was the only *sikerei* singing, but then others joined in, melding their vocals with the drums, women's chanting, and percussed floorboards.

The collaboration between musicians and dancers created a living soundscape, an orchestra of booms and clangs and charged spiritual yells. I felt it in my joints and muscles. My abdomen tightened, and my shoulders relaxed. My head began to nod. I knew the sensation intimately. I wanted to dance.

———————

This has been a book about the timeless appeal of shamanism. But it could have just as easily been about music—about how, despite our incredible differences, we devise songs with deep similarities capable of evoking common emotional tones. Music, like shamanism, is dazzlingly varied, yet there is a structure underlying that variety. Dance songs everywhere tend to exhibit certain features. So do lullabies and healing songs. Transport an Indian

American anthropologist to a remote island in Southeast Asia, and the local music would not only prove addictively catchy—it could also urge him to move.[1]

In fact, this book could have been about any number of complex, near-universal cultural traditions. Hero stories, origin myths, property norms, institutions of justice, rites of passage, beliefs in gods and souls—the list can seem endless. As with shamanism, these are cultural products. They require humans to transmit them, maturing into their spectacular forms as generations of learners shape them. Yet we hairless apes invent them with a consistency that almost looks predestined. And even across vast cultural distances, these products often still affect us, sometimes deeply. Their nature is paradoxical: malleable yet stereotyped, cultural yet ever present.

The UCLA anthropologist Clark Barrett once called these practices "super-attractors." He was riffing on another term, "cultural attractors," first developed by the French philosopher and cognitive scientist Dan Sperber. A cultural attractor is a state favored during cultural transmission—a kind of gravitational center toward which cultural evolution seems pulled. Examples of attractors abound and include the triumphant endings of hero stories, beliefs that rainbows are supernatural, and the tendency for painted portraits to stare directly at the viewer. These act as cognitive magnets, drawing ideas into familiar forms.[2]

Super-attractors are "super" for two reasons. First, they are complex packages of functionally interrelated cultural attractors. Like a machine built from an array of interacting components, shamanism involves non-ordinary states, narratives of otherworldly contact, and goal-oriented services. Hero stories include not just triumphant endings but also charming protagonists, relatable obstacles, and adventurous plots. Each of these parts might count as an attractor, but when fit together for a common purpose, they create super-attractors.

Second, whereas standard attractors are often sensitive to environmental factors, super-attractors tend to be far less constrained. Direct-gaze portraits are attractors but only in societies where people photograph faces or paint them in rich detail. Wooden spears might be an attractor if you live somewhere forested, but move to a treeless expanse, and they disappear. This is less so the case with super-attractors. Of course, shamanism and other complex, ubiquitous traditions are not insulated from all environmental variation. We saw that shamanism disappears when populations become tiny, for instance. But super-attractors are much more robust, developing almost everywhere humans have lived.

The term "super-attractors" is new, although the concept has a long history. More than a century ago, Franz Boas, the German-born pioneer of American anthropology, published an article in *Science* that began, "Modern anthropology has discovered the fact that human society has grown and developed everywhere in such a manner that its forms, its opinions and its actions have many fundamental traits in common." Later, he continued, "Many attempts have been made to discover the causes which have led to the formation of ideas 'that develop with iron necessity wherever man lives.' This is the most difficult problem of anthropology and we may expect that it will baffle our attempts for a long time to come."[3]

Even as he recognized the importance of super-attractors, however, Boas suggested that anthropologists put off studying them. Before waxing on about supposed universals, he warned, they needed to understand the societies they were comparing. They needed to conduct detailed histories and ethnographies, to devote themselves to "laying clear the complex relations of each individual culture." He concluded, "The solid work is still all before us."[4]

———————

Boas's arguments influenced generations of anthropologists. Intensive fieldwork became a rite of passage for aspiring researchers, resulting in reams of meticulous dissertations and one of the great bodies of knowledge about humanity. Boas's dream of deep engagement with different cultures materialized. At the same time, however, comparative research shriveled up. Studying patterns became taboo. The rise of postmodernism and the corresponding distrust of scientific objectivity further crippled comparative projects in the 1970s. Flipping through the field's major journals in 2019, the anthropologist Robert Borofsky reported that "comparisons are now relatively narrow, rare, and/or brief," leading him to question "to what degree cultural anthropology has made systematic intellectual progress in recent decades."[5]

Talk of universals has become especially seditious. "When universalism is mentioned in humanistic writing, it is most often denounced as a tool of oppression," wrote Patrick Hogan, a literary scholar, in 2003. I have seen this firsthand. In 2017, when colleagues and I submitted a grant proposal to build a database to study universality and diversity in music, one reviewer connected our work to "the Nazi regime's abuse of evolutionist ideas." Another later wrote that the idea of musical universals "is deeply ethnocentric and Eurocentric" and "reinforces 19th century European colonial ideology." When we published some findings in *Science* in 2019, including evidence of music's universality and common features of dance songs, healing songs, and lullabies, a prominent ethnomusicologist tweeted that our work was "pseudoscientific racist BS."[6]

I found all this confusing. Aren't violence and subjugation backed by doctrines of difference, not similarity? Which genocidal commando justified mass slaughter by citing the cross-cultural appeal of dance music or calling up the fact that people around the globe sing to fussy infants?

Once I did my homework, I had a better sense of where the critics were coming from. Non-European peoples were branded as primitive or backward when they deviated from the presumably "natural" practices of colonizers. And countless campaigns of conquest have been waged in the name of "universal" faiths. The French Wars of Religion, which pitted Catholics against Protestants and left millions dead, were underlain by the universalist mantra of *un roi, une foi, une loi* (one king, one faith, one law). "Universalism without toleration, it's clear, turns easily to murder," wrote the philosopher Kwame Anthony Appiah.[7]

Even acknowledging this history, however, the critics' reasoning is fallacious. The violence they have in mind has been linked to what Appiah calls "pseudouniversalism," or Eurocentric customs masquerading as universal norms. It's not studying cultural regularities that supports cruelty; it's the assertion that a group violates an arbitrary ideal and thus deserves to be conquered, colonized, or exterminated. If anything, careful cross-cultural research would reveal the hollowness of claimed universals. Rather than denouncing the study of patterns, we should condemn intolerance and the regressive logic defending it.[8]

After a decade of doing this kind of research, I'm convinced that these critics are not just mistaken; they have it backward. Comparison seems to dissolve cultural hubris much more than it reinforces it. A power of anthropology, remember, is in turning the strange familiar and the familiar strange, yet this reversal requires a comparative approach. The *sikerei* are unique products of Mentawai history, but they become more recognizable when analyzed together with similar practitioners around the world. Jesus and Wall Street money managers seem to exemplify Western exceptionalism—that is, until considered alongside Kalahari trance healers and countless messianic prophets. A serious global perspective helps curb cultural vanity, showing commonality where people otherwise assume difference and even superiority.

Perhaps the biggest casualty of anthropology's relativist turn has been its ability to produce generalizable knowledge. For Boas, the existence of cultural patterns was exciting because it signaled an underlying order. "The momentous discovery" of widespread traits, he wrote, "implies that laws exist which govern the development of society, that they are applicable to our society as well as to those of past times and of distant lands." Boas thought it worthwhile to identify these laws, yet his call to put off comparison led to their abandonment and to an eventual rejection of the science of society. The discipline best set up to discover the general processes shaping culture has thus made remarkably little progress.[9]

Some researchers consider this a death knell for anthropology. The study of humanity in its manifold forms is losing relevance, and a big reason, it seems, is its intellectual stagnation. Borofsky, who noted the narrowing focus of the field, wrote, "Anthropology's present difficulties—its declining membership, its limited funding, its lack of innovative perspectives that others can then build on in insightful ways, its limited positive public image, its fragmentation—are entwined with our inability to move toward broader, more comparative syntheses that provide insights that are valued by those beyond the discipline." He continued, "What is needed is the courage, the daring, to return to the comparative focus and make it vital to the field once more."

A small contingent of researchers has kept up the pursuit, however. They have embraced data collection and comparison and seek to position anthropology as a field that can contribute to and draw from other scientific disciplines, especially cognitive science and evolutionary theory. I was partly trained in this tradition, and this book reflects the community's conviction that patterns are real and comprehensible.

I hope I've demonstrated that anthropologists have done what Boas asked. They have lived and collaborated with peoples, learned their languages, compiled their histories, and sought to understand each element of culture—a song, a myth, a ritual—in its context. They have studied the unique and ephemeral, expanded our sense of cultural possibility, and assembled a prodigious archive of human experience. At the same time, the biological and behavioral sciences have flourished, illuminating our origins, our evolution, and the shared architecture of our minds.

Some 130 years after Boas's call to hold off comparison, we are equipped to reclaim anthropology's most difficult problem of charting and explaining our commonalities. The power of traditions to resonate across time and geography deserves contemplation.

————————

I wasn't the only onlooker affected by the performances that night. After about four minutes, I looked to my right and saw two women on the dance floor. Their eyes were closed. Singing and holding hands, they seemed caught in rapturous enchantment. When I turned back, the *sikerei* looked hypnotized. Some stared straight ahead; others seemed to nod drowsily. I knew what was about to happen. Aman Joji shot his arms forward and fell to the ground. Opa dissociated and scampered back and forth. A third *sikerei* seemed to lose himself, hovering around Opa but with his eyes closed and his arms flapping. The music sped up. The women's chanting turned into a falsetto trill.

The veranda felt like an orb of spirit-infused light suspended in thick darkness. And as seemingly everyone around me went into trance, I experienced the same pull. I inhaled deeply and felt my eyes turn upward under shut lids. I stood on a precipice, a pool of water beneath me. I only had to jump. I could let the sound and social environment and a deeper consciousness wash over me. I could let my body jerk and my head shake. I could give in to ecstasy.

Acknowledgments

Thank you, foremost, to the people of Madobag, Ugai, and Buttui. *Tubut masurak bagatta.*

There are many people who assisted me with my Mentawai fieldwork, most notably Maskota Delfi, Christian Hammons, Rob Henry, and Juniator Tulius. I'm especially grateful to my assistant, translator, guide, language teacher, informant, fixer, and friend, *siripokku simaeruk (simasingin tai)*, Rustam (Boroiogok) Sakaliou. My research with the Mentawai has been supported by a National Science Foundation Graduate Research Fellowship, a Sheldon Traveling Fellowship from the Harvard Committee on General Scholarships, a grant from the Mind, Brain, and Behavior Initiative at Harvard University, and a grant from the Templeton Religion Trust, as part of the "Persistence of Wild Religions" project (TRT-2021-10490).

Thank you to François-Xavier Ricaut and Robert Bégouën for organizing the trip to Trois-Frères, to Nelsa de la Hoz for the introduction to the Huottüja, to Bethany Burum for taking me to Burning Man that first time in 2015, and to Rusty Greaves for sending, and allowing me to quote from, the unpublished manuscript on yopo.

Thank you to everyone who has helped turn a zygote of an idea into this living, breathing, beautiful book, especially my agent, Max Brockman, and my U.S. and U.K. editors, Erroll McDonald and Casiana Ionita. Thank you also to everyone else at Allen Lane and Knopf who made this book a reality, including Brian Etling and Nora Reichard. My fellowship at the Institute for Advanced Study in Toulouse, funded by the French National Research Agency (ANR) under grant ANR-17-EURE-0010, allowed me to write much of this book.

Joe Henrich and Richard Wrangham have been incredible mentors and, despite my stubbornness, have supported me endlessly. This book would not exist without Luke Glowacki: The smell of animal hides wafting from your office helped transform me from a zoologist-in-training to this strange breed of anthropologist. You pushed me to learn the language, to become an ethnography nerd, and to think big while grounding ideas in observations of human behavior. You kept reminding me that I could write this book, long after it seemed a possibility.

Henry Finder deserves a special thanks, as his editorial eye at *The New Yorker* inspired me to rewrite several chapters. Angela Chen and Sarah Burke edited articles I wrote for *Wired* and *Vice* that went on to provide the foundations for chapters 10 and 11, respectively. Paul Bloom edited the article at *Behavioral and Brain Sciences* in which I advanced my theory of shamanism and has since encouraged my nonacademic writing.

For setting aside time to answer my many questions, thank you to Jeanet Bentzen, Natalie Gukasyan, Stephanie Harper, Ted Kaptchuk, Tanya Luhrmann, J. P. Millsap, Martti Nissinen, Barnaby Ruhe, Paul Seabright, Richard Sosis, Anne-Katrin Spiess, Peter Stocke, Glenn Treisman, Robert Wallis, Polly Wiessner, Michael Winkelman, and anyone else I may have missed. Many of you read passages of this book and provided helpful feedback. Others who did the same, and who also have my gratitude, include Josh Elbaum, Léo Fitouchi, Hugo Mercier, and Dimas Iqbal Romadhon, as well as Patricio Cruz y Celis Peniche, Cristina Moya, Lesley Newsom, Pete Richerson, and other members of the EEHBC Lab at U.C. Davis. My colleagues Teresa Steele, Tim Weaver, and Nicolas Zwyns looked over passages about human evolution and the Upper Paleolithic. Eli Elster and Ze

(Kevin) Hong read the book in its entirety and offered feedback; thank you, both.

Sandeep, brother, thank you for helping me see a different side of shamanism and for venturing with me. Our journey began that night in Keeney Quad and has continued for more than fifteen years, from the playa to the Orinoco to realms unseen. Your contributions resonate throughout this book, particularly in a chapter in which you're never mentioned. As you wrote in a 2012 email, quoting the Joker: "I think you and I are destined to do this forever."

An enormous, love-saturated thank-you to my mother, Rosie, and my father, Inderpal, for giving me so much, so unceasingly, and for cultivating many of the interests that have come to fruition in this book.

Most of all, thank you to my daughter, Zora, and my wife, Nina. Zori, my joy, even in the short time you've been on this planet, you've taught me so much about the human experience. You also get a shout-out given that the anticipation of your arrival motivated me to finish the manuscript on time.

And finally, Nina, Bai Zora, my fellow okapi: You've championed this project from when I started working on a proposal until I've typed the final words of these acknowledgments. You've been the best fellow adventurer I could have asked for and have urged me to continue when I've felt disheartened. You've listened to every passage of this book, often many times, with a sharp, editorial intuition. As with Sikameinan in the river and Silakkikkiou in the forest, your presence is felt throughout these pages.

Notes

INTRODUCTION

1. Balikci 1963; Evans-Pritchard 1937; Katz 1982b.
2. Silva and Lillios 1962, p. 408; Thalbitzer 1909, p. 454; Singh 2018; Evans-Pritchard 1937; Chagnon and Asch 1973. See also references in chapters 3 and 7.

CHAPTER 1   SETTING OFF

1. Tulius 2012; Tenaza and Fuentes 1995. Tenaza and Fuentes (1995) report that South Pagai received a mean annual rainfall of 4,420 millimeters between 1974 and 1985. The Greenwich Observatory (London) received 562.86 millimeters of rainfall, on average, between 1991 and 2020 (metoffice.gov.uk). According to the National Climatic Data Center, Seattle received an average of 37.07 inches (941.58 millimeters) between 1971 and 2000 (drought.unl.edu).
2. Wilting et al. 2012.
3. Tulius 2012; Hammons 2010; Bakker 1999.
4. For examples of their work, see Schefold 1988, Tulius 2012.
5. Toffelmier 1967.
6. Loeb 1929.
7. Schefold 1998; Bakker 1999; Hammons 2010.
8. Hammons 2010.
9. Lacocque 1987, p. 121; Weinberger 1986; Eliade 1981, pp. 6, 10.
10. Eliade 1964; 1988.
11. Eliade 1964, p. 5.
12. For a prominent example, see Harner 1982.

13. See, for example, Kendall 1985, I. M. Lewis 2003.
14. Siikala 1992; Anisimov 1963.
15. N. S. Price 2001, pp. 3–4.
16. Hutton 2001, pp. 60–61, 122, 123.
17. Winkelman and White 1987.
18. Winkelman 1986; Peoples, Duda, and Marlowe 2016; Putnam 1948, p. 340; B. S. Hewlett et al. 2013; Grzelczyk 2016; Minu-endajú 1946; Pilling 1958, p. 115.
19. See, for example, I. M. Lewis 2003, Winkelman 2002, Alich 2023. Lewis (2003, p. 49) defined a shaman as "a 'master of spirits,' with the implication that this inspired priest incarnates spirits, becoming possessed voluntarily in controlled circumstances." For Winkelman, shamans are charismatic social and religious leaders, mostly found in hunter-gatherer societies, who enter altered states of consciousness and tend to exhibit characteristics like healing, soul flight, animal spirit allies, and animal transformation. Alich wrote that shamanism necessarily involves the use of techniques to "temporarily step into an alternative state of consciousness" but added that "the shamanic view of the world is organized into different yet equal parts: the earth or physical world, the human world, and the stars or cosmic world."
20. Hultkrantz 1993; 1973; Hutton 2001. Hultkrantz (1973, p. 34) defined the shaman as "a social functionary who, with the help of guardian spirits, attains ecstasy in order to create a rapport with the supernatural world on behalf of his group members." Hutton (2001, p. vii) listed four common uses of the term "shamanism," the first of which was "the practice of anybody who contacts a spirit world while in an altered state of consciousness."
21. Evans-Pritchard 1937, p. 178; Desjarlais 1992, p. 235; Rodd 2006; Vitebsky 2017; Eliade 1964.
22. See the discussion in N. S. Price 2001.
23. Hutton 2001, pp. vii, 47.
24. Zieme 2008; Wallis 2003.
25. See, for example, C. F. Klein et al. 2002, Rydving 2011.

CHAPTER 2   THE MIND BEHIND THE MAGIC

1. For more about Sikameinan and the ceremonies for dealing with it, see Singh, Kaptchuk, and Henrich 2021.
2. Riesebrodt 2010.

3. Field 2009.
4. Tiffen 2009; Foley 2009; Nicholson 2009; ABC News 2009.
5. Holmgaard 2019, p. 316.
6. Holmgaard 2019, p. 317.
7. Thucydides 2009, pp. 99–100.
8. Rowland 2014, p. 28; Petrone et al. 2020; Daley 2018.
9. Eames 2021.
10. Bogoras 1909, pp. 206–7; Turnbull 1965, p. 189; Tylor 1920, chapter 8.
11. Murdock 1980.
12. Singh 2021a.
13. Boyer 2008; Bloom 2007.
14. Guthrie 1995; Barrett 2000. Barrett first referred to this cognitive mechanism as a "hyperactive agent detection device," although scholars now more often refer to it as a mechanism that detects agency, not agents.
15. Luhrmann 2012; Macfarlane 2022.
16. Luhrmann 1989; 2000; 2013.
17. Luhrmann 2020, p. 1. The quotation comes from a conversation with Luhrmann.
18. Evans-Pritchard 1956, p. 9.
19. Barton 1946, p. 210.
20. Murphy 1958, p. 21.
21. Spiro 1978, pp. 56–58.
22. Barrett 2012.
23. Dawkins 2019, p. 236.
24. Legare and Gelman 2008; Shweder et al. 1997; Astuti and Harris 2008; Mead 1956, pp. 152–53; Barlev and Shtulman 2021.
25. Kerns 1983, p. 148.
26. Luhrmann 2020.
27. Rödlach 2006, p. 65.
28. Weinman 2019; Hall 2022.
29. "Cristiano Ronaldo's Pre-Match Ritual Revealed" 2022; C. Jones 2020; Hyde 2009.
30. Vyse 2014.
31. Lopez, Matthews, and Baumer 2018; Paine 2020; Robison 2022.
32. Burger and Lynn 2005.
33. Accessed August 17, 2022.
34. Beck and Forstmeier 2007; Foster and Kokko 2009; D. D. P. Johnson et al. 2013.

35. Nesse 2019.
36. Sosis and Handwerker 2011; Lang, Krátký, and Xygalatas 2020; 2022.
37. Pinker 1997, p. 534.
38. Legare and Souza 2012; Hong 2022; Rozin and Nemeroff 2002.

CHAPTER 3   THE XENIZED

1. Singh and Henrich 2020.
2. Narby and Huxley 2001, p. 8.
3. Howard 1974; Onwuejeogwu 1969, p. 286; Reichel-Dolmatoff 1978.
4. K. Harper 1997; Pryde 1972, p. 13.
5. Pryde 1972, p. 13; K. Harper 1997; Anderson 1997.
6. Pryde 1972, pp. 112–13.
7. Pryde 1972, p. 113.
8. Wilbert 1963, p. 222; Dobrizhoffer 1822, pp. 77–78.
9. Albert and Kopenawa 2013, p. 39.
10. Stépanoff 2015. The Wikipedia page "Shamanism" was accessed on November 30, 2023.
11. McCall 2000, pp. 27–28.
12. Spencer and Gillen 1904, pp. 480–81.
13. Kendall 2016, p. 51; 1991.
14. Singh, Wrangham, and Glowacki 2017.
15. Harner 1973b, p. 118.
16. Jakobsen 2020, p. 33; Vitebsky 2017, p. 76.
17. Chagnon 1967, p. 42; Lessa 1950, p. 100.
18. Singh 2018.
19. Basso 1967, p. 78.
20. "Rare Mimeographed 1933 Booklet Sells for $47,800!" 2006.
21. Siegel and Shuster 1933.
22. Siegel and Shuster 1933.
23. Siegel and Shuster 1933.
24. Ricca 2013, p. 101; Siegel and Shuster 1938, p. 1.
25. For more on origin stories, see Romagnoli and Pagnucci 2013, pp. 109–11; Hatfield, Heer, and Worcester 2013.
26. Wellman 1991; Gelman 2004.
27. Singh 2018, p. 12; McCall 2000, p. 28.
28. Gillin 1932.

29. Blacker 1975, pp. 66, 81.
30. Singh and Henrich 2020.
31. I. M. Lewis 2003; Bourguignon 1973; Wood and Stockly 2018; Nelson 2016.
32. Adriani and Kruijt 1968, p. 361; 1969, pp. 113–15.
33. Andaya 2018.
34. Boellstorff 2005, pp. 39–40.

CHAPTER 4   DRAMAS OF OTHERNESS

1. Ott 2001; McBride 2000; Torres et al. 1991; Miller et al. 2019.
2. Torres and Repke 2006.
3. Rouget 1985, pp. 3–12; Blacker 1975, pp. 22–23.
4. Harner 1982.
5. Winkelman 2010; 2002. Winkelman, in turn, distinguishes among three "primary clusters" within the integrative state of consciousness: shamanic soul flight, meditative absorption, and mediumistic possession.
6. For example, Alich 2023; P. A. Wright 1989; Frecska, Hoppál, and Luna 2016.
7. Vaitl et al. 2005.
8. Sobiecki 2008.
9. "PsychonautWiki" 2023.
10. "Subjective Effect Index" 2023.
11. For examples of shamanic use of tobacco, ayahuasca, and datura, see Wilbert 1987, Harner 1968, Powers 1877, p. 380.
12. McMullen 2017, p. 5.
13. Blacker 1975, p. 262.
14. Blacker 1975, p. 263.
15. Blacker 1975, p. 277.
16. D. Harper 2023; *Oxford English Dictionary* 2023.
17. Winkelman 2002; Harner 2005.
18. Greaves, n.d., p. 13.
19. Greaves, n.d.
20. Albert and Kopenawa 2013, p. 43.
21. Albert and Kopenawa 2013, p. 89.
22. Gmelin 2001, p. 28.
23. Boas 1930, p. 1.
24. Lévi-Strauss 1963; Whitehead 2000.

25. Whitehead 2000, p. 161.
26. Lebra 1982, p. 305; Hallowell 1942, p. 80; Linton 1933, p. 200; Olson 1936, p. 155; Albert and Kopenawa 2013, p. 110.
27. Buckner 2022.
28. Evans-Pritchard 1937, p. 236.
29. Singh, Kaptchuk, and Henrich 2021; Gusinde 1971, p. 1069.

CHAPTER 5   BEHOLD THE BIRDHEAD

1. Heying and Weinstein 2021, p. 17.
2. Miton, Claidière, and Mercier 2015; Edgerton 1992.
3. Singh 2022.
4. Kovoor 1980, p. 5.
5. Kovoor 1976, chapter 1; 1980, pp. 176–77.
6. Kovoor 1980, pp. 177–78.
7. Kovoor 1976, preface.
8. *Scientific American* 1922, p. 389; Christopher 1975, pp. 188–89.
9. JREF Staff 2012; L. King 2001b; 2001a; M. Fox 2020.
10. "List of Prizes for Evidence of the Paranormal" 2022. Accessed on November 2, 2022.
11. Frank 1961.
12. Frank 1961.
13. Wampold 2015, although see Cuijpers, Reijnders, and Huibers 2019.
14. Specter 2011.
15. Kaptchuk, Hemond, and Miller 2020, p. 2.
16. Kaptchuk et al. 2008.
17. Kaptchuk et al. 2008.
18. Kaptchuk et al. 2009.
19. Kaptchuk et al. 2009.
20. Kaptchuk et al. 2010.
21. Jha 2010.
22. Wernsdorff et al. 2021; Faraone 2008, p. 710.
23. Kaptchuk, Hemond, and Miller 2020.
24. Singh 2021b.
25. Katz 1982b; Wiessner and Larson 1979.
26. Katz 1982a, p. 349.
27. Katz 1982a, p. 349.
28. Kaplan, Hooper, and Gurven 2009; Rueger et al. 2016; Gariépy,

Honkaniemi, and Quesnel-Vallée 2016; Holt-Lunstad, Smith, and Layton 2010.

29. McClenon 2001; 1997.
30. Reviewed in Singh 2018.
31. See, for example, Harner 1968.
32. Murphy 1958, p. 46; Burkhalter 2001, p. 42.

CHAPTER 6 THE FIRST RELIGION

1. R. Bégouën 2014; Pastoors et al. 2021. The date of 17,000 years ago is a calibrated date. Radiocarbon dating gives an uncalibrated date of approximately 13,870 BP (before present), which corresponds to 17,200 to 16,500 calibrated years before present (calBP).
2. R. Bégouën 2014.
3. R. Bégouën 2014, p. 18.
4. R. Bégouën 2014, pp. 18–19.
5. R. Bégouën 2014, p. 19.
6. Hutton 2003, pp. 33–34; La Barre 1970, p. 161; R. Bégouën 2014, p. 21.
7. Lewis-Williams and Dowson 1988; Little et al. 2016; Grosman, Munro, and Belfer-Cohen 2008; Jaubert et al. 2016.
8. Harari 2015, p. 62.
9. Bocherens 2015; Schwartz-Narbonne et al. 2019.
10. Langlais et al. 2016; El Zaatari and Hublin 2014; Posth et al. 2023.
11. J. Jones 2021; for information about the number of sites, see, for example, Bourdier 2010.
12. Clottes and Lewis-Williams 1998.
13. Campbell 1969, p. 301.
14. Lewis-Williams and Dowson 1990; Motta, Veth, and Balanggarra Aboriginal Corporation 2021; Taçon and Chippindale 2001; Lewis-Williams and Dowson 1988; Aubert et al. 2019.
15. Lewis-Williams and Dowson 1988; Lewis-Williams 2016, p. 126.
16. Halverson 1988, p. 225.
17. Helvenston and Bahn 2003; Lewis-Williams and Dowson 1988, p. 204; Vaitl et al. 2005. PsychonautWiki accessed on December 6, 2023.
18. Singh, Kaptchuk, and Henrich 2021, p. 66; unpublished data from the Anansi project.
19. Clottes and Lewis-Williams 1998, p. 95; Bahn 2010, p. 94.

20. Kellogg 1969.
21. Boas 1928.
22. Grosman, Munro, and Belfer-Cohen 2008, p. 17665.
23. Porr and Alt 2006.
24. The ubiquity of shamanism, including among hunter-gatherers, is reviewed in Singh 2018.
25. Hutton 2007, p. 123; Eliade 1964, pp. 244, 502. Eliade (1964, p. 504) acknowledged that the "ecstatic experience" is "fundamental in the human condition, and hence known to the whole of archaic humanity," yet maintained that "shamanism crystallized as an autonomous and specific complex" in "Central and North Asia."
26. Stépanoff 2021.
27. Bickerton 2008, pp. 115–34.
28. See also R. Fox 1971.
29. Henrich 2004.
30. Peoples, Duda, and Marlowe 2016; Holmberg 1969, pp. 17, 103, 223; Sharp 1969, p. xii; Mann 2005, see note on p. 363; Stearman 1984, p. 640; Walker et al. 2012.
31. Dass 1987, pp. 9–10.
32. Blevins 2007; Radcliffe-Brown 1922, p. 18; Thangaraj et al. 2003.
33. Radcliffe-Brown 1922, pp. 137–40.
34. Radcliffe-Brown 1922, pp. 48, 176–79.
35. Pilling 1958, pp. 38–39; Marlowe 2010, p. 19; Holmberg 1969, p. 12.
36. Cooper 1989; Dass 1987, pp. 8–9.
37. Radcliffe-Brown 1922, p. 176.
38. Greenhill et al. 2010; Morin 2016, p. 5.
39. Skinner 1948.
40. R. G. Klein 1992; Conard 2010; McBrearty and Brooks 2000; Sykes 2020; Fuentes et al. 2023.
41. Jaubert et al. 2016; Fuentes et al. 2023; Martinón-Torres et al. 2023.
42. Hutton 2003, pp. 33–34.
43. Hutton 2003, pp. 29, 34–35.

CHAPTER 7   THE REBEL AND THE REDEEMER

1. Behrend 1999, pp. 67–68.
2. Behrend 1999, cover.

3. Behrend 1999, pp. 131–32.
4. Behrend 1999, pp. 132–34; Allen 1991, p. 376.
5. Behrend 1999, pp. 1, 3, 43–44, 46–47.
6. Behrend 1999, p. 10; Allen 1991, p. 373.
7. Behrend 1999, pp. 3, 62.
8. Worsley 1968; J. R. Lewis 1988; Laugrand and Oosten 2010, pp. 48–57; Blacker 1975, pp. 127–39.
9. Guinn 2017.
10. Behrend 1999, pp. 57, 132.
11. Behrend 1999, pp. 23–26.
12. Nissinen 2017, pp. 173–76.
13. Nissinen 2017, pp. 15, 25–26.
14. Nissinen 2017, pp. 191–92, 195–200.
15. Nissinen 2017, pp. 27–28.
16. The original Hebrew and Greek (Swete's Septuagint) versions of Genesis 15:12 are available on Bible Hub (https://biblehub.com; last accessed on December 6, 2023).
17. Nissinen 2017, p. 189.
18. Philo 1937, p. 137.
19. Davies 1995, p. 60. The original Greek versions of Mark 11:32, Matthew 21:26, and Luke 20:6 are available on Bible Hub (last accessed on December 6, 2023).
20. See Nissinen 2020. Nissinen has argued for similarities between shamanism and classical Near Eastern prophecy, yet based on supposed features of shamanism such as soul journeying and belonging to "traditional small-scale societies," he has concluded that they are distinct. This book maintains that these are not valid definitive criteria of shamanism—that the emphasis on soul journeying, which began with Eliade, reflects a historical misrepresentation of Siberian practices, while the impulse to restrict shamanism to "traditional small-scale societies" reflects, in part, long-standing primitivist biases.
21. Shantz 2009, p. 27.
22. Shantz 2009, p. 20.
23. Shantz 2009; May 1956.
24. Origen 1907, p. 615.
25. For more on how scholars reconstruct the life of Jesus, see Ehrman 1999.
26. Meier is quoted in Davies 1995, p. 44.
27. Davies 1995; Craffert 2008.

28. A digitized version of Strong's Concordance is available on Bible Hub (https://biblehub.com; last accessed on December 7, 2023). The Greek word *existémi* was assigned number 1839. See also Strong 1890.
29. The Greek versions of Luke 4:18 and Acts 19:6 both refer to the Spirit (*Pneuma*) upon (*ep'*) someone.
30. Pick 1909, p. 182; Ehrman 1999, pp. 21–22; Davies 1995, pp. 7–8.
31. Behrend 1999, pp. 89–90.
32. Behrend 1999, p. 90.
33. Behrend 1999, pp. 82, 89–90.
34. Behrend 1999, pp. 90, 93; Associated Press 2007.
35. Behrend 1999, pp. 96–97.
36. Behrend 1999, p. 97.
37. Behrend 1999, pp. 174–78.
38. Behrend 1999, pp. 179–88; Arieff, Blanchard, and Husted 2015; USAID 2006.

CHAPTER 8 OUROBOROS

1. Howard-Browne 2014.
2. Hayes 2012.
3. R. Wright 2009, pp. 29, 31–32, 45.
4. Hultkrantz 1991, p. 18; Dunbar 2022.
5. Assmann 2019.
6. Hyatt 2002, pp. 24–26; Potts 2009, pp. 61–63.
7. Potts 2009, pp. 66–73; Hyatt 2002, pp. 26–30; Garrett 1987, pp. 8–9.
8. Hyatt 2002, pp. 27–28; Garrett 1987, p. 9.
9. Knox 1950, p. 1.
10. Thomas 1988; Eliade 1964, p. 373.
11. Thomas 1988.
12. Bell 2005, p. 11.
13. Brodie 1995, pp. 427–35.
14. Brodie 1995, pp. 37–49.
15. Southerton 2004.
16. Vogel and Dunn 1993, p. 2.
17. Vogel and Dunn 1993, p. 8.
18. Vogel and Dunn 1993, p. 24; "Gift of Tongues," n.d.
19. Trevett 2017.

20. Meeks 2011, pp. 213–14.
21. Meeks 2011, pp. 250–52.
22. Meeks 2011, pp. 232, 255–59.
23. Wariboko and Oliverio 2020; A. H. Anderson 2013, p. 1.
24. Madigan 2021, pp. 16, 36, 105.
25. Madigan 2021, pp. 36, 89, 104.
26. Madigan 2021, pp. 9, 197, 203, 211.
27. Cohn 1976; Manning 2009; Newell 2008.
28. Zanini 2015.
29. Zanini 2015.
30. McConnell 2000; Dickson 1995.
31. Grim 2009; Majumdar and Crawford 2024.
32. Flaherty 1992, p. 123.

CHAPTER 9   MEET THE SHAMANISTAS

1. Lipka and Gecewicz 2017; Pew Research Center 2023; 2018.
2. Alich 2023; Ramsdale 2020; Barnes, Bloom, and Nahin 2008; Pew Research Center 2014, p. 115.
3. Wallis 2003.
4. Aldred 2000, p. 333.
5. Townsend 2004, pp. 5–6; Scuro and Rodd 2015.
6. Stuckard 2005, p. 744; Harner 1982, p. 2.
7. Harner 2005, p. 161.
8. See Harner 1982, pp. 1–22 for his accounts of his experiences with ayahuasca and datura.
9. Harner 2005, p. 161.
10. Harner 2005, p. 165.
11. Harner 2005, p. 165; 1973a, p. xii.
12. Harner 1968.
13. Harner 1982; 2005.
14. Harner 1982, pp. 57–58.
15. Harner 1982, p. 27.
16. Rodd 2006, p. 49.
17. Harner 1982, p. 20.
18. Stuckard 2005.
19. Stuckard 2005; Foundation for Shamanic Studies 2001; 2023.
20. Wallis 2003, p. 46.
21. Wallis 2003, p. 51.

22. Harner 1982; Siikala 1992; Anisimov 1963.
23. Harner 1973b. According to the electronic Human Relations Area Files, forty-seven paragraphs in *The Jívaro* are about "Shamans and Psychotherapists," OCM code 756 (https://ehrafworldcultures .yale.edu; last accessed on December 8, 2023).
24. Harner 1973b, pp. 119–22, 124, 154–56, 202.
25. Priklonski and Krauss 1888, p. 171.
26. For more information, see Shamandome 2011.
27. Braun 2010.

CHAPTER 10   HEDGE WIZARDS

1. Bakker 1999; Schefold 1998.
2. Sheppard and Schefold 1974.
3. Bakker 1999; for more, see Schefold 1988, Hammons 2010.
4. Weber 1946.
5. Weber 1946.
6. Pew Research Center 2023; Hamplová and Nešpor 2009.
7. Malkiel 1995; 2005.
8. M. King 2013.
9. Fernando 2010; "Most Successful Chimpanzee on Wall Street" 2023.
10. Dunn 2023, p. 245; Malkiel 2005, pp. 1–2; see also Malkiel 2003.
11. "Bloomberg Billionaires Index" 2023 (retrieved December 13, 2023); E. Price 2017.
12. Martin 2019; Holm 2016.
13. Millsap 2020, introduction.
14. R. Wright 2009; S. G. B. Johnson 2018.
15. Millsap 2020, chapter 6.
16. O'Donnell 2022.
17. Millsap 2020, chapter 2.
18. S. G. B. Johnson 2018; S. A. Hewlett and Luce 2006.
19. Basu 2018; Jackson 2023; Colvin 2015.
20. Isaacson 2011, pp. 43, 486, 548; Darby 2019; Solon 2017; Bilton 2021.
21. Auletta 2014.
22. Auletta 2014; Weingus 2019; Shiffer 2019; Stieg 2019.
23. Bilton 2021.
24. Khurana 2002a, p. 68; 2002b, p. 62.
25. Khurana 2002a, pp. 69, 152.

26. Khurana 2002a, pp. 51–80.
27. Khurana 2002a, p. 73.
28. Khurana 2002a, p. 13.
29. Davydova et al. 2022.
30. There is a large literature on impression management and identity. For examples, see Milinski 2016, Goffman 1959, Engelmann and Rapp 2018.
31. M. Lewis 2023; Wilser 2022.
32. Yaffe-Bellany 2022; Bekiempis 2023.
33. Friedman 2022.
34. Sheppard and Schefold 1974.

CHAPTER 11   ARCHAIC REVIVAL

1. "Iowaska Information" 2023 (last accessed on December 13, 2023).
2. Brabec de Mori 2011.
3. Brabec de Mori 2011.
4. Brabec de Mori 2011; Gow 1994.
5. Joiner 2020; Illing 2019; Pollan 2018, p. 334.
6. Letcher 2006, pp. 72–80.
7. Letcher 2006, pp. 81–83; R. G. Wasson 1957.
8. R. G. Wasson 1957, p. 102; V. P. Wasson and Wasson 1957, p. 289.
9. R. G. Wasson 1957; V. P. Wasson 1957; Mangini 2021.
10. Letcher 2006, pp. 96–98.
11. R. G. Wasson 1957, pp. 113–14.
12. La Barre 1979; 1972; Muraresku 2020; McKenna 1992.
13. A link to Martin Fortier's writings is available in the article that inspired this chapter; see Singh 2020.
14. Letcher 2006; 2011.
15. See, for example, Samorini 2019, Winkelman 2019.
16. Hernandez-Santiago et al. 2017.
17. Letcher 2006, pp. 76–77; for examples, see de Borhegyi 1961, 1963, Lowy 1971.
18. Winkelman 2019; Letcher 2006, p. 33.
19. Winkelman 2019, p. 57; "Chucuito Temple of Fertility" 2012; Kummer 2006.
20. McKenna 1992.
21. Letcher 2006, pp. 37–38.
22. Winkelman 2019, p. 43.
23. Human Relations Area Files, n.d.; Ember 1997.

24. Editors of Goop and Grob 2019.
25. Chagnon and Asch 1973.
26. Chagnon and Asch 1973.
27. Albert and Kopenawa 2013; Brabec de Mori 2021; Harner 1973a; Rodd 2006.
28. Dobkin de Rios and Rumrrill 2008, p. 7.
29. Dobkin de Rios and Rumrrill 2008.
30. Dobkin de Rios and Rumrrill 2008, pp. 45, 48.
31. Dobkin de Rios and Rumrrill 2008, p. 12.
32. Bourzat and Hunter 2019, pp. 15–17.
33. Bourzat and Hunter 2019.
34. Ovies and Bautista 2021, pp. 321–22.
35. Gearin 2022, p. 502.

CONCLUSION

1. Singh and Mehr 2023; Mehr et al. 2018; 2019.
2. Sperber 1996; Claidière, Scott-Phillips, and Sperber 2014.
3. Boas 1896, pp. 901–2.
4. Boas 1896, p. 908.
5. Borofsky 2019.
6. Hogan 2003, p. 8; Mehr et al. 2019, supplementary materials, p. 9.
7. Appiah 2006, pp. 140–41.
8. Appiah 1992, p. 58.
9. Boas 1896, p. 901.

Bibliography

ABC News. 2009, October 3. "Samoa Tsunami Death Toll Rises."

Adriani, Nicolaus, and Albertus Christiaan Kruijt. 1968. *The Bare'e-Speaking Toradja of Central Celebes (the East Toradja)*, vol. 1. Human Relations Area Files.

———. 1969. *The Bare'e-Speaking Toradja of Central Celebes (the East Toradja)*, vol. 2. Human Relations Area Files.

Albert, Bruce, and Davi Kopenawa. 2013. *The Falling Sky: Words of a Yanomami Shaman.* Harvard University Press.

Aldred, Lisa. 2000. "Plastic Shamans and Astroturf Sun Dances: New Age Commercialization of Native American Spirituality." *American Indian Quarterly* 24 (3): 329–52.

Alich, Alexander. 2023, January 3. "Shamanism: What You Need to Know About the Fastest-Growing 'Religion' in England and Wales." The Conversation.

Allen, Tim. 1991. "Understanding Alice: Uganda's Holy Spirit Movement in Context." *Africa* 61 (3): 370–99.

Andaya, Leonard Y. 2018. "The Bissu: Study of a Third Gender in Indonesia." In *Gender in Focus: Identities, Codes, Stereotypes and Politics*, ed. Andreea Zamfira, Christian de Montlibert, and Daniela Radu. Verlag Barbara Budrich.

Anderson, Allan Heaton. 2013. *To the Ends of the Earth: Pentecostalism and the Transformation of World Christianity.* Oxford University Press.

Anderson, Sarah. 1997, December 30. "Obituary: Duncan Pryde." *The Independent.*

Anisimov, Arkadiy F. 1963. "The Shaman's Tent of the Evenks and the Origin of the Shamanistic Rite." In *Studies in Siberian Shamanism*. ed. Henry N. Michael. University of Toronto Press.

Appiah, Kwame Anthony. 1992. *In My Father's House: Africa in the Philosophy of Culture*. Oxford University Press.

———. 2006. *Cosmopolitanism: Ethics in a World of Strangers*. W. W. Norton & Company.

Arieff, Alexis, Lauren Ploch Blanchard, and Tomas F. Husted. 2015. "The Lord's Resistance Army: The U.S. Response." Congressional Research Service.

Assmann, Jan. 2019. "Ouroboros: The Ancient Egyptian Myth of the Journey of the Sun." *Aegyptiaca* 4: 19–32.

Associated Press. 2007, January 19. "Alice Lakwena, Ugandan Rebel, Dies." *The New York Times*.

Astuti, Rita, and Paul L. Harris. 2008. "Understanding Mortality and the Life of the Ancestors in Rural Madagascar." *Cognitive Science* 32 (4): 713–40.

Aubert, Maxime, Rustan Lebe, Adhi Agus Oktaviana, et al. 2019. "Earliest Hunting Scene in Prehistoric Art." *Nature* 576 (7787): 442–45.

Auletta, Ken. 2014, December 8. "Blood, Simpler." *The New Yorker*.

Bahn, Paul G. 2010. *Prehistoric Rock Art: Polemics and Progress*. Cambridge University Press.

Bakker, Laurens. 1999. "Tiele! Turis! The Social and Ethnic Impact of Tourism in Siberut (Mentawai)." MA thesis. Leiden University.

Balikci, Asen. 1963. "Shamanistic Behavior Among the Netsilik Eskimos." *Southwestern Journal of Anthropology* 19 (4): 380–96.

Barlev, Michael, and Andrew Shtulman. 2021. "Minds, Bodies, Spirits, and Gods: Does Widespread Belief in Disembodied Beings Imply That We Are Inherent Dualists?" *Psychological Review* 128 (6): 1007–21.

Barnes, Patricia M., Barbara Bloom, and Richard L. Nahin. 2008. "Complementary and Alternative Medicine Use Among Adults and Children: United States, 2007." *National Health Statistics Reports*, vol. 12.

Barrett, Justin L. 2000. "Exploring the Natural Foundations of Religion." *Trends in Cognitive Sciences* 4 (1): 29–34.

———. 2012. *Born Believers: The Science of Children's Religious Belief*. Atria Books.

Barton, Roy Franklin. 1946. *The Religion of the Ifugao*. American Anthropological Association.

Basso, Keith H. 1967. "Heavy with Hatred: An Ethnographic Study of Western Apache Witchcraft." PhD dissertation. Stanford University.

Basu, Tanya. 2018, August 11. "CEOs like PepsiCo's Indra Nooyi Brag They Get 4 Hours of Sleep. That's Toxic." *The Daily Beast*.

Beck, Jan, and Wolfgang Forstmeier. 2007. "Superstition and Belief as Inevitable By-Products of an Adaptive Learning Strategy." *Human Nature* 18 (1): 35–46.

Bégouën, Henri. 1920. "Un Dessin Relevé dans la Caverne des Trois-Frères, à Montesquieu-Avantès (Ariège)." *Comptes Rendus des Séances de l'Académie des Inscriptions et Belles-Lettres* 64 (4): 303–10.

Bégouën, Robert. 2014. "Historique." In *La Caverne des Trois-Frères: Anthologie d'un Exceptionnel Sactuaire Préhistorique*, ed. Robert Bégouën, Jean Clottes, Valérie Feruglio, and Andreas Pastoors. Association Louis Bégouën, 14–45.

Behrend, Heike. 1999. *Alice Lakwena & the Holy Spirits: War in Northern Uganda 1986–97*. Ohio University Press.

Bekiempis, Victoria. 2023, October 13. "Caroline Ellison's Testimony Against Sam Bankman-Fried: Five Key Takeaways." *The Guardian*.

Bell, Kirsten. 2005. "The Trouble with Charisma: Religious Ecstasy in Ch'ŏndogyo." *Asian Studies Review* 29: 3–18.

Bickerton, Derek. 2008. *Bastard Tongues: A Trailblazing Linguist Finds Clues to Our Common Humanity in the World's Lowliest Languages*. Farrar, Straus and Giroux.

Bilton, Nick. 2021, April. "'They Present a Version of Themselves That Isn't Real': Inside the Dark, Biohacked Heart of Silicon Valley." *Vanity Fair*.

Blacker, Carmen. 1975. *The Catalpa Bow: A Study of Shamanistic Practices in Japan*. George Allen & Unwin Ltd.

Blevins, Juliette. 2007. "A Long Lost Sister of Proto-Austronesian? Proto-Ongan, Mother of Jarawa and Onge of the Andaman Islands." *Oceanic Linguistics* 46 (1): 154–98.

Bloom, Paul. 2007. "Religion Is Natural." *Developmental Science* 10 (1): 147–51.

"Bloomberg Billionaires Index." 2023. Bloomberg.

Boas, Franz. 1896. "The Limitations of the Comparative Method of Anthropology." *Science* 4 (103): 901–8.

———. 1928. *Primitive Art*. Harvard University Press.

———. 1930. *The Religion of the Kwakiutl Indians*. Part 2: *Translations*. Columbia University Press.

Bocherens, Hervé. 2015. "Isotopic Tracking of Large Carnivore Palaeoecology in the Mammoth Steppe." *Quaternary Science Reviews* 117: 42–71.

Boellstorff, Tom. 2005. *The Gay Archipelago: Sexuality and Nation in Indonesia*. Princeton University Press.

Bogoras, Waldemar. 1909. *The Chukchee*. Part 1: *Material Culture*. Leiden and New York: E. J. Brill Ltd. and G. E. Stechert.

Borhegyi, Stephan de. 1961. "Miniature Mushroom Stones from Guatemala." *American Antiquity* 26 (4): 498–504.

———. 1963. "Pre-Columbian Pottery Mushrooms from Mesoamerica." *American Antiquity* 28 (3): 328–38.

Borofsky, Robert. 2019, September 10. "Where Have the Comparisons Gone? (Should We Blame the Grinch?)." *Fieldsites*.

Bourdier, Camille. 2010. "Paléogéographie Symbolique du Magdalénien Moyen: Apport de l'Étude des Productions Graphiques Pariétales des Abris Occupés et Sculptés de l'Ouest Français (Roc-Aux-Sorciers, Chaire-à-Calvin, Reverdit, Cap-Blanc)." Doctoral thesis. Université Bordeaux.

Bourguignon, Erika. 1973. *Religion, Altered States of Consciousness, and Social Change*. The Ohio State University Press.

Bourzat, Françoise, and Kristina Hunter. 2019. *Consciousness Medicine: Indigenous Wisdom, Entheogens, and Expanded States of Consciousness for Healing and Growth*. North Atlantic Books.

Boyer, Pascal. 2008. "Religion: Bound to Believe?" *Nature* 455 (7216): 1038–39.

Brabec de Mori, Bernd. 2011. "Tracing Halluncinations: Contributing to a Critical Ethnohistory of Ayahuasca Usage in the Peruvian Amazon." In *The Internationalization of Ayahuasca*, ed. Beatriz Caiuby Labate and Henrik Jungaberle. Lit Verlag, 23–48.

———. 2021. "The Power of Social Attribution: Perspectives on the Healing Efficacy of Ayahuasca." *Frontiers in Psychology* 12: 748131.

Braun, Shelly Beth. 2010. "Neo-Shamanism as a Healing System: Enchanted Healing in a Modern World." PhD dissertation. The University of Utah.

Breuil, Henri. 1930. "Un Dessin de la Grotte des Trois Frères (Montesquieu-Avantès) Ariège." *Comptes Rendus des Séances de l'Académie des Inscriptions et Belles-Lettres* 74 (3): 261–64.

Brodie, Fawn M. 1995. *No Man Knows My History*. Vintage Books.

Buckner, William. 2022. "A Deceptive Curing Practice in Hunter-Gatherer Societies." *Humans* 2 (3): 95–103.

Burger, Jerry M., and Amy L. Lynn. 2005. "Superstitious Behavior Among American and Japanese Professional Baseball Players." *Basic and Applied Social Psychology* 27 (1): 71–76.

Burkhalter, Steve Brian. 2001. *Amazon Gold Rush: Markets and the Mundurucu Indians*. University Microfilms International.

Campbell, Joseph. 1969. *The Masks of God: Primitive Mythology*. The Viking Press.

Chagnon, Napoleon A. 1967. "Yanomamö Warfare, Social Organization and Marriage Alliances." PhD dissertation. University of Michigan.

Chagnon, Napoleon A., and Timothy Asch. 1973. *Magical Death*. United States: Documentary Education Resources.

Christopher, Milbourne. 1975. *Mediums, Mystics and the Occult*. Thomas Y. Crowell Company.

"Chucuito Temple of Fertility." 2012. Atlas Obscura. https://www.atlas obscura.com/places/chucuito.

Claidière, Nicolas, Thomas C. Scott-Phillips, and Dan Sperber. 2014. "How Darwinian Is Cultural Evolution?" *Philosophical Transactions of the Royal Society B* 369: 20130368.

Clottes, Jean, and James David Lewis-Williams. 1998. *The Shamans of Prehistory: Trance and Magic in the Painted Caves*. Harry N. Abrams, Inc.

Cohn, Norman. 1976. *Europe's Inner Demons*. Frogmore: Paladin.

Colvin, Geoff. 2015, November 18. "Do Successful CEOs Sleep Less Than Everyone Else?" *Fortune*.

Conard, Nicholas J. 2010. "Cultural Modernity: Consensus or Conundrum?" *Proceedings of the National Academy of Sciences of the United States of America* 107 (17): 7621–22.

Cooper, Zarine. 1989. "Analysis of the Nature of Contacts with the Andaman Islands During the Last Two Millennia." *South Asian Studies* 5 (1): 134–47.

Craffert, Pieter F. 2008. *The Life of a Galilean Shaman: Jesus of Nazareth in Anthropological-Historical Perspective*. Cascade Books.

"Cristiano Ronaldo's Pre-Match Ritual Revealed." 2022, October 22. MARCA.

Cuijpers, Pim, Mirjam Reijnders, and Marcus J. H. Huibers. 2019. "The Role of Common Factors in Psychotherapy Outcomes." *Annual Review of Clinical Psychology* 15: 207–31.

Daley, Jason. 2018, October 10. "Mount Vesuvius Boiled Its Victims' Blood and Caused Their Skulls to Explode." *Smithsonian.*

Darby, Luke. 2019, April 19. "Jack Dorsey Only Eats One Meal a Day." *GQ.*

Dass, F. A. M. 1987. *The Andaman Islands.* Bangalore: The Good Shepherd Convent Press.

Davies, Stevan. 1995. *Jesus the Healer: Possession, Trance, and the Origins of Christianity.* Continuum.

Davydova, Daria, Rüdiger Fahlenbrach, Leandro Sanz, and René M. Stulz. 2022, October. "The Unicorn Puzzle." *NBER Working Paper Series.*

Dawkins, Richard. 2019. *Outgrowing God: A Beginner's Guide.* Random House.

Desjarlais, Robert R. 1992. *Body and Emotion: The Aesthetics of Illness and Healing in the Nepal Himalayas.* University of Pennsylvania Press.

Dickson, Brice. 1995. "The United Nations and Freedom of Religion." *The International and Comparative Law Quarterly* 44 (2): 327–57.

Dobkin de Rios, Marlene, and Roger Rumrrill. 2008. *A Hallucinogenic Tea, Laced with Controversy: Ayahuasca in the Amazon and the United States.* Praeger.

Dobrizhoffer, Martin. 1822. *An Account of the Abipones, an Equestrian People of Paraguay*, vol. 2. John Murray.

Dunbar, Robin. 2022. *How Religion Evolved: And Why It Endures.* Oxford University Press.

Dunn, James. 2023. *Share Investing for Dummies.* John Wiley & Sons Australia.

Eames, Christopher. 2021, August 23. "Pompeii: Echoes of Sodom and Gomorrah." Armstrong Institute of Biblical Archaeology.

Edgerton, Robert. 1992. *Sick Societies: Challenging the Myth of Primitive Harmony.* Free Press.

Editors of Goop and Charles Grob. 2019, January 10. "The Science and Shamanism of Psychedelics." Goop.

Ehrman, Bart D. 1999. *Jesus: Apocalyptic Prophet of the New Millennium.* Oxford University Press.

El Zaatari, Sireen, and Jean Jacques Hublin. 2014. "Diet of Upper Paleolithic Modern Humans: Evidence from Microwear Texture Analysis." *American Journal of Physical Anthropology* 153 (4): 570–81.

Eliade, Mircea. 1964. *Shamanism: Archaic Techniques of Ecstasy.* Princeton University Press.

———. 1981. *Autobiography*. Vol. 1: *1907–1937, Journey East, Journey West*. Harper & Row.

———. 1988. *Autobiography*. Vol. 2: *1937–1960, Exile's Odyssey*. The University of Chicago Press.

Ember, Melvin. 1997. "Evolution of the Human Relations Area Files." *Cross-Cultural Research* 31 (1): 3–15.

Engelmann, Jan M., and Diotima J. Rapp. 2018. "The Influence of Reputational Concerns on Children's Prosociality." *Current Opinion in Psychology* 20: 92–95.

Evans-Pritchard, E. E. 1937. *Witchcraft, Oracles, and Magic Among the Azande*. Clarendon Press.

———. 1956. *Nuer Religion*. Clarendon Press.

Faraone, Stephen V. 2008. "Interpreting Estimates of Treatment Effects: Implications for Managed Care." *Pharmacy and Therapeutics* 33 (12): 700–703, 710–11.

Fernando, Vincent. 2010, January 14. "Russian Fund Managers Rush to Control the Damage as Circus Chimp Kicks Their Collective Asses." *Business Insider*.

Field, Michael. 2009, December 4. "Pacific Tsunami Four Storeys High." *Stuff*.

Flaherty, Gloria. 1992. *Shamanism and the Eighteenth Century*. Princeton University Press.

Foley, Meraiah. 2009, September 30. "Scores Are Killed as Tsunami Hits Samoa Islands." *The New York Times*.

Foster, Kevin R., and Hanna Kokko. 2009. "The Evolution of Superstitious and Superstition-like Behaviour." *Proceedings. Biological Sciences / The Royal Society* 276 (1654): 31–37.

Foundation for Shamanic Studies. 2001. "Shamanism: Foundation for Shamanic Studies."

———. 2023. "Core Shamanism Workshops, Training, and Courses." https://shamanism.org/workshops/index.php.

Fox, Margalit. 2020, October 30. "James Randi, Magician Who Debunked Paranormal Claims, Dies at 92." *The New York Times*.

Fox, Robin. 1971. "The Cultural Animal." In *Man and Beast: Comparative Social Behavior*, ed. J. F. Eisenberg and Wilton S. Dillon. Smithsonian Institution Press, 273–96.

Frank, Jerome D. 1961. *Persuasion and Healing: A Comparative Study of Psychotherapy*. The Johns Hopkins University Press.

Frecska, Ede, Mihály Hoppál, and Luis E. Luna. 2016. "Nonlocality and the Shamanic State of Consciousness." *NeuroQuantology* 14 (2): 155–65.

Friedman, Vanessa. 2022, December 13. "Hey Silicon Valley, Maybe It's Time to Dress Up, Not Down." *The New York Times.*

Fuentes, Agustin, Marc Kissel, Penny Spikins, et al. 2023. "Burials and Engravings in a Small-Brained Hominin, *Homo naledi,* from the Late Pleistocene: Contexts and Evolutionary Implications." *BioRxiv.* 2023.06.01.543135.

Gariépy, Geneviève, Helena Honkaniemi, and Amélie Quesnel-Vallée. 2016. "Social Support and Protection from Depression: Systematic Review of Current Findings in Western Countries." *British Journal of Psychiatry* 209 (4): 284–93.

Garrett, Clarke. 1987. *Spirit Possession and Popular Religion: From the Camisards to the Shakers.* The Johns Hopkins University Press.

Gearin, Alex K. 2022. "Primitivist Medicine and Capitalist Anxieties in Ayahuasca Tourism Peru." *Journal of the Royal Anthropological Institute* 28 (2): 496–515.

Gelman, Susan A. 2004. "Psychological Essentialism in Children." *Trends in Cognitive Sciences* 8 (9): 404–9.

"Gift of Tongues." n.d. The Church of Jesus Christ of Latter-Day Saints. https://www.churchofjesuschrist.org/study/history/topics/gift-of-tongues?lang=eng. Accessed December 14, 2023.

Gillin, John. 1932. "Crime and Punishment Among the Barama River Carib of British Guiana." *American Anthropologist* 36: 331–44.

Gmelin, Johann Georg. 2001. "Shamans Deserve Perpetual Labor for Their Hocus-Pocus." In *Shamans Through Time: 500 Years on the Path to Knowledge,* ed. Jeremy Narby and Francis Huxley. Penguin Putnam, 27–28.

Goffman, Erving. 1959. *The Presentation of Self in Everyday Life.* Doubleday Anchor Books.

Gow, Peter. 1994. "River People: Shamanism and History in Western Amazonia." In *Shamanism, History, and the State,* ed. Nicholas Thomas and Caroline Humphrey. University of Michigan Press, 90–113.

Greaves, Russell D. n.d. "Description of the Use of *Anadenanthera peregrina* Snuff Among the Savanna Pumé of the Llanos of Venezuela." Unpublished manuscript, 1–24.

Greenhill, S. J., Q. D. Atkinson, A. Meade, and R. D. Gray. 2010. "The Shape and Tempo of Language Evolution." *Proceedings of the Royal Society B: Biological Sciences* 277 (1693): 2443–50.

Grim, Brian J. 2009. "Pentecostalism's Growth in Religiously Restricted Environments." *Society* 46 (6): 484–95.

Grosman, Leore, Natalie D. Munro, and Anna Belfer-Cohen. 2008. "A 12,000-Year-Old Shaman Burial from the Southern Levant (Israel)." *Proceedings of the National Academy of Sciences of the United States of America* 105 (46): 17665–69.

Grzelczyk, Maciej. 2016. "Rituals and Sacred Places of the Sandawe People (Kondoa Region, Tanzania) in the Past and the Present." *Revista Santuários, Cultura, Arte, Romarias, Peregrinações, Paisagens e Pessoas*, 1–6.

Guinn, Jeff. 2017. *The Road to Jonestown: Jim Jones and Peoples Temple.* Simon and Schuster.

Gusinde, Martin. 1971. *The Fireland Indians.* Vol. 1: *The Selk'nam, on the Life and Thought of a Hunting People of the Great Island of Tierra Del Fuego.* Trans. Frieda Schütze. Human Relations Area Files.

Guthrie, Stewart Elliot. 1995. *Faces in the Clouds: A New Theory of Religion.* Oxford University Press.

Hall, Jamie. 2022, December 13. "Why Does Tiger Woods Wear Red on Sunday?" *Bunkered.*

Hallowell, A. Irving. 1942. *The Role of Conjuring in Saulteaux Society.* University of Pennsylvania Press.

Halverson, John. 1988. "Commentary on Lewis-Williams and Dowson." *Current Anthropology* 29 (2): 225–26.

Hammons, Christian S. 2010. "Sakaliou: Reciprocity, Mimesis, and the Cultural Economy of Tradition in Siberut, Mentawai Islands, Indonesia." PhD dissertation. University of Southern California.

Hamplová, Dana, and Zdeněk R. Nešpor. 2009. "Invisible Religion in a 'Non-Believing' Country: The Case of the Czech Republic." *Social Compass* 56 (4): 581–97.

Harari, Yuval Noah. 2015. *Sapiens: A Brief History of Humankind.* Vintage.

Harner, Michael. 1968. "The Sound of Rushing Water." *Natural History* 77 (6): 28–33, 60–61.

———. 1973a. "Introduction." In *Hallucinogens and Shamanism*, ed. Michael Harner. Oxford University Press, xi–xv.

———. 1973b. *The Jívaro: People of the Sacred Waterfalls.* University of California Press.

———. 1982. *The Way of the Shaman: A Guide to Power and Healing.* Bantam Books.

———. 2005. "Tribal Wisdom: The Shamanic Path." In *Higher Wis-*

dom: Eminent Elders Explore the Continuing Impact of Psychedelics, ed. Roger Walsh and Charles S. Grob. State University of New York Press, 159–79.

Harper, Douglas. 2023. "Inspiration." Etymoline: Online Etymology Dictionary.

Harper, Kenn. 1997, November 21. "Duncan Pryde an Appreciation." *Nunatsiaq News*.

Hatfield, Charles, Jeet Heer, and Kent Worcester. 2013. "Historical Considerations." In *The Superhero Reader*, ed. Charles Hatfield, Jeet Heer, and Kent Worcester. Jackson: University Press of Mississippi, 3–6.

Hayes, Phil. 2012, March 30. "Pastor Kerney Thomas—The CURE for Depression!!" YouTube.

Helvenston, Patricia A., and Paul G. Bahn. 2003. "Testing the 'Three Stages of Trance' Model." *Cambridge Archaeological Journal* 13 (2): 213–24.

Henrich, Joseph. 2004. "Demography and Cultural Evolution: How Adaptive Cultural Processes Can Produce Maladaptive Losses— The Tasmania Case." *American Antiquity* 69 (2): 197–214.

Hernandez-Santiago, Faustino, Magdalena Martínez-Reyes, Jesús Pérez-Moreno, and Gerardo Mata. 2017. "Pictographic Representation of the First Dawn and Its Association with Entheogenic Mushrooms in a 16th Century Mixtec Mesoamerican Codex." *Scientia Fungorum* 46: 19–28.

Hewlett, Barry S., Justin S. Mongosso, Roxanna King, and Arthur C. Lehmann. 2013. "Searching for the Truth: The Poison Oracle Among Central African Foragers and Farmers." In *Magic, Witchcraft and Religion: A Reader in the Anthropology of Religion*, ed. Pamela A. Mero. McGraw Hill, 316–22.

Hewlett, Sylvia Ann, and Carolyn Buck Luce. 2006, December. "Extreme Jobs: The Dangerous Allure of the 70-Hour Workweek." *Harvard Business Review*.

Heying, Heather, and Bret Weinstein. 2021. *A Hunter-Gatherer's Guide to the 21st Century: Evolution and the Challenges of Modern Life*. Penguin.

Hogan, Patrick Colm. 2003. *The Mind and Its Stories: Narrative Universals and Human Emotion*. Cambridge University Press.

Holm, Erik. 2016, May 2. "Warren Buffett's Epic Rant Against Wall Street." *The Wall Street Journal*.

Holmberg, Allan R. 1969. *Nomads of the Long Bow: The Siriono of Eastern Brazil.* The Natural History Press.

Holmgaard, Sanne Bech. 2019. "The Role of Religion in Local Perceptions of Disasters: The Case of Post-Tsunami Religious and Social Change in Samoa." *Environmental Hazards* 18 (4): 311–25.

Holt-Lunstad, Julianne, Timothy B. Smith, and J. Bradley Layton. 2010. "Social Relationships and Mortality Risk: A Meta-Analytic Review." *PLoS Medicine* 7 (7): e1000316.

Hong, Ze. 2022. "A Cognitive Account of Manipulative Sympathetic Magic." *Religion, Brain and Behavior,* 12 (3): 254–70.

Howard, James H. 1974. "The Arikara Buffalo Society Medicine Bundle." *Plains Anthropologist* 19 (66): 241–71.

Howard-Browne, Rodney. 2014, March 11. "Steel Plate in Neck Healing Miracle and Testimony." YouTube.

Hultkrantz, Åke. 1973. "A Definition of Shamanism." *Temenos* 9: 25–37.

———. 1991. "The Drum in Shamanism: Some Reflections." *Scripta Instituti Donneriani Aboensis* 14: 9–27.

———. 1993. "Introductory Remarks on the Study of Shamanism." *Shaman* 1 (1–2): 5–16.

Human Relations Area Files. n.d. "EHRAF World Cultures."

Hutton, Ronald. 2001. *Shamans: Siberian Spirituality and the Western Imagination.* Hambledon Continuum.

———. 2003. *Witches, Druids and King Arthur.* Hambledon Continuum.

———. 2007. *Shamans: Siberian Spirituality and the Western Imagination.* Hambledon Continuum.

Hyatt, Eddie L. 2002. *2000 Years of Charismatic Christianity.* Charisma House.

Hyde, Marina. 2009, June 30. "Obsessive? Compulsive? That's an Order at Wimbledon." *The Guardian.*

Illing, Sean. 2019, March 8. "The Extraordinary Therapeutic Potential of Psychedelic Drugs, Explained." *Vox.*

"Iowaska Information." 2023. Ayahuasca Foundation.

Isaacson, Walter. 2011. *Steve Jobs.* Simon & Schuster.

Jackson, Ashton. 2023, May 18. "Elon Musk Says He's Upped His Sleep to 6 Hours per Night—And That His Old Routine Hurt His Brain." CNBC.

Jakobsen, Merete Demant. 2020. *Shamanism: Traditional and Contemporary Approaches to the Mastery of Spirits and Healing.* Berghahn.

Jaubert, Jacques, Sophie Verheyden, Dominique Genty, et al. 2016.

"Early Neanderthal Constructions Deep in Bruniquel Cave in Southwestern France." *Nature* 534 (7605): 111–14.

Jha, Alok. 2010, December 22. "Placebo Effect Works Even If Patients Know They're Getting a Sham Drug." *The Guardian.*

Johnson, Dominic D. P., Daniel T. Blumstein, James H. Fowler, and Martie G. Haselton. 2013. "The Evolution of Error: Error Management, Cognitive Constraints, and Adaptive Decision-Making Biases." *Trends in Ecology & Evolution* 28 (8): 474–81.

Johnson, Samuel G. B. 2018. "Financial Alchemists and Financial Shamans." *Behavioral and Brain Sciences* 41: e78.

Joiner, Whitney. 2020, September 21. "Who Will Benefit from Psychedelic Medicine?" *The Washington Post Magazine.*

Jones, Colton. 2020, April 30. "Knock on Hardwood: NBA Players a Superstitious Lot." *Sports Illustrated.*

Jones, Jonathan. 2021, April 23. "Did Art Peak 30,000 Years Ago? How Cave Paintings Became My Lockdown Obsession." *The Guardian.*

JREF Staff. 2012. "The James Randi Educational Foundation Million Dollar Paranormal Challenge 'FAQ.'" James Randi Educational Foundation.

Kaplan, Hillard S., Paul L. Hooper, and Michael Gurven. 2009. "The Evolutionary and Ecological Roots of Human Social Organization." *Philosophical Transactions of the Royal Society B: Biological Sciences* 364 (1533): 3289–99.

Kaptchuk, Ted J., Elizabeth Friedlander, John M. Kelley, et al. 2010. "Placebos Without Deception: A Randomized Controlled Trial in Irritable Bowel Syndrome." *PLoS ONE* 5 (12): e15591.

Kaptchuk, Ted J., Christopher C. Hemond, and Franklin G. Miller. 2020. "Placebos in Chronic Pain: Evidence, Theory, Ethics, and Use in Clinical Practice." *British Medical Journal* 370: m1668.

Kaptchuk, Ted J., John M. Kelley, Lisa A. Conboy, et al. 2008. "Components of Placebo Effect: Randomised Controlled Trial in Patients with Irritable Bowel Syndrome." *British Medical Journal* 336 (7651): 999–1003.

Kaptchuk, Ted J., Jessica Shaw, Catherine E. Kerr, et al. 2009. "'Maybe I Made Up the Whole Thing': Placebos and Patients' Experiences in a Randomized Controlled Trial." *Culture, Medicine and Psychiatry* 33 (3): 382–411.

Katz, Richard. 1982a. "Accepting 'Boiling Energy': The Experience of !Kia-Healing Among the !Kung." *Ethos* 10 (4): 344–68.

————. 1982b. *Boiling Energy: Community Healing Among the Kalahari Kung*. Harvard University Press.

Kellogg, Rhoda. 1969. *Analyzing Children's Art*. National Press Books.

Kendall, Laurel. 1985. *Shamans, Housewives, and Other Restless Spirits: Women in Korean Ritual Life*. University of Hawaii Press.

————. 1991. *An Initiation "Kut" for a Korean Shaman*. University of Hawaii Press.

————. 2016. "Initiating Performance: The Story of Chini, a Korean Shaman." In *The Performance of Healing*, ed. Carol Laderman and Marina Roseman. Routledge, 17–58.

Kerns, Virginia. 1983. *Women and the Ancestors: Black Carib Kinship and Ritual*. University of Illinois Press.

Khurana, Rakesh. 2002a. *Searching for a Corporate Savior: The Irrational Quest for Charismatic CEOs*. Princeton University Press.

————. 2002b. "The Curse of the Superstar CEO." *Harvard Business Review*. September 2002.

King, Larry. 2001a. "Spiritual Medium Versus Paranormal Skeptic (Featuring Rosemary Altea and James Randi)." *Larry King Live*. CNN, June 5.

————. 2001b. "Are Psychics Real? (Featuring Sylvia Browne and James Randi)." *Larry King Live*. CNN, September 3.

King, Mark. 2013, January 13. "Investments: Orlando Is the Cat's Whiskers of Stock Picking." *The Observer*.

Klein, Cecelia F., Eulogio Guzman, Elisa C. Mandell, and Maya Stanfield-Mazzi. 2002. "The Role of Shamanism in Mesoamerican Art: A Reassessment." *Current Anthropology* 43 (3): 383–419.

Klein, Richard G. 1992. "The Archeology of Modern Human Origins." *Evolutionary Anthropology: Issues, News, and Reviews* 1 (1): 5–14.

Knox, R. A. 1950. *Enthusiasm: A Chapter in the History of Religion, with Special Reference to the XVII and XVIII Centuries*. Oxford University Press.

Kovoor, Abraham T. 1976. *Begone Godmen! Encounters with Spiritual Frauds*. Jaico Publishing House.

————. 1980. *Gods, Demons and Spirits*. Jaico Publishing House.

Kummer, Luke Jerod. 2006, March 21. "How Real Is That Ruin? Don't Ask, the Locals Say." *The New York Times*.

La Barre, Weston. 1970. *The Ghost Dance: Origins of Religion*. Garden City, NY: Doubleday.

————. 1972. "Hallucinogens and the Shamanic Origins of Religion."

In *Flesh of the Gods: The Ritual Use of Hallucinogens*, ed. Peter T. Furst. Praeger, 261–78.

———. 1979. "Shamanic Origins of Religion and Medicine." *Journal of Psychedelic Drugs* 11 (1–2): 7–11.

Lacocque, Pierre-Emmanuel. 1987. "Mircea Eliade Remembered." *McGill Journal of Education / Revue des Sciences de l'Éducation de McGill* 22 (002): 117–30.

Lang, Martin, Jan Krátký, and Dimitris Xygalatas. 2020. "The Role of Ritual Behaviour in Anxiety Reduction: An Investigation of Marathi Religious Practices in Mauritius." *Philosophical Transactions of the Royal Society B: Biological Sciences* 375 (1805): 20190431.

———. 2022. "Effects of Predictable Behavioral Patterns on Anxiety Dynamics." *Scientific Reports* 12: 19240.

Langlais, Mathieu, Anthony Sécher, Solène Caux, et al. 2016. "Lithic Tool Kits: A Metronome of the Evolution of the Magdalenian in Southwest France (19,000–14,000 Cal BP)." *Quaternary International* 414: 92–107.

Laugrand, Frédéric B., and Jarich B. Oosten. 2010. *Inuit Shamanism and Christianity: Transitions and Transformations in the Twentieth Century.* McGill–Queen's University Press.

Lebra, William P. 1982. "Shaman-Client Interchange in Okinawa: Performative Stages in Shamanic Therapy." In *Cultural Conceptions of Mental Health and Therapy*, ed. A. J. Marsella and G. M. White. Springer.

Legare, Cristine H., and Susan A. Gelman. 2008. "Bewitchment, Biology, or Both: The Co-Existence of Natural and Supernatural Explanatory Frameworks Across Development." *Cognitive Science* 32 (4): 607–42.

Legare, Cristine H., and André L. Souza. 2012. "Evaluating Ritual Efficacy: Evidence from the Supernatural." *Cognition* 124 (1): 1–15.

Lessa, William Armand. 1950. *The Ethnography of Ulithi Atoll.* University of California.

Letcher, Andy. 2006. *Shroom: A Cultural History of the Magic Mushroom.* Faber and Faber.

———. 2011, September 17. "Taking the Piss: Reindeer and Fly Agaric." *Andy Letcher: Folk Paganism, Psychedelics, Animism and All Manner of Wyrdlore* (blog).

Lévi-Strauss, Claude. 1963. "The Sorcerer and His Magic." In *Structural Anthropology*, vol. 1. Basic Books, 167–85.

Lewis, Ioan M. 2003. *Ecstatic Religion: A Study of Shamanism and Spirit Possession.* 3rd ed. Routledge.

Lewis, James R. 1988. "Shamans and Prophets: Continuities and Discontinuities in Native American New Religions." *American Indian Quarterly* 12 (3): 221–28.

Lewis, Michael. 2023. *Going Infinite: The Rise and Fall of a New Tycoon.* W. W. Norton.

Lewis-Williams, James David. 2016. *The Mind in the Cave: Consciousness and the Origins of Art.* Thames & Hudson.

Lewis-Williams, James David, and Thomas A. Dowson. 1988. "The Signs of All Times: Entoptic Phenomena in Upper Paleolithic Art." *Current Anthropology* 29 (2): 201–45.

———. 1990. "Through the Veil: San Rock Paintings and the Rock Face." *The South African Archaeological Bulletin* 45 (151): 5–16.

Linton, Ralph. 1933. *The Tanala: A Hill Tribe of Madagascar.* Field Museum Press.

Lipka, Michael, and Claire Gecewicz. 2017, September 6. "More Americans Now Say They're Spiritual but Not Religious." Pew Research Center.

"List of Prizes for Evidence of the Paranormal." 2022. Wikipedia.

Little, Aimée, Benjamin Elliott, Chantal Conneller, et al. 2016. "Technological Analysis of the World's Earliest Shamanic Costume: A Multi-Scalar, Experimental Study of a Red Deer Headdress from the Early Holocene Site of Star Carr, North Yorkshire, UK." *PLoS ONE* 11 (4): 1–10.

Loeb, Edwin M. 1929. "Shaman and Seer." *American Anthropologist* 31 (1): 60–84.

Lopez, Michael J., Gregory J. Matthews, and Benjamin S. Baumer. 2018. "How Often Does the Best Team Win? A Unified Approach to Understanding Randomness in North American Sport." *Annals of Applied Statistics* 12 (4): 2483–516.

Lowy, B. 1971. "New Records of Mushroom Stones from Guatemala." *Mycologia* 63 (5): 983–93.

Luhrmann, Tanya M. 1989. *Persuasions of the Witch's Craft: Ritual Magic in Contemporary England.* Harvard University Press.

———. 2000. *Of Two Minds: An Anthropologist Looks at American Psychiatry.* Vintage.

———. 2012. *When God Talks Back: Understanding the American Evangelical Relationship with God.* Vintage.

———. 2013, October 15. "Conjuring Up Our Own Gods." *The New York Times.*

———. 2020. *How God Becomes Real: Kindling the Presence of Invisible Others.* Princeton University Press.

Macfarlane, Alan. 2022. "Interview of Tanya Luhrmann." YouTube. August 1, 2022. https://www.youtube.com/watch?v=GYWg2K8 ZIsg.

Madigan, Kevin. 2021. *The Popes Against the Protestants: The Vatican and Evangelical Christianity in Fascist Italy.* Yale University Press.

Majumdar, Samirah, and Sarah Crawford. 2024, March 5. "Globally, Government Restrictions on Religion Reached Peak Levels in 2021, While Social Hostilities Went Down." Pew Research Center.

Malkiel, Burton G. 1995. "Returns from Investing in Equity Mutual Funds 1971 to 1991." *Journal of Finance* 50 (2): 549–72.

———. 2003. "The Efficient Market Hypothesis and Its Critics." *Journal of Economic Perspectives* 17 (1): 59–82.

———. 2005. "Reflections on the Efficient Market Hypothesis: 30 Years Later." *The Financial Review* 40 (1): 1–9.

Mangini, Mariavittoria. 2024. "Unseen Women in Psychedelic History." *Journal of Humanistic Psychology* 64 (4): 635–52.

Mann, Charles C. 2005. *1491: New Revelations of the Americas Before Columbus.* Knopf.

Manning, David. 2009. "Accusations of Blasphemy in English Anti-Quaker Polemic, c. 1660–1701." *Quaker Studies* 14 (1): 27–56.

Marlowe, Frank W. 2010. *The Hadza: Hunter-Gatherers of Tanzania.* University of California Press.

Martin, Emmie. 2019, February 27. "Warren Buffett Wants 90 Percent of His Wealth to Go to This One Investment After He's Gone." CNBC.

Martinón-Torres, María, Diego Garate, Andy I. R. Herries, and Michael D. Petraglia. 2023. "No Scientific Evidence That *Homo naledi* Buried Their Dead and Produced Rock Art." *Journal of Human Evolution,* in press.

May, L. Carlyle. 1956. "A Survey of Glossolalia and Related Phenomena in Non-Christian Religions." *American Anthropologist* 58 (1): 75–96.

McBrearty, Sally, and Alison S. Brooks. 2000. "The Revolution That Wasn't: A New Interpretation of the Origin of Modern Human Behavior." *Journal of Human Evolution* 39 (5): 453–563.

McBride, Michael C. 2000. "Bufotenine: Toward an Understanding of

Possible Psychoactive Mechanisms." *Journal of Psychoactive Drugs* 32 (3): 321–31.

McCall, John Christensen. 2000. *Dancing Histories: Heuristic Ethnography with the Ohafia Igbo.* University of Michigan Press.

McClenon, James. 1997. "Shamanic Healing, Human Evolution, and the Origin of Religion." *Journal for the Scientific Study of Religion* 36 (3): 345–54.

———. 2001. *Wondrous Healing: Shamanism, Human Evolution, and Origin of Religion.* Northern Illinois University Press.

McConnell, Michael W. 2000. "Why Is Religious Liberty the First Freedom?" *Cardozo Law Review* 21: 1243–65.

McKenna, Terence. 1992. *Food of the Gods: The Search for the Original Tree of Knowledge.* Bantam Books.

McMullen, James. 2017. "Carmen Elizabeth Blacker 1924–2009: Biographical Memoir." In *Carmen Blacker: Scholar of Japanese Religion, Myth, and Folklore: Writings and Reflections,* ed. Hugh Cortazzi. Amsterdam University Press, 4–27.

Mead, Margaret. 1956. *New Lives for Old: Cultural Transformation—Manus, 1927–1953.* Morrow.

Meeks, Lori. 2011. "The Disappearing Medium: Reassessing the Place of Miko in the Religious Landscape of Premodern Japan." *History of Religions* 59 (2): 208–60.

Mehr, Samuel A., Manvir Singh, Dean Knox, et al. 2019. "Universality and Diversity in Human Song." *Science* 366: eaax0868.

Mehr, Samuel A., Manvir Singh, Hunter York, et al. 2018. "Form and Function in Human Song." *Current Biology* 28 (3): 356–68.

Milinski, Manfred. 2016. "Reputation, a Universal Currency for Human Social Interactions." *Philosophical Transactions of the Royal Society B: Biological Sciences* 371: 20150100.

Miller, Melanie J., Juan Albarracin-Jordan, Christine Moore, and José M. Capriles. 2019. "Chemical Evidence for the Use of Multiple Psychotropic Plants in a 1,000-Year-Old Ritual Bundle from South America." *Proceedings of the National Academy of Sciences* 116 (23): 11207–12.

Millsap, J. P. 2020. *The Shamans of Wall Street: Shh, Finance Professionals Don't Know Anything.* Self-published.

Minuendajú, Curt. 1946. "Social Organization and Beliefs of the Botocudo of Eastern Brazil." *Southwestern Journal of Anthropology* 2 (1): 93–115.

Miton, Helena, Nicolas Claidière, and Hugo Mercier. 2015. "Universal

Cognitive Mechanisms Explain the Cultural Success of Bloodletting." *Evolution and Human Behavior* 36 (4): 303–12.

Morin, Olivier. 2016. *How Traditions Live and Die.* Oxford University Press.

"Most Successful Chimpanzee on Wall Street." 2023. Guinness World Records.

Motta, Ana Paula, Peter M. Veth, and Balanggarra Aboriginal Corporation. 2021. "Relational Ontologies and Performance: Identifying Humans and Nonhuman Animals in the Rock Art from North-Eastern Kimberley, Australia." *Journal of Anthropological Archaeology* 63: 101333.

Muraresku, Brian C. 2020. *The Immortality Key: The Secret History of the Religion with No Name.* St. Martin's Press.

Murdock, George P. 1980. *Theories of Illness: A World Survey.* University of Pittsburgh Press.

Murphy, Robert. 1958. "Mundurucu Religion." *Publications in American Archaeology and Ethnology* 49: 1–154.

Narby, Jeremy, and Francis Huxley, eds. 2001. *Shamans Through Time: 500 Years on the Path to Knowledge.* Penguin Putnam.

Nelson, Sarah Milledge. 2016. *Shamanism and the Origin of States: Spirit, Power, and Gender in East Asia.* Routledge.

Nesse, Randolph M. 2019. "The Smoke Detector Principle: Signal Detection and Optimal Defense Regulation." *Evolution, Medicine and Public Health* 2019 (1): 1.

Newell, David D. 2008. "'Late Recruits for Britain': Anti-Shaker Propaganda During the American Revolution." *American Communal Societies Quarterly* 2 (3): 103–14.

Nicholson, Brendan. 2009, September 30. "South Pacific Tsunami Toll Rises: Three Australians Among Dead, Grave Fears for Others." *The Age.*

Nissinen, Martti. 2017. *Ancient Prophecy: Near Eastern, Biblical, and Greek Perspectives.* Oxford University Press.

———. 2020. "Why Prophets Are (Not) Shamans?" *Vetus Testamentum* 70 (1): 124–39.

O'Donnell, James. 2022, April 6. "How to Become a Billionaire: These Industries Have the Most People on the 2022 Forbes List." *Forbes.*

Olson, Ronald L. 1936. *The Quinault Indians.* The University of Washington.

Onwuejeogwu, Michael. 1969. "The Cult of the Bori Spirits Among the Hausa." In *Man in Africa*, ed. Mary Douglas and Phyllis M. Kaberry. Tavistock Publications, 279–305.

Origen. 1907. "Against Celsus." In *The Ante-Nicene Fathers: The Writings of the Fathers down to A.D. 325*. Vol. 4: *Tertullian, Part Fourth; Minucius Felix; Commodian; Origen, Parts First and Second*, ed. Alexander Roberts and James Donaldson. Charles Scribner's Sons, 395–696.

Ott, Jonathan. 2001. "Pharmañopo—Psychonautics: Human Intranasal, Sublingual, Intrarectal, Pulmonary and Oral Pharmacology of Bufotenine." *Journal of Psychoactive Drugs* 33 (3): 273–81.

Ovies, Diego Hannon, and Juan Jorge Rodriguez Bautista. 2021. "Commodified Spirituality: Tourism and Indigenous Heritage Practices in Huautla de Jimenez, Mexico." *Tourism, Culture and Communication* 21 (4): 313–29.

Oxford English Dictionary. 2023. "Genius, n. & adj., etymology." Oxford University Press.

Paine, Neil. 2020, June 24. "60 Games Aren't Enough to Crown the Best MLB Team. But Neither Are 162 Games." FiveThirtyEight.

Pastoors, Andreas, Tilman Lenssen-Erz, Tsamgao Ciqae, et al. 2021. "Episodes of Magdalenian Hunter-Gatherers in the Upper Gallery of Tuc d'Audoubert (Ariège, France)." In *Reading Prehistoric Human Tracks: Methods and Material*, ed. Andreas Pastoors and Tilman Lenssen-Erz. Springer, 211–49.

Peoples, Hervey C., Pavel Duda, and Frank W. Marlowe. 2016. "Hunter-Gatherers and the Origins of Religion." *Human Nature* 27: 261–82.

Petrone, Pierpaolo, Piero Pucci, Massimo Niola, et al. 2020. "Heat-Induced Brain Vitrification from the Vesuvius Eruption in C.E. 79." *New England Journal of Medicine* 382 (4): 383–84.

Pew Research Center. 2014. "The Shifting Religious Identity of Latinos in the United States."

———. 2018. "Being Christian in Western Europe."

———. 2023. "Spirituality Among Americans."

Philo. 1937. *On the Decalogue; on the Special Laws*, vol. 7, trans. F. H. Colson. Harvard University Press.

Pick, Bernhard. 1909. *The Apocryphal Acts of Paul, Peter, John, Andrew and Thomas*. The Open Court Publishing Co.

Pilling, Arnold Remington. 1958. "Law and Feud in an Aboriginal Society of North Australia." PhD dissertation. University of California, Berkeley.

Pinker, Steven. 1997. *How the Mind Works.* W. W. Norton & Company.

Pollan, Michael. 2018. *How to Change Your Mind: What the New Science of Psychedelics Teaches Us About Consciousness, Dying, Addiction, Depression, and Transcendence.* Penguin Press.

Porr, M., and K. W. Alt. 2006. "The Burial of Bad Dürrenberg, Central Germany: Osteopathology and Osteoarchaeology of a Late Mesolithic Shaman's Grave." *International Journal of Osteoarchaeology* 16 (5): 395–406.

Posth, Cosimo, He Yu, Ayshin Ghalichi, et al. 2023. "Palaeogenomics of Upper Palaeolithic to Neolithic European Hunter-Gatherers." *Nature* 615 (7950): 117–26.

Potts, John. 2009. *A History of Charisma.* Palgrave Macmillan.

Powers, Stephen. 1877. *Tribes of California.* Government Printing Office.

Price, Emily. 2017, December 13. "Warren Buffett Just Won a $1 Million Bet." *Fortune.*

Price, Neil S. 2001. "An Archaeology of Altered States: Shamanism and Material Culture." In *The Archaeology of Shamanism*, ed. Neil Price. London: Routledge, 3–16.

Priklonski, Vasilij, and Friedrich S. Krauss. 1888. "Shamanism Among the Yakut." *Mittheilungen der Anthropologischen Gesellschaft in Wien,* 165–82.

Pryde, Duncan. 1972. *Nunaga: My Land, My Country.* M. G. Hurtig Ltd.

"PsychonautWiki." 2023. PsychonautWiki.

Putnam, Patrick. 1948. "The Pygmies of the Ituri Forest." In *A Reader in General Anthropology*, ed. Carleton S. Coon. Henry Holt and Company, 322–42.

Radcliffe-Brown, A. R. 1922. *The Andaman Islanders: A Study in Social Anthropology.* Cambridge University Press.

Ramsdale, Suzannah. 2020, October 15. "Are You Having a Spiritual Meltdown? Best Shamans in London." *Evening Standard.*

"Rare Mimeographed 1933 Booklet Sells for $47,800!" 2006, September 25. Comicdom.

Reichel-Dolmatoff, Gerardo. 1978. *Beyond the Milky Way: Hallucinatory Imagery of the Tukano Indians.* UCLA Latin American Center Publications.

Ricca, Brad. 2013. *Super Boys: The Amazing Adventures of Jerry Siegel and Joe Shuster—The Creators of Superman.* St. Martin's Press.

Riesebrodt, Martin. 2010. *The Promise of Salvation: A Theory of Religion.* University of Chicago Press.

Robison, Robert. 2022, November 17. "How Often Does the Best Team Win the Title?" *Elder Research.*

Rodd, Robin. 2006. "Piaroa Sorcery and the Navigation of Negative Affect: To Be Aware, to Turn Away." *Anthropology of Consciousness* 17 (1): 35–64.

Rödlach, Alexander. 2006. *Witches, Westerners, and HIV: AIDS and Cultures of Blame in Africa.* Left Coast Press.

Romagnoli, Alex S., and Gian S. Pagnucci. 2013. *Enter the Superheroes: American Values, Culture, and the Canon of Superhero Literature.* The Scarecrow Press.

Rouget, Gilbert. 1985. *Music and Trance: A Theory of the Relations between Music and Possession.* The University of Chicago Press.

Rowland, Ingrid D. 2014. *From Pompeii: The Afterlife of a Roman Town.* Harvard University Press.

Rozin, Paul, and Carol Nemeroff. 2002. "Sympathetic Magical Thinking: The Contagion and Similarity 'Heuristics.'" In *Heuristics and Biases: The Psychology of Intuitive Judgment,* ed. Thomas Gilovich, Dale Griffin, and Daniel Kahneman. Cambridge University Press, 201–16.

Rueger, Sandra Yu, Christine Kerres Malecki, Yoonsun Pyun, et al. 2016. "A Meta-Analytic Review of the Association Between Perceived Social Support and Depression in Childhood and Adolescence." *Psychological Bulletin* 142 (10): 1017–67.

Rydving, Håkan. 2011. "Le Chamanisme Aujourd'hui: Constructions et Déconstructions d'une Illusion Scientifique." *Études Mongoles et Siberiennes, Centrasiatiques et Tibétaines* 45: 2–23.

Samorini, Giorgio. 2019. "The Oldest Archeological Data Evidencing the Relationship of *Homo sapiens* with Psychoactive Plants: A Worldwide Overview." *Journal of Psychedelic Studies* 3 (2): 63–80.

Schefold, Reimar. 1988. *Lia: Das Grosse Ritual auf den Mentawai-Inseln (Indonesien).* Dietrich Reimer Verlag.

———. 1998. "The Domestication of Culture: Nation-Building and Ethnic Diversity in Indonesia." *Bijdragen Tot de Taal-, Land- en Volkenkunde* 154 (2): 259–80.

Schwartz-Narbonne, R., F. J. Longstaffe, K. J. Kardynal, et al. 2019. "Reframing the Mammoth Steppe: Insights from Analysis of Isotopic Niches." *Quaternary Science Reviews* 215: 1–21.

Scientific American. 1922, December. "Announcing $5000 for Psychic Phenomenon."

Scuro, Juan, and Robin Rodd. 2015. "Neo-Shamanism." In *Encyclopedia of Latin American Religions,* ed. H. Gooren. Springer.

Shamandome. 2011. "Shamandome at Burning Man [Archived]."

Shantz, Colleen. 2009. *Paul in Ecstasy: The Neurobiology of the Apostle's Life and Thought.* Cambridge University Press.

Sharp, Lauriston. 1969. "Foreword." In *Nomads of the Long Bow: The Siriono of Eastern Bolivia.* The Natural History Press.

Sheppard, John, and Reimar Schefold. 1974. *The Sakuddei.* Royal Anthropological Institute.

Shiffer, Emily J. 2019, March 22. "Elizabeth Holmes' Diet of Green Juice and Salads Comes Under Scrutiny After New HBO Doc." *Women's Health.*

Shweder, Richard A., N. C. Much, M. Mahapatra, and L. Park. 1997. "The 'Big Three' of Morality (Autonomy, Community, Divinity) and the 'Big Three' Explanations of Suffering." In *Morality and Health,* ed. A. Brand and Paul Rozin. Routledge, 119–69.

Siegel, Jerry, and Joe Shuster. 1933. "The Reign of the Superman." *Science Fiction* 3.

———. 1938. "Superman." *Action Comics* 1: 1–13.

Siikala, Anna-Leena. 1992. "Siberian and Inner Asian Shamanism." In *Studies on Shamanism,* ed. Anna-Leena Siikala and Mihály Hoppal. Finnish Anthropological Society and Akadémiai Kiadó, 1–14.

Silva, Alcionilio Bruzzi Alves da, and Ivana Lillios. 1962. *The Indigenous Civilization of the Uaupés.* Centro de Pesquisas de Iauareté and Human Relations Area Files.

Singh, Manvir. 2018. "The Cultural Evolution of Shamanism." *Behavioral and Brain Sciences* 41: e66.

———. 2020, December 10. "Psychedelics Weren't as Common in Ancient Cultures as We Think." *Vice.*

———. 2021a. "Magic, Explanations, and Evil: The Origins and Design of Witches and Sorcerers." *Current Anthropology* 62 (1): 2–29.

———. 2021b. "The Sympathetic Plot, Its Psychological Origins, and Implications for the Evolution of Fiction." *Emotion Review* 13 (3): 183–98.

———. 2022. "Subjective Selection and the Evolution of Complex Culture." *Evolutionary Anthropology* 31: 266–80.

Singh, Manvir, and Joseph Henrich. 2020. "Why Do Religious Leaders Observe Costly Prohibitions? Examining Taboos on Mentawai Shamans." *Evolutionary Human Sciences* 2: e32.

Singh, Manvir, Ted J. Kaptchuk, and Joseph Henrich. 2021. "Small Gods, Rituals, and Cooperation: The Mentawai Water Spirit Sikameinan." *Evolution and Human Behavior* 42 (1): 61–72.

Singh, Manvir, and Samuel Mehr. 2023. "Universality, Domain-Specificity, and Development of Psychological Responses to Music." *Nature Reviews Psychology* 2: 333–46.

Singh, Manvir, Richard W. Wrangham, and Luke Glowacki. 2017. "Self-Interest and the Design of Rules." *Human Nature* 28: 457–80.

Skinner, B. F. 1948. "'Superstition' in the Pigeon." *Journal of Experimental Psychology* 38 (2): 168–72.

Sobiecki, J. F. 2008. "A Review of Plants Used in Divination in Southern Africa and Their Psychoactive Effects." *Southern African Humanities* 20 (1): 333–51.

Solon, Olivia. 2017, September 4. "The Silicon Valley Execs Who Don't Eat for Days: 'It's Not Dieting, It's Biohacking.'" *The Guardian*.

Sosis, Richard, and W. Penn Handwerker. 2011. "Psalms and Coping with Uncertainty: Religious Israeli Women's Responses to the 2006 Lebanon War." *American Anthropologist* 113 (1): 40–55.

Southerton, Simon G. 2004. *Losing a Lost Tribe: Native Americans, DNA, and the Mormon Church*. Signature Books.

Specter, Michael. 2011, December 4. "The Power of Nothing." *The New Yorker*.

Spencer, Baldwin, and F. J. Gillen. 1904. *The Northern Tribes of Central Australia*. Macmillan and Co.

Sperber, Dan. 1996. *Explaining Culture: A Naturalistic Approach*. Blackwell Publishers Ltd.

Spiro, Melford E. 1978. *Burmese Supernaturalism*. Institute for the Study of Human Issues.

Stearman, Allyn MacLean. 1984. "The Yuqui Connection: Another Look at Siriono Deculturation." *American Anthropologist* 86 (3): 630–50.

Stépanoff, Charles. 2015. "Transsingularities: The Cognitive Foundations of Shamanism in Northern Asia." *Social Anthropology* 23 (2): 169–85.

———. 2021. "Shamanic Ritual and Ancient Circumpolar Migrations: The Spread of the Dark Tent Tradition Through North Asia and North America." *Current Anthropology* 62 (2): 239–46.

Stieg, Cory. 2019, March 19. "Elizabeth Holmes' Very Particular Green Juice Diet, Explained." Refinery29.

Strong, James. 1890. *The Exhaustive Concordance of the Bible*. Eaton and Mains.

Stuckard, Kocku von. 2005. "Harner, Michael—And the Foundation for Shamanic Studies." In *The Encyclopedia of Religion and Nature*, ed. Bron R. Taylor. Thoemmes Continuum, 743–44.

"Subjective Effect Index." 2023. PsychonautWiki.

Sykes, Rebecca Wragg. 2020. *Kindred: Neanderthal Life, Love, Death and Art*. Bloomsbury.

Taçon, Paul S. C., and Christopher Chippindale. 2001. "Transformation and Depictions of the First People: Animal-Headed Beings of Arnhem Land, N.T., Australia." In *Theoretical Perspectives in Rock Art Research: ACRA: The Alta Conference on Rock Art*, ed. Knut Helskog. Instituttet for Sammenlignende Kulturforskning, 175–210.

Tenaza, Richard R., and Agustín Fuentes. 1995. "Monandrous Social Organization of Pigtailed Langurs (*Simias concolor*) in the Pagai Islands, Indonesia." *International Journal of Primatology* 16 (2): 295–310.

Thalbitzer, W. 1909. "The Heathen Priests of East Greenland (Angakut)." In *Verhandlungen des XVI. Internationalen Amerikanisten-Kongresses*. A. Hartleben's Verlag, 447–64.

Thangaraj, Kumarasamy, Lalji Singh, Alla G. Reddy, et al. 2003. "Genetic Affinities of the Andaman Islanders, a Vanishing Human Population." *Current Biology* 13 (2): 86–93.

Thomas, Nicholas. 1988. "Marginal Powers: Shamanism and the Disintegration of Hierarchy." *Critique of Anthropology* 8: 53–73.

Thucydides. 2009. *The Peloponnesian War*. Oxford University Press.

Tiffen, Rachel. 2009, October 1. "Up to Six NZers Feared Dead in Tsunami." *The New Zealand Herald*.

Toffelmier, Gertrude. 1967. "Edwin Meyer Loeb 1894–1966." *American Anthropologist* 69 (2): 200–203.

Torres, Constantino Manuel, and David B. Repke. 2006. *Anadenanthera: Visionary Plant of Ancient South America*. Haworth Press.

Torres, Constantino Manuel, David B. Repke, Kelvin Chan, et al. 1991. "Snuff Powders from Pre-Hispanic San Pedro de Atacama: Chemical and Contextual Analysis." *Current Anthropology* 32 (5): 640–49.

Townsend, Joan B. 2004. "Individualist Religious Movements: Core and Neo-Shamanism." *Anthropology of Consciousness* 15 (1): 1–9.

Trevett, Christine. 2017. "Montanism." In *The Early Christian World*, ed. Philip E. Esler. Routledge, 867–84.

Tulius, Juniator. 2012. "Family Stories: Oral Tradition, Memories of the Past, and Contemporary Conflicts over Land in Mentawai-Indonesia." PhD diss. Leiden University.

Turnbull, Colin M. 1965. *The Mbuti Pygmies: An Ethnographic Survey. Anthropological Papers of the American Museum of Natural History*, vol. 50. The American Museum of Natural History.

Tylor, Edward B. 1920. *Primitive Culture: Researches into the Development of Mythology, Philosophy, Religion, Language, Art and Custom*, vol. 1, 6th ed. John Murray.

USAID. 2006. "Uganda—Complex Emergency (Situation Report #3, Fiscal Year [FY] 2006)."

Vaitl, Dieter, Niels Birbaumer, John Gruzelier, et al. 2005. "Psychobiology of Altered States of Consciousness." *Psychological Bulletin* 131 (1): 98–127.

Van der Merwe, B., A. Rockefeller, A. Kilian, et al. 2024. "A Description of Two Novel *Psilocybe* Species from Southern Africa and Some Notes on African Traditional Hallucinogenic Mushroom Use." *Mycologia*, 1–14.

Vitebsky, Piers. 2017. *Living Without the Dead: Loss and Redemption in a Jungle Cosmos*. University of Chicago Press.

Vogel, Dan, and Scott C. Dunn. 1993. "'The Tongue of Angels': Glossolalia Among Mormonism's Founders." *Journal of Mormon History* 19 (2): 1–34.

Vyse, Stuart. 2014. *Believing in Magic: The Psychology of Superstition*. Oxford University Press.

Walker, Robert S., Søren Wichmann, Thomas Mailund, and Curtis J Atkisson. 2012. "Cultural Phylogenetics of the Tupi Language Family in Lowland South America." *PLoS ONE* 7 (4): e35025.

Wallis, Robert J. 2003. *Shamans/Neo-Shamans: Ecstasy, Alternative Archaeologies and Contemporary Pagans*. Routledge.

Wampold, Bruce E. 2015. "How Important Are the Common Factors in Psychotherapy? An Update." *World Psychiatry* 14 (3): 270–77.

Wariboko, Nimi, and L. William Oliverio. 2020. "The Society for Pentecostal Studies at 50 Years: Ways Forward for Global Pentecostalism." *Pneuma* 42 (4): 327–33.

Wasson, R. Gordon. 1957, May 13. "Seeking the Magic Mushroom." *Life*.

Wasson, Valentina Pavlovna. 1957, May 9. "I Ate the Sacred Mushrooms." *This Week*.

Wasson, Valentina Pavlovna, and R. Gordon Wasson. 1957. *Mushrooms, Russia and History*. Pantheon Books.

Weber, Max. 1946. "Science as a Vocation." In *Max Weber: Essays in Sociology*. Trans. and ed. H. H. Gerth and C. Wright Mills. Oxford University Press, 129–56.

Weinberger, Eliot. 1986. "Mircea Eliade." *Sulfur* 17: 108–10.

Weingus, Leigh. 2019, March 21. "Nutritionists Weigh In on Elizabeth Holmes' Ultra-Restrictive Diet." *HuffPost*.

Weinman, Sam. 2019, February 12. "Here Are a Few of Tiger Woods' Fairly Odd Superstitions." *Golf Digest*.

Wellman, Henry M. 1991. "Insides and Essences: Early Understandings of the Non-Obvious." *Cognition* 38: 213–44.

Wernsdorff, Melina von, Martin Loef, Brunna Tuschen-Caffier, and Stefan Schmidt. 2021. "Effects of Open-Label Placebos in Clinical Trials: A Systematic Review and Meta-Analysis." *Scientific Reports* 11 (1): 1–14.

Whitehead, Harry. 2000. "The Hunt for Quesalid: Tracking Lévi-Strauss' Shaman." *Anthropology and Medicine* 7 (2): 149–68.

Wiessner, Polly, and Flemming T. Larson. 1979. "'Mother! Sing Loudly for Me!': The Annotated Dialogue of a Basarwa Healer in Trance." *Botswana Notes and Records* 11: 25–31.

Wilbert, Johannes. 1963. *Indios de la Región Orinoco-Ventuari*. Fundación La Salle de Ciencias Naturales.

———. 1987. *Tobacco and Shamanism in South America*. New Haven, CT, and London: Yale University Press.

Wilser, Jeff. 2022, April 14. "Sam Bankman-Fried: The Man, the Hair, the Vision." CoinDesk.

Wilting, Andreas, Rahel Sollmann, Erik Meijaard, et al. 2012. "Mentawai's Endemic, Relictual Fauna: Is It Evidence for Pleistocene Extinctions on Sumatra?" *Journal of Biogeography* 39 (9): 1608–20.

Winkelman, Michael. 1986. "Trance States: A Theoretical Model and Cross-Cultural Analysis." *Ethos* 14 (2): 174–203.

———. 2002. "Shamanism and Cognitive Evolution." *Cambridge Archaeological Journal* 12: 71–101.

———. 2010. *Shamanism: The Neural Ecology of Consciousness and Healing*. Praeger.

———. 2019. "Introduction: Evidence for Entheogen Use in Prehistory and World Religions." *Journal of Psychedelic Studies* 3 (2): 43–62.

Winkelman, Michael, and Douglas White. 1987. "A Cross-Cultural

Study of Magico-Religious Practitioners and Trance States: Database." *HRAF Research Series in Quantitative Cross-Cultural Data III.*

Wood, Connor, and Kate Stockly. 2018. "Complexity and Possession: Gender and Social Structure in the Variability of Shamanic Traits." *Behavioral and Brain Sciences* 41: e91.

Worsley, Peter. 1968. *The Trumpet Shall Sound: A Study of "Cargo" Cults in Melanesia.* Schocken Books.

Wright, Peggy Ann. 1989. "The Nature of the Shamanic State of Consciousness: A Review." *Journal of Psychoactive Drugs* 21 (1): 25–33.

Wright, Robert. 2009. *The Evolution of God.* Little, Brown and Company.

Yaffe-Bellany, David. 2022, May 14. "A Crypto Emperor's Vision: No Pants, His Rules." *The New York Times.*

Zanini, Paolo. 2015. "Twenty Years of Persecution of Pentecostalism in Italy: 1935–1955." *Journal of Modern Italian Studies* 20 (5): 686–707.

Zieme, Peter. 2008. "A Note on the Word 'Shaman' in Old Turkic." *Shaman* 16: 137–42.

Index

Page numbers of tables appear in italics.

Manvir Singh is an assistant professor of anthropology at the University of California, Davis. He holds a bachelor's degree from Brown University and a PhD from Harvard University. A frequent contributor to *The New Yorker*, he has also published work in *Wired*, *Vice*, *Aeon*, and *The Guardian*, as well as leading academic journals including *Science, Nature Human Behaviour*, and *Behavioral and Brain Sciences*. He has studied psychedelic use in the Orinoco River basin of Colombia and, since 2014, has conducted ethnographic fieldwork with Mentawai communities on Siberut Island, Indonesia, focusing on shamanism and justice. He lives with his wife, Nina, and daughter, Zora, in Davis, California.

A NOTE ON THE TYPE

This book was set in Janson, a typeface long thought to have been made by the Dutchman Anton Janson, who was a practicing typefounder in Leipzig during the years 1668–1687. However, it has been conclusively demonstrated that this type is actually the work of Nicholas Kis (1650–1702), a Hungarian, who most probably learned his trade from the master Dutch typefounder Dirk Voskens. The type is an excellent example of the influential and sturdy Dutch types that prevailed in England up to the time William Caslon (1692–1766) developed his own incomparable designs from them.

Composed by North Market Street Graphics,
Lancaster, Pennsylvania